# Political Economy
of Fairness

# Political Economy of Fairness

Edward E. Zajac

The MIT Press
Cambridge, Massachusetts
London, England

First MIT Press paperback edition, 1996

© 1995 Massachusetts Institute of Technology

This book was set in Palatino by Asco Trade Typesetting Ltd., Hong Kong and was printed and bound in the United States of America.

Library of Congress Cataloging-in-Publication Data

Zajac, Edward E.
  Political economy of fairness / Edward E. Zajac.
    p.   cm.
  Includes bibliographical references and index.
  ISBN 0-262-24038-6 (HB), 0-262-74019-2 (PB)
    1. Economics—Moral and ethical aspects.  2. Fairness.  3. Social justice.
  4. United States—Economic policy—Moral and ethical aspects.  I. Title.
HB72.Z29   1995
330—dc20                                                              94-42414
                                                                          CIP

To My Family
Brooky, Bonnie, John, and Leah

# Contents

# Acknowledgments

Like most authors of academic books, I have relied on the help of a number of people to correct errors in the manuscript, to make suggestions for its improvement, to provide me with data from their area of expertise, and, most important, to give me the courage to persevere. I wish to take this opportunity to thank them. No less than nine anonymous referees did me the honor of reading a draft manuscript and providing many helpful suggestions; I am indebted to them all. Among colleagues at the University of Arizona, I received help from Corinne Bronfman, Dan Dhaliwal, John Drabicki, Brad Hansen, Don Heckerman, Mark Isaac, Jeff LaFrance, Deborah Mathieu, Lyn Ragsdale, Vernon Smith, and Gordon Tullock. Others who helped me were Gerry Faulhaber of the University of Pennsylvania; Dick Jankowski of the State University of New York at Fredonia; Mary-Olson of Washington University; Robert Patrick of Stanford; Peter Linhart, Roy Radner, and Frank Sinden of AT&T Bell Laboratories; Bob Rosenthal, Ingo Vogelsang, and Andy Weiss of Boston University; Gerry Bierwag of Florida International University; Tracy Murray of the University of Arkansas; Frederick Murphy of Temple University; Allen Soyster of Pennsylvania State University; Richard Cabe of New Mexico State University; Catherine Eckel of Virginia Polytechnic Institute; Jeffrey Rohlfs of Strategic Policy Research; Bill Taylor of National Economic Research Associates; and Nancy Davis, Scott McClellan, Robert McKenna, and Mary Wybenga of U.S. West. I am also grateful for the feedback I have gotten from students over the years as I have expounded the ideas in this book. In fall 1993, I was especially fortunate to have as students in my "Economics of Regulation" class three graduate students, Gary Davis, Gene Mesher, and Bernard Ruhl. They brought the perspective of mature students with considerable work experience earning graduate degrees in public administration, management information systems, and business administration, respectively. All three provided insightful comments on the manuscript.

Some of the material in the book was presented at seminars at the Universities of Arizona and Maryland, and at the Wharton School, University of Pennsylvania; I would like to thank the participants for their comments.

When I was thinking of what to call this book, my son John suggested the title. I wish to thank him for it.

Jennifer Boice and Charlotte Kenan of the *Tucson Citizen* graciously arranged access to the *Citizen*'s library, and provided me with the clippings of news stories needed to refresh my memory of the events recounted in chapter 22. Alison Habel's deft hand produced the illustrations. I am thankful not only for her skill, but for her forbearance as she patiently dealt with a seemingly endless stream of modifications and corrections.

The staff of The MIT Press has been a delight to work with, and I greatly appreciate their help. Terry Vaughn and Ann Sochi provided guidance and hand-holding during preparation of the manuscript; Melissa Vaughn expertly excised needless words, recast wording to make it more understandable, and caught errors; and Brooke Stevens prepared concise yet accurate promotional materials.

Also, I would like to thank Edgar Gilbert of AT&T Bell Labs and his son, Peter, for the quote at the beginning of chapter 1.

Finally, I am indebted to my present and former employers. The University of Arizona granted me a sabbatical leave during the 1991–92 academic year, which enabled me to start this book; its allowing me to go on leave during the Spring 1994 semester enabled me to finish it. Several passages in this book were adapted from my *Fairness or Efficiency: An Introduction to Public Utility Pricing* (Zajac, 1978), written while I was employed by AT&T Bell Laboratories. I am greatly appreciative of Bell Labs' liberal policy of encouraging its employees to write books, and especially thankful for Bell Labs' assigning me the copyright of *Fairness or Efficiency*.

The conventional statement applies with force: I am immensely grateful for all of the help I have received, but final responsibility for errors is solely mine.

# I

# Basic Economic Concepts and Ideas

# 1  Introduction and Overview

*A great book is like a great misfortune.*

Callimachus (poet employed at the great library of Alexandria, ca. 305–240 B.C.)

## 1.1  This Book's Goals

This book started out as a second edition of my *Fairness or Efficiency: An Introduction to Public Utility Pricing* (1978). My notion was to expand the first edition to reflect research advances made since it was published fifteen years ago, especially the considerable advances in fairness theory. However, anonymous reviewers of my draft suggested that I broaden the book's outlook to extend beyond public utility economics. As one reviewer put it, my draft contained a "coherent discourse" of fairness and efficiency, one that was germane to all sorts of current policy debates.

When I read the reviews, it dawned on me that within my draft was a new book struggling to get out, a book that reflected the way I actually teach a course on the economics of regulation and antitrust to senior undergraduate economics majors and graduate students in business, public administration, and law. The course does not focus on public utility regulation; during some semesters I don't even mention it. Instead, it deals in general terms with regulation and government intervention.

The general issues I consider in the course are not new. They were on society's center stage during my childhood in the Great Depression, and, with the end of the cold war, they again occupy center stage. But they have been the staple of controversies in public utility regulation since its inception at the end of the last century.

And public utility regulation is where I first met them, when in late 1965 I was assigned from the Mathematics Research Center at Bell Laboratories to a task force at AT&T. The task force's job was to a plan a strategy for coping with a comprehensive investigation of AT&T's pricing policies by the Federal Communications Commission (FCC). Subsequently I returned to Bell Labs and changed careers, moving from engineering and applied mathematics to economics. But I continued be in the thick of regulatory policy advising and research until I left Bell Labs at the end of 1983 to come to the University of Arizona.

The format of my course reflects my experience of watching and being involved for almost twenty years in a parade of regulatory dramas. The typical drama had a number of stakeholders; the arguments were rarely about economic efficiency; rather they were intense disagreements about "fairness" to the general public. To the cynic, the stakeholders appeared to be using public-interest arguments to justify their self-interest. But the cynical view is an oversimplification. Usually the stakeholders wholeheartedly and sincerely believed in the righteousness of their cause. In the end, in the typical regulatory drama, the economic efficiency consequences were all over the map and only dimly perceived.

For example, in the Bell System we were intensely proud of providing the "best telephone service in the world" and highly motivated by the thought that we were performing a great public service. Those opposing us we felt were either misguided, ill informed, or just plain evil. Of course it just so happened that the stakeholders, Bell or non-Bell, would also benefit should the stakeholders advocated position be adopted. And the considerable literature on economically efficient public utility pricing and policy usually had little influence in determining regulatory outcomes.

After I left Bell Labs I realized that this structure—stakeholders-fairness-efficiency—is general and not confined to the regulation of telephone services. In the debate about putting limits on tort awards in medical malpractice suits, trial lawyers sincerely cite cases of persons who have suffered terrible harms at the hands of bad doctors—the implication being that you too could be one of these poor souls and the limits would deprive you of due process. The doctors equally sincerely point to the huge costs of malpractice insurance because of tort awards that are out of control. At this level, the debate is commonplace in the media. However, actual calculations of the benefits and costs are much harder to come by. Still rarer is a reasoned discussion of the trade-off in this case between the rights of individuals who have been damaged and the rights of society.

The reviewers' comments tipped the balance. I scrapped the idea of a second edition and started over. I abandoned the idea of educating non-economists on how economists think of public utility regulation for the broader goal of educating noneconomists on how economists think about government intervention into a market economy. At the same time, I wanted to educate economists on the main advances of fairness theory and its importance in policy analysis. Although fairness theory is currently primitive compared to economic theory, it still has a lot of structure. I am convinced that, just as economic theory can offer nonobvious insights and have predictive power, so can fairness theory. And together the two can yield more powerful theories and insights than could each alone.

My main goal was to write a book to help raise the level of the fairness–economic efficiency debate, and to provide a vocabulary of concepts and terms that will allow people to communicate more quickly and deeply about policy. A second goal is both to illustrate the importance of getting the economic theory right and to show how this is not always easy and has taken society a long time. An excellent example, taken up in chapter 20, is the struggle of the Supreme Court to put meaning into the Sherman and Clayton Acts. If one takes the term *restraint of trade* literally, it means the death of the free market, because every entrepreneur is trying to restrain the trade of rivals. But how does one distinguish between a good and a bad restraint of trade? From a strict economic efficiency point of view, this is not a trivial problem, and the Supreme Court struggled with it for years following the passage of the Sherman Act, and again after passage of the Cellar-Kefauver amendment to the Clayton Act. And of course it also raises the question, To what extent should society protect the small entrepreneur from the economic power of giant firms? That is, to what extent should "fairness" enter into a discussion of antitrust issues? These questions are perennial and will undoubtedly be revisited in the Clinton administration.

A third goal is to show both the pervasiveness of the government interference in the marketplace and the generality of the stakeholder-fairness-efficiency paradigm as an organizing framework of analysis. I stress to my students that regulation and government intervention extends to every nook and cranny of the U.S. economy. No book can possibly treat all regulations or even all classes of regulation. In assigning term papers, I encourage students to select a topic from their own experience. If they work or have worked, I urge them to write on some aspect of regulation of the firm for which they worked. When they explore this possibility, they are often surprised to find just how regulated their employer is. For instance, a student who worked in a beauty parlor did not realize that the Food and Drug Administration (FDA) regulated cosmetics, nor did a student salesman at an auto supply store realize the full consequences of the government's program to replace the refrigerants in automobile air conditioners. In both cases there were of course stakeholders, accusations and counteraccusations of unfair treatment, and overall costs and benefits to society to be analyzed.

Another major change of this book from the draft is the intended readership. Instead of noneconomists lawyers, engineers, and regulators, I now have in mind a primary readership like my students—seniors and beginning graduate students. But I have tried to make the book accessible to a much broader readership than economics students and professional economists. "Policy" courses are taught in all sorts of departments. To reach students in these courses and professionals in other social sciences, I have tried to keep the book as elementary as possible, assuming only some rudimentary familiarity with the elements of supply and demand analysis. As a secondary readership I have in mind policy makers and their staffs.

## 1.2   This Book's Point of View

A while ago, my automobile got sick. When I started it, a red light on the dashboard glared "brake" and the temperature needle was stuck at the right end of the red zone labeled "overheated." Worst of all in the Tucson summer, there was no power to open the windows or run the air conditioner. Of course I envisioned spending thousands of dollars on repair bills in order to track down what was wrong and fix it.

I drove as quickly as I could to my auto repair shop, hoping the overheated engine wouldn't bind before I could get there and say, "I have no appointment, but this car is dangerous to drive. Fix it as soon as you can." When I explained the symptoms to the mechanic, he said simply, "Sounds like the ignition lock." To my amazement, the mechanic called within a few hours and said my car was ready. He explained that when one turns the key, several things happen. The dashboard warning lights flicker "on," and some of the dashboard needles momentarily swing to full range. This is to allow the driver to check that they all indicator lights and needles work. In addition, all of the power except that necessary to turn the starter is shut off. This is to allow the battery to concentrate its full attention on getting the engine started, because once the engine gets going, it can provide abundant power for everything.

What had happened was that a linkage between the ignition key and the ignition switch had bound. As a result, all of the indicator lights and needles would hang up and the power would be shut off, even though the engine was running. It only required a little lubrication to unbind the linkage and cure the problem. My bill was not the expected thousands, but only a few dollars for the small amount of time it took to get at the linkage and apply the necessary lubrication.

Why am I telling this story? Because it illustrates the importance of *positive* theory—social sciences jargon for a theory that describes *what is*. A valid positive theory not only can explain, but most important, it can predict. Newton's laws in physics are a good example: they predict the orbits of satellites with great accuracy. By way of contrast, *normative* theory specifies what *ought to be*, such as a theory of good architectural design or good art, or of how society ought to be structured in order to be just.

In the case of my sick automobile, I had no positive theory of how it worked, but luckily, my mechanic had a very good one. If a mysterious disease had carried off all of the mechanics in the world, I could have spent countless hours trying to figure out what was wrong and how to cope with it. My mechanic spent about fifteen seconds diagnosing my problem and perhaps a half an hour curing it. Without a good positive theory of my own, I was also at the mechanic's mercy. If he had not been honest, he could have easily concocted an involved tale of why the problem had been difficult to diagnose, how it had taken many hours of labor and expensive parts to fix it, and he could have bilked me out of the many dollars I was expecting to pay.

This book tries to make positive theory. In the social sciences, we generally cannot hope to find positive theories that have the explanatory and predictive power of my mechanic's theory, much less of Newton's laws. We have to be satisfied with theories that predict trends or average tendencies. And then, we often find that two or three theories have equal explanatory and predictive power. Nevertheless, as is discussed in more detail in chapter 10, even a crude positive theory with limited power to predict can be useful as compared to no positive theory at all or a positive theory that is false, has no predictive power, and only misleads.

I have resisted prescribing "what should be done" about specific fairness-efficiency problems facing the American or global society. Such a normative approach would require me to impose my ethical views on the reader, which is contrary to the spirit of the book. In fact, the reader who finishes this book may very well conclude that the basic ethical dilemmas facing American and European societies are more complicated and difficult than he or she realized.

Economists will not find unusual my reluctance to take ethical stances—economics courses usually avoid any discussion of ethics. Instead, they will probably find it idiosyncratic that an economist devotes roughly one-fourth of his book to a serious discussion of fairness and economic justice.

On the other hand, although the stress on fairness may be idiosyncratic, the book's behavioral assumptions are very much mainstream economics; the book unabashedly assumes that economic agents tend to follow their self-interest. Many social scientists who are not economists consider this a jarring and even outrageous assumption, one they challenge on both empirical and ethical grounds. They argue that people don't behave this way, that people are altruistic and charitable, and, furthermore, that self-serving, selfish behavior should be condemned on moral grounds.

These objections have validity but miss the point. In making positive theory, we want the behavioral model that, out of all the alternatives, has the best predictive power (see chapter 10 for a discussion of this point). Of course, people are to a degree altruistic and charitable, and some persons are selflessly willing to give their lives for a cause. But by and large, if the stakes are high enough, models based on self-interest have distressingly good predictive power, at least in the sense of predicting aggregate trends and average tendencies. As I write, Congress has just begun to debate President Clinton's proposal for health care reform. It takes no genius to predict which principal interest groups will be for or against adoption of the proposal, or how they will try to modify it to their own ends. Likewise, 1993 saw the passage of a tax bill by two votes in the House of Representatives and one vote (Vice President Gore's) in the Senate. The predicted attempt by the wealthy to shift assets so as to escape taxes immediately began with a vengeance, and many articles on exactly how they are doing it have already appeared in the business press.

Hence, although the predictive power of self-interest-based economic theories is modest, it is still better than competing theories. This means that there is great room for improvement. A central thesis of this book is that improvement lies in the direction of modifying standard economic theory to take fairness into account.

## 1.3   Overview

I should make clear that this book is an introduction to not only one subject, but to a number of subjects treated at length in economics, moral philosophy, political science, public choice, and social psychology. I have decided to the minimize the use of phrases like "further consideration of this topic is beyond the scope of this book." Instead the reader will find references to a larger literature, usually in the notes at the end of each chapter. Thus the reader who expects to find a "great" book that comprehensively surveys all of these areas in depth will be disappointed (but as the quote at the beginning of this chapter indicates, the reader should also be happy). Instead, my hope is that the reader will find a concise treatment that introduces main ideas and gives new insights, a treatment that at first glance is inviting rather than threatening.

The book is divided into four parts. Part I summarizes basic economic ideas and concepts that are used in the rest of the book. For students with a strong background in economics, part I may be skipped. But much of the material, such as principal-agent theory and incentive compatible regulatory design, has come into economics only in the last decade or two and has yet to work its way into the standard elementary and intermediate economics courses. For that matter, some of the older material (notably economic efficiency or economywide Pareto optimality), is still treated only lightly because it depends on a general equilibrium analysis. So even undergraduate economics majors may find some new material in part I. Noneconomists will find all of it new, but if they have had a rudimentary exposure to supply-demand analysis, they should also find it accessible.

Part II then presents the elements of fairness theory, covering both positive and normative theory. I usually teach this material right after chapter 2 on economic efficiency; unless students have taken courses in moral philosophy, they have no familiarity with it. And knowledge of this material is essential for the term paper or class project that they must start near the semester's beginning. In this book, however, I have placed it where it logically belongs—after a development of basic economic ideas.

Next, in part III, I discuss the economists' normative and positive theories of regulation and government intervention, including lump-sum taxes as first best, Ramsey taxes and regulated prices, regulation to cure market failures, public choice, and rent seeking. This part culminates with a discussion of incentive-compatible regulation as the economist's current candidate for the best way to approach regulation and government intervention.

Finally, part IV presents a series of case studies, each organized according to the stakeholder-fairness-efficiency framework. Some of the cases, such as the development of antitrust law for horizontal mergers, have a long history. Others, like the adoption of incentive-compatible regulation of telephone companies, are current, in a state of flux, and still very controversial. However, the purpose of the case studies is not to give a comprehensive overview of all of U.S. regulation and policies of government intervention. Rather, the purpose is to illustrate recurrent themes and to present examples of the application of the stakeholders-fairness-efficiency framework. Instructors should find it easy to write up their own cases in the same framework and thus to present material that is tailor-made to the needs of their students.

# 2       The Concept of Economic Efficiency

*[T]he propensity to truck, barter, and exchange one thing for another . . . is common to all men, and to be found in no other race of animals . . . Nobody ever saw a dog make a fair and deliberate exchange of one bone for another with another dog.*

Adam Smith, *Wealth of Nations*

## 2.1   Economic Efficiency and General Equilibrium of an Economy

When I ask students what they think "economic efficiency" means to an economist, they usually answer something like "making things at least cost" or "minimizing the resources needed for production." Environmentally sensitive students sometimes answer that "economic efficiency" means "making things without wasting any resources."

Of course, definitions of technical terms are arbitrary and we can attach any specific definition to a technical term that we wish, as long as all of us use the definition in a consistent way. But if we are to streamline communication, we need terms that convey important concepts and ideas and that can lead to new insights. A few examples usually convince the students that definitions like those I have just given fall short of the mark; they don't convey the main idea we need if we are to talk sensibly about how to make an entire economy "efficient."

Suppose, for one example, there was an economy in which all of the shoe factories were superbly engineered to make shoes at absolutely the minimum cost. But suppose that the factories made *only left shoes*. We would not consider this economy to be very efficient. So the notion of minimum cost or minimum use of resources, by itself, isn't adequate. What about the notion that economic efficiency means no "waste"? After all, the output of the shoe factories producing only left shoes would be wasted because no one would buy them. Maybe the environmental student was right—zero "waste" should be the definition of *economic efficiency*. But this, too, has limitations. Consider the following proposals to eliminate "waste":

• Require everyone to time-share bedrooms, taking turns sleeping eight hours, thereby eliminating the two-thirds of bedrooms that are currently "wasted."

• Standardize colors of shirts and blouses to a single color, perhaps blue, chosen by majority vote, thereby eliminating the "waste" of resources currently used to manufacture different colors.

• Standardize styles of clothes to a single style, perhaps a tunic, again chosen by majority vote, thereby eliminating the "waste" of excessive number of styles.

• Eliminate needless gas stations as seen in large cities where sometimes two gas stations are located at the same intersection, thereby eliminating the "waste" of having too many gas stations.

• Eliminate people choosing a hotel when they travel to a distance city, a practice which results in occupancy rates of 60–70 percent and an uneven distribution of occupants among the available hotels. Instead, have hotel rooms assigned by a central authority, thereby eliminating the "waste" of hotel rooms being vacant.

• Eliminate movies, television, the production of all art, and so forth, thereby eliminating the "waste" of resources devoted to activities not necessary for the sustenance of life.

You get the idea. Each of above cases eliminates "waste" by running roughshod over the desires and preferences of members of the economy.

And that's the fundamental point—an adequate definition of *efficiency* for an entire economy must take into account *both consumption and production*, or, in other terms, *both the demand and supply sides* of the economy.

At first glance, coming up with such a definition may seem impossible; indeed, as chapter 7 discusses at length, it took economists several centuries to crystallize the modern concept of economic efficiency. But, in fact, the modern concept is based on a simple idea—exploit gains through trade or exchange. The concept is also powerful and useful in analysis. It's easiest to see how it works if we proceed from simple to more complicated examples, starting with the illustration of a prisoner-of-war camp economy and building to the case of a modern, complex economy.

## 2.2   Economic Efficiency in a Prisoner-of-War Camp Economy

Imagine a World War II German prisoner-of-war camp, populated by captured British and French soldiers. Imagine further that each week the prisoners get identical packages of food rations consisting of tea, coffee,
mutton, veal, oats to make porridge, bread, various kinds of fruit, and the
like. What would we expect to happen after the rations are distributed? Undoubtedly, the soldiers would begin to trade with each other. French soldiers who abhor tea might trade tea to British soldiers in return for the
coffee they abhor. Mutton lovers/veal haters might trade with veal lovers/
mutton haters; porridge lovers/bread haters might trade with bread lovers/
porridge haters; and so on. These trades would be mutually advantageous
to both trading partners. If the prisoners were to negotiate mutually advantageous trades until all possible remaining trades would result in a good
deal for one partner but a poor deal for the other, we would say that our
prisoner-of-war camp economy had arrived at an *economically efficient equilibrium* (also known as an "allocatively efficient equilibrium," "Pareto equilibrium," or a "Pareto-optimal state").[1]

The idea of mutually advantageous actions or "gains in trade" is at the
heart of Pareto or economic efficiency. In spite of its simplicity, this hypothetical example illustrates three key properties of economic efficiency that
always must be borne in mind: (1) its *nonuniqueness*, (2) its *dependence on
resource or income distribution*, and (3) its being at best only a necessary or
*minimum condition for justice*.

More specifically in terms of our prisoner-of-war camp economy, first
suppose that both prisoner B and prisoner C preferred coffee to tea, while
the reverse were true for prisoner A. If A traded all of A's excess coffee for
B's excess tea, A would not be interested in a coffee-for-tea trade with C.
A and C could no longer mutually gain by a trade, and of course should A
choose to trade instead with C, A and B could not mutually benefit from
a trade. After either trade, the prisoner-of-war camp economy might be
economically efficient, but the compositions of the resulting food rations
owned by A, B, and C would depend on which of the two trades were
made.

Second, the economically efficient state that is reached after mutually
beneficial trades are exhausted depends on the initial endowment of the
economy's agents. Suppose that instead of identical weekly rations, the
German authorities distributed the same total amounts of different food-
stuffs but in diverse rations based on a survey of prisoners' individual

tastes. If the survey reflected tastes perfectly, there might be no incentive to trade. The economy would also be in a Pareto optimal state, but the state would probably be different from the Pareto optimality achieved by trading from identical rations.

Third, economic efficiency does not necessarily satisfy intuitive notions of justice, fairness, or equity. For example, suppose the German authorities gave all of the rations to a single prisoner, chosen because of his strength and brutality. The chosen prisoner might decide that none of the other prisoners had anything to offer in trade and might choose to trade with no one, keeping all of the rations to himself and allowing the other prisoners to starve. The other prisoners might think that this process of distributing rations was grossly unfair, but it would result in economic efficiency nevertheless.

In spite of these drawbacks and others discussed in chapter 7, Pareto or economic efficiency is an important concept to be considered in deciding fairness questions. For example, it also seems obviously unfair to *prevent* exchanges that advantage some without hurting others. Thus all other factors being equal, one might consider economic efficiency to be a necessary fairness condition in any reasonable definition of fairness, while granting that, depending on the definition of fairness, some economically efficient allocations may be fairer than others. The relationship of economic (Pareto) efficiency to fairness is a crucial issue—one that will occupy us throughout this monograph.

## 2.3   Economic Efficiency in a Simple Barter Economy

In our simple, prisoner-of-war camp economy the problem was to allocate a finite amount of food to the inmates. In a real economy we are again faced with finite resources—a finite amount of labor and a finite amount of natural resources. With infinite resources we would have no economic problem; each person in the economy could consume resources to the point of satiation. But if resources are not infinite, we have the problem that is often called "the fundamental problem of economics": how to allocate finite resources to the individuals who make up the economy. As in the prisoner-or-war camp example, we can imagine the individuals' starting with some initial endowment, their natural endowments of labor plus whatever they may have acquired through inheritance, marriage, or gifts. Similarly, we can again imagine an allocation built on mutual gains in trade.

Indeed, in a simple barter economy, resources may be allocated by a gains-in-trade mechanism akin to that at work in our hypothetical prisoner-of-war camp economy. In the ancient rural village the cobbler might shoe the baker's family in return for bread. By such specialization of labor, both shoes and bread are produced at a minimum expenditure of man-hours and other resources. Likewise, the mutton-loving cobbler who has accumulated a lot of pork might trade with the pork-loving baker who has accumulated a lot of mutton. Through such trades, goods are consumed so as best to accord with differing tastes or preferences. Finally, barter or trades may *coordinate* production with consumption. For suppose the villagers are individually indifferent between a pound of mutton and a pound of pork, while a rearrangement of resources will allow a farmer to produce three more pounds of mutton for every pound less of pork. In such a case, for every forgone trade of a pound of pork the farmer could substitute the trade of a pound of mutton and still have two pounds of mutton available for further barter. Thus gains in trade would provide incentives to produce more mutton and less pork, to the benefit of consumers and farmers but to no one's harm. By trades throughout the village and the incentives toward specialization of labor and production processes that minimize resource expenditures and that maximize individual consumer satisfactions, we might expect the village to be brought to an efficient allocation of resources. With an efficient allocation, no further adjustments in production or consumption are possible that advantage some without disadvantaging others.

## 2.4  Economy Efficiency in a Money Economy

The United States economy consists of about 90 million households and about 14 million businesses. At first glance, it may seem that any relationship between the barter economy of an ancient rural village and a modern, complex market economy like that of the United States is far-fetched. In fact, a barter economy consisting only of direct exchanges would be extremely inefficient. Each of us would have to spend time gathering information about the trustworthiness of those with whom we are bartering, the quality of the products being offered, our trading partners' bargaining strength as measured by the amount of goods they have available, and so on. To a large extent, in a money economy, prices gather a large part of this information for us, a topic we discuss in greater detail in chapter 3; in addition, the banking and financial institutions, with their power to issue currency and credit, facilitate indirect exchanges. So, when I buy a dozen eggs at my local supermarket, I indirectly exchange my labor for the eggs, but I don't know, nor will I ever meet, the person who produces the eggs, and that person does not know me. Moreover, I may pay for my eggs with a credit card or by writing a check.

If we imagine our simple barter economy extended to include money and a rudimentary financial system, we see how prices, acting in indirect exchanges, work to bring the economy to economic efficiency. For example, consider again the above case where villagers are individually indifferent between a pound of mutton and pound of pork, but a rearrangement of resources will allow farmers to produce three more pounds of mutton for every pound less of pork. We would expect mutton prices to fall with respect to pork prices because additional mutton could be produced at a relatively small decrease in pork output. This in turn might stimulate increased mutton and decreased pork demand and result in a new equilibrium, with both farmers' income and consumers' satisfaction increased.

Thus in spite of the greater complexity of a modern market economy, we might hope that through the price mechanism and the action of supply and demand, Pareto or economic efficiency would be achieved. The standard theory demonstrates that this will be the case when certain conditions in the economy prevail, for example, when the economy's agents individually have so little effect in markets that they do not significantly influence the prices of either what they produce or what they consume, and when there are no serious impediments to the action of supply and demand.[2]

The theoretical conditions are said to describe a *perfectly competitive economy*. They are often interpreted to mean that, for the perfectly competitive model to have validity, thousands of firms must be competing in a market. This might lead one to conclude that the theory of perfect competition is so unrealistic as to be useless. But laboratory experiments show this to be far too pessimistic a view. In repeatedly replicated experiments, it turns out as few as six to eight firms in a rivalrous situation can lead to the competitive equilibrium predicted by the theory, and rarely are many more firms needed.[3] The perfectly competitive model is thus much more than a theoretical benchmark; it contains predictive power for real-life situations when only a handful of firms are competing with one another.

Finally, note that the perfectly competitive economy exhibits the key efficiency properties of the prisoner-of-war camp economy and the barter economy. The economically efficient allocation of resources is (1) not unique, in part, because (2) the economically efficient allocation depends on the initial endowments of resources held by the individuals in the economy, and (3) efficient allocations do not necessarily accord with intuitive ideas of fairness or justice.

## 2.5   Properties of a Market Economy

In the discussion so far of the ideal market economy, I have stressed economic efficiency because of its importance in the rest of the book. But focusing on efficiency may obscure other properties of a market economy. For example, a modern market economy allows us to make choices, unencumbered by the heavy hand of the state in every economic transaction. The combination of each one of us seeking to promote our self-interest and the action of prices to convey information (we consider this below) and to facilitate trades and exchanges daily leads to millions of Pareto improvements. Buying a week's groceries at our favorite supermarket alone leads to dozens of them. In this way, a market economy moves toward Pareto optimality without its members giving the matter a second's thought—in Adam Smith's famous words, "led by an invisible hand."

Still another important feature of a modern market economy is its ability to efficiently fulfill almost every conceivable customer need. My supermarket is never out of eggs or milk or bread or coffee. At the same time, Tucson, where I live, has no warehouses filled with excesses of these items; rather, there is a continual flow of all of them into Tucson, a flow that is self-calibrated to be as large as necessary, but no larger.

Finally, a modern market economy has built-in incentives for its agents to innovate. For example, when I lived in the East, I had a marvelous idea for an invention—put some funnels holding lime on the two sides of my fertilizer spreader. That way, when I spread fertilizer, the lime deposited from the funnels would make tracks that would show me where I had been, so I would leave no unfertilized areas and would not waste fertilizer by going over the same area twice. When I went to the hardware store to buy the funnels and find ways to attach them to my spreader, the clerk pointed to spreaders on display that had such funnels built into them. My idea had occurred to someone else years before and had been made into a commercial product! This is not an isolated case, and as I write, countless inventors and designers, driven by the self-interest of making a profit are trying to find new market niches, heretofore unexploited, that, when developed, will fill a customer need.

## 2.6   Economic Efficiency and Partial Equilibrium: Consumers' and Producers' Surpluses

Thus far, I have couched our discussion of economic efficiency in what economists call a "general equilibrium" setting. That is, for both the case of a simple barter economy and the case of a modern, complex money economy, we have considered economic efficiency and related matters for the economy as a whole, including both its production and consumption sides and the coordination of these two sides. However, because of its complexity, a full-blown general equilibrium analysis is very hard to do, so hard that many undergraduate economics majors never encounter one and are never exposed to the idea of economic efficiency (economywide Pareto optimality).

Instead, most teaching of undergraduate economics is in a *partial equilibrium* context. The analysis is always of a single market, ignoring the interaction of that market with the rest of the economy or implicitly assuming the interaction to be negligible. In spite of the obvious limitations of partial equilibrium analyses, they are extremely valuable, indeed, they form the bulwark of applied economics. We consider next the partial equilibrium approach to economic efficiency in terms of consumers' and producers' surpluses, starting with the first of these.

Suppose when you went to buy eggs, only one egg per week were available and the weekly purchase of this egg was put up for auction. What would you bid? Perhaps you would bid $10 per week to obtain your weekly egg (you really *love* eggs). Now, suppose your bid wins, but after a few weeks of enjoying your egg, a second egg per week becomes available. You might be willing to bid only $9 per week to obtain a weekly ration of an additional egg. And so it would go. Your *willingness to pay* for a weekly egg would steadily decrease with each extra weekly egg that became available. We can graph this as shown in figure 2.1. The vertical axis shows

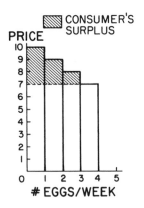

**Figure 2.1**
Willingness to pay for eggs; consumer's surplus

the maximum price that you are willing to pay for a weekly egg, and the horizontal axis the number of weekly eggs that you consume.

Of course, eggs are typically not auctioned off to the highest bidder, but are sold to all who wish to buy them at a uniform price. Suppose this uniform price is $7 per week. Figure 2.1 shows that you would then buy 4 eggs per week. But the important point is that only the last egg had a value to you of $7. All the others had a value in excess of $7. In fact, you would receive an excess or surplus of $10 − $7 = $3 of value on the first egg, a surplus of $9 − $7 = $2 of value on the second egg, and a surplus of $8 − $7 = $1 of value on the third egg, for a total of $3 + $2 + $1 = $6 of surplus value. This total amount of surplus is called the "consumer's surplus". Figure 2.1 represents consumer's surplus by the sum of the areas of the bars above the dotted line at P = $7/week.

A similar situation exists on the producer's side. Presumably, the producer will find it cheapest to produce the first egg, perhaps the additional or *marginal cost* (see next chapter) of the first egg will be $1 per week. The marginal cost of the second egg will be somewhat more, perhaps $2 per week, and so on. Figure 2.2 plots these marginal costs. If the uniform market price is $4 per week, figure 2.2 indicates that the producer will sell 4 eggs per week. But again, the surplus value to the producer will be the amount received for each egg over and above its marginal cost. For the first egg, this surplus value will be $4 − $1 = $3, for the second egg it will be $4 − $2 = $2, for the third egg $4 − $3 = $1, and no surplus value for the fourth egg. The total *producer's surplus* of value will be $3 + $2 + $1 = $6. Figure 2.2 represents the producer's surplus by the sum of the areas of the bars between P = $4/week and the height of the respective marginal costs.

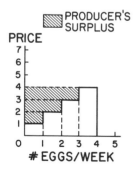

**Figure 2.2**
Marginal cost of eggs; producer's surplus

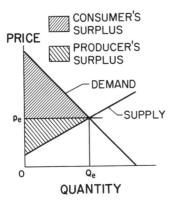

**Figure 2.3**
Consumer's and producer's surplus for continuous demand and supply schedules

The sequence of willingnesses to pay forms the consumer's demand schedule, while the sequence of marginal costs forms the producer's supply schedule. Moreover, to explain the concepts of consumer's and producer's surpluses, I have used an artificial example of eggs, with artificially high prices so that the graphs would be easy to read.

The usual procedure is to abstract even further to consider continuous, rather than discrete, consumption and production and further, to aggregate individual consumer's and producer's surpluses into overall consumers' and producers' surpluses. The demand and supply schedules then become demand and supply *curves*, often depicted as straight lines for conceptual and drawing simplicity. Thus we arrive at figure 2.3, where DEMAND denotes the demand curve, SUPPLY the supply curve, and the indicated triangular areas represent consumers' and producers' surpluses.

The supply and demand curves of figure 2.3 are familiar to anyone who has taken an elementary economics course. If there are no impediments to the workings of the market, as will theoretically be the case in perfect competition, the intersection of the supply and demand curves will determine an equilibrium, called the *perfectly competitive equilibrium*. At this equilibrium, the market price will be $p_e$ and the quantity produced will be $Q_e$, as shown on figure 2.3. Moreover, the equilibrium price will just equal marginal cost, the cost of the last unit produced. In symbols, $p_e = mc$, where $p_e$ is the equilibrium price and $mc$ is the marginal cost. We shall repeatedly refer to this fact throughout this book.

Less familiar but highly significant for our purposes is another fact. When a product is sold at the market price, both the buyers *and* sellers gain, the *buyers* by the amount of the *consumers'* surplus and the *sellers* by the amount of the *producers'* surplus. Thus we see illustrated in another form the basic principle behind economic activity in a free market: all *voluntary* economic transactions are *win-win* or *Pareto-improving*; all parties to them gain or at least do not lose.

## 2.7 Some Caveats

In the paragraphs above I have tried to explain the basic concept of economic efficiency and to stress its importance. Although in my view the material presented represents the current mainstream view of economists, the reader should be aware that some economists stress other concepts and ideas and even use the term *economic efficiency* in different ways. For example, the mainstream view focuses on a static concept, Pareto optimality, wherein the economy has settled into a state where no further win-win or Pareto-improving transactions are possible. This minimizes the dynamic, ever-changing nature of a modern economy, especially its ability to generate inventions, innovations, and technological change.

Schumpeter, a great economist of this century, stressed the dynamic aspect of modern economies, in particular, their continual creation of new products and new methods of production and organization, accompanied by their continual destruction of old ones. Economists who focus on a static aspect of an economy run the danger of doing beautiful work on the wrong problem. Schumpeter (1950, 84) argued that the relevant problem was not how existing structures operate, but how an economy creates and destroys them. A definition of economic efficiency incorporating Schumpeter's ideas has to cope with basic dynamic, rather than static, processes of an economy and with some notion of the efficiency of its creation and destruction of institutions.

Still another view focuses on the apparent ills of society and how they should be remedied. This view argues that once one embraces the mainstream methodologies of economic analysis couched in terms like *economic efficiency* and *Pareto optimality*, one has already slanted the agenda away from what needs to be done to correct society's apparent injustices. In past years, supporters of this view have included numerous Marxists, but this is no longer the case; perhaps other adherents will invent another structure to take the place of the Marxian perspective.

In any event, in spite of alternative views like these, the mainstream of economic analysis and methodology remains intact. The principal technical economic journals are replete with references to Pareto optimality and analyses that attempt to characterize it in a plethora of scenarios. Likewise, the aim of giving new Ph.D.s the methodological tools to continue the mainstream tradition drives graduate training in economics in the leading universities.

**Exercises**

1. *Webster's Ninth New Collegiate Dictionary* defines *efficiency* as "effective operation as measured by a comparison of production with cost (as in energy, time, and money)." Discuss why this definition is inadequate as a definition of efficiency for an entire economy.

2. Discuss the concept of economic efficiency. Include a discussion of the strengths and weaknesses of this concept from the point of view of the policy maker.

3. What is wrong with the statement "Pareto optimality in consumption and in production means that the economy as a whole is in a Pareto-optimal state"?

4. Describe consumer's and producer's surpluses.

# 3                                More Economic Concepts

*Prices are the scouts and guides for resources as they seek their highest valued uses.*
Anonymous

## 3.1   Costs and Choice, Planning

Conceivably, in a money economy we could agree to use only the word "price" and never use the word "cost." After all, doesn't the word "cost" simply mean the price that a buyer pays for something? Why do we need both words? We need both because "cost" typically embodies not only "what you paid for it" but some consideration of choice. Except for routine items like coffee, milk, bread, and so forth, that you may buy daily at the same store, choosing the same brands, you probably gave some thought to what you bought. You made a choice from among several alternatives.

Economists have developed a vocabulary to characterize not only what you paid for something but some property of the choice that you made before you paid for it. The vocabulary consists of the word "cost" modified by some adjective. For example, there is the term *marginal cost*. What is the element of choice embodied in this term? It refers to the cost of the last unit that a producer made. For one thing, the cost of this unit doesn't appear unless the producer chooses to make it. Further, in a perfectly competitive market, the producer will choose to continue producing until the cost of the last unit—its *marginal cost* just equals the prevailing price.

By the way, the term *marginal* embodies a notion of choice that goes beyond cost. In the discussion of trades, in both the prisoner-of-war camp example and the example of a barter economy, I had the economy's agents trading until the last trade exhausted all possibilities of mutual gain through trade. At this point, a Pareto-optimal equilibrium had set in. An economist would say that the agents traded until the marginal or last trade exhausted all possible gains through trade. Alternatively, the economist might say that trades continued until, *at the margin*, all gains through trade had been exhausted. We'll encounter *at the margin* a number of times throughout this book.

Other frequently used terms are *short-run cost* and *long-run cost*. The former refers to alternatives that are in your choice set now; the latter to alternatives that will eventually be in your choice set. For example, you may be stuck with a twenty-year lease for the store out of which you operate your business. Your lease payments do not enter into your current business decisions; unless you declare bankruptcy, or your landlord wants to buy you out, or some other unforseen event happens, there is nothing you can do about them. Of course, eventually you will have to consider whether or not to renew the lease. On the other hand, how many employees you hire is something under your present control, as is the amount that you spend on advertising. Your leasing expenses are *long-run costs*; your employee and advertising expenses are *short-run costs*.

Still another useful term is *opportunity cost*. To illustrate it, suppose that Robinson Crusoe and Friday are stranded on a desert island that only has mango trees. Crusoe and Friday have only two sources of food—fish and mangoes—which they obtain through their own labor. There is a trade-off between the production of fish and mangoes. Crusoe and Friday can devote all of their energies to producing fish, which, if they work as efficiently as they can, will yield them 50 fish a week. Or they can devote all of their energies to producing mangoes, with a maximum yield of 150 mangoes per week. Or, they can divide their energies between fish and mango production to get something in between. Figure 3.1 depicts the result.

The curve shown in figure 3.1 is called "the production possibilities frontier" or PPF. It is the boundary of all the fish-mangoes production possibilities attainable by the Crusoe-Friday economy when the economy is at Pareto optimality in production. All of the points within the shaded area below the PPF are attainable, while all of the points above the PPF are unattainable.

Suppose now that Crusoe and Friday are producing at point P, below the PPF and thus within the attainable region. At this point, a Pareto improvement is possible. They don't have to give up the production of mangoes to produce more fish; by rearranging the amount of time each devotes to producing mangoes and fish, Crusoe and Friday can increase the output of both. In colloquial terms, there is a free lunch in this economy. However,

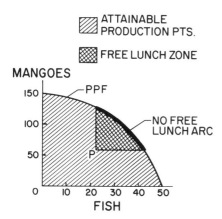

Figure 3.1
Free lunch zone within the production possibilities frontier

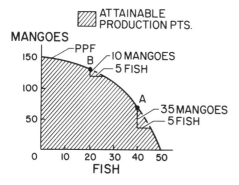

Figure 3.2
Opportunity cost on the production possibilities frontier

starting at point P, they can capitalize on their free lunch opportunity only until they reach the "no free lunch arc" on the PPF.

Once they are on the PPF, Crusoe and Friday can produce more of mangoes only by producing less of fish, or the reverse, as shown in figure 3.2. For example, at point A in figure 3.2, the economy has to forgo the production of 35 mangoes in order to increase its fish production by 5. In economists' jargon, the opportunity cost of 5 fish is 35 mangoes. On the other hand, at point B in figure 3.2, the economy has to forgo only 10 mangoes in order to produce 5 more fish. The opportunity cost of 5 fish is then 10 mangoes; as fish production decreases, so does the opportunity cost of the 5 fish.

In a nutshell, opportunity cost is simply a forgone benefit. The concept reflects the popular saying, "there is no free lunch." Resources are always finite and limited. This means that free lunches—Pareto improvements or win-win trades—will ultimately be exhausted, and economic activities must ultimately face a resource constraint. At that point, to get something, the economy or individuals in it will have to forgo something else.

Finally, note that as soon as we entertain choice among alternatives, we are planning. And, in a market economy, all sorts of planning goes on, starting at the level of the household and individual firm. If we are going to talk about policy, especially at the level of local or federal government, we must factor in planning. In economists' jargon, this means that *future costs* are relevant. Which is to say, bygones are bygones and are of interest only insofar as they affect the future. Thus, if gasoline prices next year are expected to be $1.50/gallon, truckers will act differently from how they would act if they expected gasoline prices to be $1/gallon. And they couldn't care less what gasoline prices were last year.

As obvious as this fact is, we find that regulatory and governmental policy has a difficult time coping with it. Policy that must take costs into account must be able to resist attack, which drives it to be based on concrete numbers. Past and present costs can be determined by consulting the accounting department; future ones are speculative and a matter of opinion. So it is that, distressingly often, we find policy decisions made with exquisite precision, but based on past costs. This is fine if historic costs accurately predict future costs, but if historic costs are poor predictors of future costs, such policy decisions may be based on foundations of sand.

## 3.2  Fixed, Variable, and Sunk Costs

In this book we shall have occasion to use the notions of fixed and variable costs, and it is important to understand the difference. *Fixed costs* are costs that do *not* vary with the quantity produced; *variable costs* are costs that *do* vary with the quantity produced. Thus, in order to operate an airline, I must buy or lease an airplane. I must bear the purchase or lease cost of the airplane regardless of the number of passengers I carry, and this represents a fixed cost. On the other hand, there are expenses, such as those of providing meals, handling luggage, and issuing tickets, that will depend on the number of passengers that my airline carries. These are variable costs.

Another important cost concept is reflected in the term *sunk cost*. This is an expenditure that, once made, cannot be recouped. Ordinary operating expenses, such as electricity, heat, and employees' wages are sunk costs, as is the cost of an asset that becomes obsolete and cannot be sold to anyone else. On the other hand, if there is a ready secondhand market for an asset, only a portion of its purchase price will represent a sunk cost. If one is fortunate, one may acquire an asset that does not lose its market value at all, or that may even appreciate in value over time. At certain periods in history, Steinway pianos have had this property, as have diamonds and paintings by well-known artists. The outlay for such an asset is not a sunk cost.

## 3.3   Prices as Carriers of Information in a Market Economy

I AM A LEAD PENCIL ... And, ... I am a mystery.

*Not a single person on the face of this earth knows how to make me.*
My family tree begins with a cedar of straight grain that grows in Northern California and Oregon. Now contemplate all the saws and trucks and rope and countless other gear used in harvesting and carting the cedar logs ... Think of all the persons and the numberless skills that went into their fabrication: the mining of ore, the making of steel and its refinement into saws, axes, motors, ... Why untold thousands of persons had a hand in every cup of coffee the loggers drink!

... The cedar logs are cut into small, pencil-length slats less than one-fourth of an inch in thickness.... Once in the pencil factory ... each slat is given eight grooves by a complex machine, after which another machine lays leads in every other slat, applies glue, and places another slat on top ...

My "lead" itself ... is complex. The graphite is mined in Ceylon.... [It] is mixed with clay from Mississippi ... Then wetting agents are added such as sulfonated tallow—animal fats chemically reacted with sulfuric acid.... To increase their strength and smoothness the leads are then treated with a hot mixture which includes candelilla wax from Mexico.

My cedar receives six coats of lacquer. Do you know all of the ingredients of lacquer? My bit of metal—the ferrule—is made of brass ... Those black rings on my ferrule are black nickel. What is black nickel and how is it applied? The complete story ... would take pages to explain.

Then there is my crowning glory, ... "the plug," the part man uses to erase the errors he makes with me. An ingredient called "factice" is what does the erasing. It is ... made by reacting rape seed oil from the Dutch East Indies with sulfur chloride.

Does anyone wish to challenge my earlier assertion that no single person on the face of this earth knows how to make me?

There is a fact still more astounding: The absence of a master mind, of anyone dictating or forcibly directing these countless actions which bring me into being. No trace of such a person can be found. Instead, we find the Invisible Hand at work. This is the mystery to which I earlier referred.

— Leonard E. Read, "I, Pencil: My Family Tree"

Leonard E. Read's famous "I, Pencil" (1958) dramatically illustrates a point stressed by Hayek (1945) in an even more famous paper. Knowledge is extensive and diffuse; each of us knows only a minuscule fraction of all knowledge. Yet, in a market economy, the immense amount of knowledge that is needed to make something as simple as an ordinary lead pencil is brought together through the action of prices.

If the price is right, there will be a demand for iron ore to feed steel furnaces to produce the steel that produces saws. If the price is right, the saws will be bought by lumber mills in the Northwest. If the price is right, these saws will be used to cut the cedar trees that are needed in lead pencils, and so on. The steel maker doesn't care what the saws are going to be used for, nor does the saw maker care about how the cedar logs will be used.

At each stage in the process of making a lead pencil, economic agents have access to, and, most important, have *need* for only a limited amount of information—what their suppliers are charging or apt to charge, what their customers are willing to pay, the prices of rival products, and so on. Likewise, in a market economy, the limited amount of information possessed by each economic agent suffices to direct resources to their highest-valued uses.

If, for example, workers mining iron ore go on a prolonged strike that raises the price of iron ore, this will increase the price of steel, which will increase the price of saws, the price of cedar logs, and so forth, all the way to increasing the price of a lead pencil. The buyers of lead pencils know only that the price has risen. They aren't interested in why, and, even if they were, they might have a hard time tracing back the cause of the price rise. But the price rise will curtail the demand for pencils, which in turn will curtail the demand for intermediate products, back to the curtailment of demand for iron ore. If the miners' strike continues indefinitely, the economy will adjust and come to a new equilibrium, with substitute products produced.

Thus two principal functions of prices in a market economy are to be carriers of information and to direct resources to their highest-valued uses. Centralized, command and control economies learned this lesson the hard way. They tried to replace the information-carrying and resource-directing function of prices by an army of bureaucrats. The army wasn't big enough and quickly developed its own agendas. The replacement system simply did not work.

Unfortunately, it's still the case that only trained economists seem fully to appreciate the information-carrying and resource-directing functions of prices. In the regulated sector this may make it difficult to mobilize prices to carry out their role. An example is charging for "directory assistance" telephone calls (calls to the information operator). Until the 1970s such calls were "free"—there was no explicit charge for them. Of course, the directory assistance service consumed resources, which had to be paid for from general telephone revenues. At the beginning of the 1970s the costs for local directory assistance services were growing at about three times the growth of most other costs of providing telephone service.[1] Levying an explicit charge for such calls was an obvious way to curtail this cost. But telephone company executives found it very difficult to persuade regulators and consumer groups that such a charge was not an underhanded way for Bell to make extraordinary profits. Finally, a trial demonstration was arranged in Cincinnati. In the trial the first three directory assistance calls were free; thereafter, each call was charged $0.20. The result was a reduction in the number of directory assistance calls from 80,000 to 20,000 per month. Further, it was found that only 6 percent of subscribers made more than three directory assistance calls per month. As a result of the charge, residential customers saved an average of $0.65 and business customers an average of $1.25 on their monthly phone bills. The Cincinnati trial demonstration started a chain reaction, and, one after the other, regulatory authorities throughout the United States instituted charges for local directory assistance, with most adopting a similar plan—three calls without charge, subsequent calls at a small charge.[2]

## 3.4 Opportunity Cost of Capital, Accounting and Economic Profit, and Barriers to Entry and Exit

So far we have concentrated on prices and costs faced by the individual consumer, household, or firm. In order to analyze the profitability of firms, we must also consider (1) what we mean by a firm's "profit," and (2) the conditions of entry into or exit out of the industry where the firm operates.

Opportunity Cost of Capital, Accounting and Economic Profit

Suppose your aunt has died and left you $100,000. Your first impulse is simply to invest your inheritance in U.S. Treasury bills, which pay 5 percent interest, for a total of $5,000/year. But you soon change your mind and invest it in a McDonald's franchise instead. At the end of the first year of operation your profit and loss statement looks like this:

| Revenues:          | $1,000,000 |
|--------------------|-----------:|
| Operating Expenses: | 997,500   |
| Profit             | 2,500      |

Your accountant informs you that you will have to pay federal taxes on your "profit" of $2,500.

Economists call the "profit" so calculated the "accounting profit" from your business. Why the adjective "accounting"? Because this is what appears on your firm's books of account and is what the IRS bases taxes on. However, you could have earned $5,000 by investing your inheritance in treasury bills. In other words, there was an opportunity cost associated with your decision to invest your capital in a McDonald's franchise. In the view of economists, this *opportunity cost of capital* is just as real as the costs of electricity, rent, employee's wages, and the like and should be subtracted from the accounting profit to determine your real profit, what economists call your "economic profit." Thus, we define

economic profit = accounting profit − opportunity cost of capital

In this case, although your accounting profit is $2,500 and you have to pay taxes on it, your *economic profit* is

$$\$5,000 - \$2,500 = -\$2,500,$$

and, in reality, you have lost money.

Note what happens if your firm makes *zero* economic profit. This means that your accounting profit is exactly equal to the opportunity cost of the capital that you have invested. In other terms, your accounting profit is then what you would expect to earn on your money investing it in the best available alternative. It is what you would normal expect to make, and, for this reason, economists sometimes refer to a zero economic profit as a "normal economic profit" and to anything more than a zero economic profit as a "supernormal economic profit."

Barriers to Entry and/or Exit

An important concept is that of barriers to entry and/or exit. Generally speaking, an incumbent firm, one that is already in a business, likes to keep other firms from entering into the same business. How can it do this? Here are some of the ways:

- Get patents, copyrights, or trade secrets
- Mobilize economies of scale, that is, decrease average costs by operating at a bigger size
- Get the government to regulate your industry, with regulations that allow no other firms to enter
- Develop a superior technology that takes a long time to imitate
- Develop superior marketing and advertising strategies
- Be in a business where "learning by doing" is important, in other words, work down the learning cost curve before anyone has a chance to enter your business
- Be in a business where it will be expensive for your customers to switch from you to another vendor

These are all *barriers to entry* that you might erect to keep other firms from encroaching on your business.

As an incumbent firm, you may also face *barriers to exit* should you wish to go out of business. Some of these are

- costs of discharging employees should your firm's regulations call for separation payments
- cost of selling assets
- regulatory costs (e.g., in some states, the costs of getting an environmental inspection to certify that you have not buried toxic substances on your property)

The standard assumption in economics is that if a firm enjoys no barriers to entry and/or exit, it will not be able to sustain large profits. Why? Because it will be costless for a rival to enter the firm's business and offer the same product at a lower price. The incumbent will then have to respond by lowering *its* price and so on. The result will be that neither the incum bent nor the rival is making money. At best, each will earn the opportuni cost of its capital—what it must pay in interest charges on the money it borrowed from lenders or its stockholders in order to go into business. In economists' jargon, in equilibrium, both the firm and its rival will operate at *zero economic profit*.

But barriers to entry or exit make the firm do more than respond to rivals after they appear. The firm must anticipate possible rivals, which brings us to the concept of contestability.

## 3.5   Contestable Markets

A business person's nightmare—one that can easily lead to paranoia—is that suddenly, out of nowhere, will spring a rival firm that can offer the same product or a close substitute at lower prices, higher quality, better service, and so forth, and thus take away all of the market. The businessman who has seen his firm flourish and decides to rest on his laurels does so at his peril. He must continually ask himself questions like Can a rival duplicate my technology? Can a clever engineer invent around my patents and duplicate my product at my cost or even less? Is my market vulnerable to a slightly more expensive, but much higher quality product, or a slightly lower quality but much cheaper product? and so on. He must not only worry about present rival firms, ones that he probably has carefully studied and carefully keeps track of, but also *potential* rivals. In a word, he must worry whether or not the barriers to entry that he has erected around his business will keep out not only the rivals that he knows about but the ones that he doesn't know about.

By the same token, firms that are contemplating entering new markets, already occupied by well-established firms, will consider carefully the probabilities of success, should they enter, and the cost of entering and then having to exit, should their attempt to enter be a failure. The ideal case is one where the potential entrant has nothing to lose. The firm can invest to enter a new market, try its luck, and if it is unsuccessful, recoup all of its investment and withdraw without loss. In the current jargon, such a market is called a "perfectly contestable market." Baumol, Panzar, and Willig (1982), the inventors of the concept of contestability, characterize a perfectly contestable market as one that is vulnerable to costless hit-and-run entry and exit.

Of course, no real market is perfectly contestable, and perfect contestability is a theoretical construct. Nevertheless, many markets requiring only a small entry and/or exit cost approximate a perfectly contestable market. As is the case with most theoretical constructs in economics or science, that the theoretical ideal is not realized does not diminish its importance.

A consequence of the contestability notion has been to focus attention on the importance of sunk costs in determining whether or not a market is a "natural monopoly." The earlier notion was that economies of scale were the determinative factor—with sufficient economies of scale, the largest firm would have a cost advantage, drive rivals off the scene, and occupy the entire market.

In turn, the basis of economies of scale was large fixed costs. To be efficient, a power generating station had to be of a minimum size, and the entire cost of constructing the station had to be borne before the first kilowatt-hour was generated. The higher the output, the lower the firm's average costs, and unless a rival could capture more than half the incumbent's market, the rival was doomed to have higher average costs and thus be forced to charge higher prices. Thus the market was a "natural monopoly," most efficiently served by a single provider.

The cost of a jumbo jet is also large and must be borne by a nascent airline before it carries its first passenger; there are obviously large economies to scale in airline passenger carriage. But airlines are not natural monopolies. What is the difference?

Imagine that both the power company and the airline lose all of their customers. Perhaps a deep recession has hit both the community where the power company is situated and the communities served by the airline. Suppose only a small fraction of the generating station's equipment can be sold, the buildings housing them have limited resale value, and the transmission lines and poles have only scrap value. Suppose, on the other hand, that there is an active resale market for jumbo jets, as is presently the case. The airline might then be able to recover almost all of its cost. In the case of an established power company, the full costs of a round trip—entry followed by exit—would be carefully considered by any potential entrant. Only if the profit opportunities were sufficient to cover them in a reasonably short period of time would entry occur, and we would rarely expect to see this. On the other hand, if the high resale value of jumbo jets made the round-trip costs small, we might expect to see relatively frequent entries of new airlines. In fact, we do.

The crucial difference then is the magnitude of the round-trip, *sunk* costs. Where these are large, we can expect little potential for entry, the possibility of the incumbent reaping monopoly profits, and a case to be made for government regulation. By contrast, where the round-trip sunk costs are small, even if economies of scale are substantial and a single provider minimizes costs, there may be little need for governmental regulation. The single provider who would reap large monopoly profits can expect entry in short order.[3]

## Exercises

1. Why does the term *cost* mean something more than "what you paid for it"?

2. Discuss the terms *marginal cost, opportunity cost, long-run cost,* and *short-run cost.*

3. Discuss the role of prices as carriers of information in a market economy.

4. Name some barriers to entry and exit.

5. What is a perfectly contestable market?

6. Discuss the roles of fixed and sunk costs in determining whether or not a market is contestable.

# 4  Externalities and Public Goods

*Walk down any street and you will be confronted with a vast number of external effects: the pleasing sight of a well-kept garden—the noise of children playing—exhaust fumes from passing cars—the smell of cooking—a pretty girl passing by—the roar of traffic— canine deposits underfoot—the jostle of the crowd—advertisements on billboards ... — and so on.*

John Burton

## 4.1  The Idea of an Externality

You buy season tickets to the theater. When you attend the first performance, you find that, luckily for you, the seats directly in front of you are occupied by very short people, and you have a particularly good, unobstructed view. Unfortunately, at the next performance, seated directly in front of you is a 6'9" person, who blocks your view. You have to tilt your head to one side throughout the performance, and you go home with a stiff neck. If only the short people had also subscribed for the entire season!

These are examples of *externalities*. In the case of short people occupying the seats in front you, you benefited from a *positive externality*; in the case of the 6'9" person seated in front of you, you suffered the consequences of a *negative externality*. In this chapter we briefly consider the fundamental theory of externalities and the related theory of public goods.

## 4.2  Basic Theory of Externalities

From an economic point of view, what is significant about the examples of your obstructed and unobstructed view in the theater? First of all, you had no control over who sat in front of you. You entered into an economic transaction with the producers of the performance, perhaps picking out the seat that you wanted, but something outside of your choice set, the person in front of you, either imposed a cost or conferred a benefit on you. Second, the cost or benefit was not the result of any market transaction that you entered into. For example, when you purchased your ticket, suppose you had access to a list of all those who had already purchased a seat, together with their respective heights? You could then have contacted the supertall person who had purchased the seat in front of you and offered to pay him or her to purchase another seat. But that opportunity was unavailable, and you had to accept whatever seating fate had assigned.

In the economy positive and negative externalities abound in both consumption and production. In addition to those of the quote at the beginning of this chapter, some examples are

*Consumption:* Neighbors' dogs bark and keep you awake; a fidgety child in the seat next to you makes your airplane trip miserable; the division of your favorite restaurant into smoking and nonsmoking sections greatly reduces the burden on your asthma and finally makes dining the pleasure it is for most people.

*Production:* Manufacturing firms pollute a river and reduce the fish available to fisheries located downstream; a rancher's cattle break through a fence and eat the neighboring farmer's wheat crop; an orchard's neighbor is a beekeeper whose bee's pollinate the fruit, to the benefit of both.

What effect do externalities have on economic efficiency? From the above discussion, one would suspect that the issue of control will loom large in the answer. This is indeed the case, as we can see from a simple example—a rancher whose cattle stray into the neighboring farmer's land and graze on his emerging wheat crop.

Assume that the rancher's land is only marginally able to sustain his cattle. He thus gets a lot of benefit from one of his cattle grazing on the farmer's land, since this frees up some of his own land for the remaining cows. However, the benefit is less for the second cow that strays, and still less from each additional cow that strays. Finally, if six cows stray over, the seventh will follow the herd and also stray over to join a crowd in grazing on less nourishing land than the ranch, and the benefit to the rancher of the seventh stray cow is negative.

Likewise, assume that the cost to the farmer of the first stray cow is not too much, but as the number of cows eating the wheat sprouts increase, the likelihood of their germination decreases. As a result, the marginal cost to

**Table 4.1**
Benefits and costs of rancher's cows grazing on farmer's land

| No. of cows | $TNB_R$ | $TD_F$ | $MNB_F$ | $MD_F$ | SB |
|---|---|---|---|---|---|
| 0 | 0 | 0 | 0 | 0 | 0 |
| 1 | 50 | 10 | 50 | 10 | 40 |
| 2 | 90 | 30 | 40 | 20 | 60 |
| 3 | 120 | 59 | 30 | 29 | 61 |
| 4 | 140 | 99 | 20 | 40 | 41 |
| 5 | 150 | 148 | 10 | 49 | 2 |
| 6 | 152 | 205 | 2 | 57 | −53 |
| 7 | 145 | 240 | −7 | 35 | −95 |

the farmer of each additional stray cow increases with the number of strays. This gives us the data in table 4.1. That is, if there is only one cow that could graze on the farmer's land, it would realize a total net benefit ($TNB_R$ = revenues minus costs) of \$50/year to the rancher, while doing \$10/year total damage to the farmer ($TD_F$). If we think of the rancher and farmer as forming a "minisociety," then the first cow would yield a social benefit (SB) of \$40/year (last column, table 4.1), consisting of its \$50/year benefit to the rancher less its \$10/year damage to the farmer ($TNB_R$ − $TD_F$). With two cows the rancher would realize a total net benefit of \$90/year, and thus, a marginal net benefit ($MNB_R$) for the second cow of \$90 − \$50 = \$40. At the same time, the total damage to the farmer would increase to \$30/year, with a corresponding marginal damage to the farmer ($MD_F$) for the second cow of \$20, and the social benefit (SB) of two cows would be $SB = TNB_R − TD_F = \$90 − \$30 = \$60$.

We see from table 4.1 that the social benefit of cows to this minisociety reaches a maximum of \$61/year at 3 cows; ideally, this is the number of cows this society should have. Will the rancher choose to buy 3 cows? It depends. Consider three different scenarios:

*Scenario I* The rancher is unambiguously liable and, should his cows graze on the farmer's wheat land, the rancher will have to reimburse the farmer for the damage that they cause. In this case, in computing the net benefit of his cows, the rancher will have to take into account the damages he will have to pay to the farmer. The rancher's net benefit becomes the same as the social benefit; the rancher will buy three cows, the socially optimal number, for a net benefit of \$61, and pay the farmer \$59 for the damage that they do to his crop.

*Scenario II* The rancher is unambiguously *not* liable. So every time the rancher contemplates the purchase of still another cow, the farmer decides to try to bribe him to prevent the purchase. The farmer first offers a $10/year bribe, the damage done by a single cow, to keep the rancher from buying the first cow. The rancher refuses because the benefit of $50/year of his first cow well exceeds the $10 bribe. When the rancher contemplates buying a second cow, the farmer offers a $20/year bribe, the amount of damage of a second cow. Again the rancher refuses, because to him the benefit of the second cow is $40/year, and so on, with the farmer unsuccessfully offering a $29 bribe to prevent the rancher's purchase of a third cow. Finally, the farmer is able to keep the rancher from buying his fourth cow by offering a $40/year bribe. Because the fourth cow is only worth an additional benefit of $20/year to the rancher, the rancher accepts. The bargaining is concluded; the outcome is again the social optimum of 3 cows.

*Scenario III* The farmer and the rancher consult lawyers and find that the law is ambiguous as to the rancher's liability. The rancher's lawyer tells the rancher that, although the results of litigation can never be guaranteed, the rancher has a good chance of winning a law suit and being able to graze six cows, which as table 4.1 shows, yields the rancher the maximum benefit of 152. The farmer's lawyer tells the farmer that, although the results of litigation can never be guaranteed, the farmer has a good chance of winning if he sues to prevent any rancher's cows from grazing on the farmer's land. Presented with the evidence—the alternatives of zero or six cows advocated by the farmer and the rancher, the benefits to the rancher, and the costs to the farmer—the legal process ends up splitting the difference. The rancher is allowed to graze 3 cows but must pay the farmer the damages that they cause. The rancher's legal costs alone turn out to be much more than his cost had he simply paid the farmer for the damage his cows caused. Likewise, the farmer ends up paying much more in legal fees than if he had simply bribed the rancher to keep the cows off of his land.

Thus, in both scenarios I and II, where the rancher is either unambiguously liable or not liable, we get the socially or economically efficient outcome. However, in scenario III, where liability is ambiguous, we get an uncertain outcome and the possibility of large transactions costs, borne by both the rancher and the farmer.

This example typifies the economic situation when externalities are present. In scenario III no one was in charge, so to speak, of preventing damage to the farmer's wheat crop. The rancher felt no responsibility for the damage; the farmer felt that the law should be on his side, and made no attempt to bribe the rancher. Strict liability assigned to the rancher evoked the socially optimal outcome, but as morally repugnant as it may seem, so did a lack of liability and the farmer's willingness to bribe.

In scenario III property rights were not clearly specified, whereas in scenarios I and II they were. This is a general finding of the literature on externalities, usually referred to as "Coase's theorem"[1]: *When property rights are unambiguous and clearly specified and there are no transactions costs, unencumbered markets can be expected to generate economically efficient outcomes, even in the presence of externalities.*

## 4.3   Some Further Insights

By examining the example in more detail, we can get some further insights about externalities.

Income Effects of Different Property Rights Assignments

Although different assignments of property rights can lead to efficient outcomes, even the same efficient outcome as in the example, the income consequences can be quite different. For instance, assume that both the rancher and farmer have incomes of $100/year. Then, scenarios I and II have the income consequences shown in table 4.2, where $R$ stands for "rancher" and $F$ for "farmer." In scenario I the rancher's income is reduced to $41/year while the farmer's income increases to $159/year, but their combined income remains at $200/year. In scenario II, the rancher's income is increased to $140/year, the farmer's is reduced to $60/year, but again, their combined income remains at $200/year. From the point of view of their minisociety, the payments from the rancher to the farmer are a wash; they are transfer payments, important only in that they facilitate the attainment of economic efficiency.

**Table 4.2**
Income effects of scenarios I, II, and III

|             | $R$ | $F$ | $R + F$ |
|-------------|-----|-----|---------|
| Scenario I  | 41  | 159 | 200     |
| Scenario II | 140 | 60  | 200     |

Internalization of Externalities

Suppose the rancher buys out the farmer to form a single entity, RF Inc. How many cows will the new entity buy? Table 4.1 makes it clear that RF Inc. will buy 3 cows; its profit is the social benefit when the rancher and farmer were separate entities, which reaches a maximum of $61/year at three cows. The merging of the rancher and farmer into one unit eliminates the externality problem; what were formerly social benefits become RF Inc.'s private benefits. In economists' jargon, the externality problem has been *internalized*.

Note we assumed that the rancher bought out the farmer, but we could equally well have assumed the reverse, that the farmer bought out the rancher, or that they formed a partnership. What's important from the standpoint of internalizing the externalities is that they form a single unit, but merger is not the only way to achieve internalization. In fact, the farmer's willingness to bribe can be viewed as another way. And of course the bribe needn't be a blatant money payment. The farmer could offer to help the rancher by lending him equipment, by contributing labor to the building of his barn, or in a myriad number of other ways, all of which can serve to internalize the externality of the rancher's cattle eating the farmer's wheat sprouts.

Information Effects

The example implicitly assumed a particular information structure—what the rancher knew and what the farmer knew. Different information structures yield different outcomes. For instance, scenario II implicitly assumed that the farmer knew only his damages and not the rancher's detailed schedule of benefits. At each stage, the farmer's proffered bribe was his marginal damages from an additional cow. If, instead, the farmer knew that the fourth cow would bring the rancher only an additional $20/year benefit, the farmer would offer the rancher $21/year rather than $40/year to forgo its benefit. But whether the rancher accepted would depend on whether he knew that the farmer was willing to pay a bribe as large as $40/year. And so on.

Transactions Costs

To illustrate ideas, we assumed in scenarios I and II that all transactions were costless; in reality, this would be far from the case. A bribe in kind rather than money can be expensive; the farmer could lend the rancher equipment only to find it improperly maintained or otherwise abused. Should any litigation be involved in reaching an outcome, transactions costs can be enormous, as scenario III brings out. The costs of transactions can vary widely with the form of property rights assignments adopted and can greatly influence outcomes. Most importantly, rather than being a sideshow in a controversy, transactions costs can occupy center stage. For this reason, some economists feel that Coase's work on externalities was important mainly because it drew attention to the economic role of transactions costs.

Pigovian Taxes

In response to numerous farmers' complaints, suppose the town fathers decide to tax ranchers' cattle as a way of preventing the ranchers' creation of negative externalities. If every rancher-farmer pair had exactly the same benefit and damage schedules, then the tax ought to be $21/year. This would just be enough to give the ranchers the proper incentives to forgo their fourth cows. The idea of levying a tax in order to prevent negative externalities was proposed at the beginning of this century by the British economist A. C. Pigou; such a tax is often called a "Pigovian tax."

Pigovian taxes suffer from at least three problems. First is the information problem of knowing how large to make the tax. As the example shows, either too small or too large a tax will result in a nonoptimal provision of the externality. Second, because a Pigovian tax is morally based (it's supposed to prevent "bad" things from happening), it may be inefficient. Finally, Pigovian taxes introduce a third party to the transactions—the governmental entity that is to receive the tax. This immediately means that any investigation of efficiency consequences must consider the government as well as the original parties. For example, what happens to the tax that is collected? Who benefits from it?

For instance, suppose in our example, the farmer's land is such that he can easily fence off part of it for $15, while the rest of it, which is very difficulty to fence in, has a capacity for only 3 cows. If the farmer builds his fence, three of the rancher's cows will end up grazing on his land—the socially optimum number. At the same time, assume that if a tax of $21 is levied, the $21 will simply be dissipated in bureaucratic waste. If the government did nothing, and the farmer had no recourse, he would presumably build the fence. The social cost would be his cost—$15. However, a Pigovian tax to do the same thing would have a social cost of $21, which would be dissipated in waste. From society's viewpoint, doing nothing is cheaper, and more efficient, than taxing the rancher to force him to do the morally right thing.

Obviously, the farmer might disagree with the argument that his paying $15 is the socially efficient outcome. The farmer might even complain bitterly of how unjust and morally repugnant is the very notion that the farmer should pay anything at all to protect the farmer's crops from the rancher's destructive cattle. But this again illustrates an important point that we considered briefly in chapter 2 and that we consider in more detail in part II: what is economically efficient is not necessarily what most people would consider to be just.

## 4.4  Public Goods

A consumption externality may benefit or harm more than one person. Both the farmer and rancher "consumed" the wheat crop; when your neighbor's dog barks, both you and the neighbor "consume" the barking; when someone at the next table in a restaurant smokes, both you and the smoker "consume" the smoke, and so forth. A limiting case of a consumption externality is a *public good*, a good consumed collectively by a large number of people.

Examples of a public good are national defense, police protection, the court system, parks, and lighthouses. For example, once a lighthouse is built to serve a particular ship, it is available for all ships that can see it.

What are the properties of a good that make it into a public good? There are two; a *public good* is (1) nonexcludable and (2) nondepletable. So it is not possible to exclude ships that want to use a lighthouse from using it, and if ship A benefits from using it, this doesn't reduce the lighthouse's benefit to ship B. By contrast, a *private good* is both excludable and depletable. If I buy an apple, I can exclude others from eating it; once I eat part of it, that part has been depleted and is unavailable for someone else to eat.

Because the number of people who benefit from a public good is typically very large and they cannot be excluded from benefiting from the public good, the problem of divergence between private and collective benefits becomes particularly difficult. For example, the benefits that a particular ship obtains from a lighthouse may not justify the lighthouse's cost. If this is true for all ships, no one will have an incentive to build it. Each ship will have an incentive to urge the other ships to build the lighthouse and then to free ride—to take advantage of the fact that it cannot be excluded from using the lighthouse.

The free rider problem results in many public goods being financed by taxes, and public goods are one of the primary justifications for having a taxation system.

## Exercises

1. Give an example of a consumption externality and a production externality.

2. When property rights are unambiguous and clearly specified, what effect will externalities have on the efficiency of market outcomes?

3. When externalities are present, discuss
a. income effects of different assignments of property rights
b. the internalization of externalities
c. information effects
d. effects of transactions costs
e. Pigovian taxes

4. What two properties characterize a pure public good?

5. What is meant by the notion of free riding in the consumption of public goods?

# 5                             On Firms (Private or Public Organizations)

*Heaven forbid that students should cease to read books on the science of public or business administration—provided only that these works are classified as fiction.*

C. Northcote Parkinson, *Parkinson's Law*

## 5.1    The Size of Organizations

We live in a society of many corporations, each organized into a hierarchy. At the top is a president, chairman of the board, or chief executive officer. Reporting to him or her are various vice presidents, reporting to them are heads of departments or divisions, and so on, down to the ordinary worker at the bottom. This structure is not confined to for-profit corporations, but exists in nonprofit organizations, as well as in governmental agencies, and in the military. We might characterize it as a hierarchical, command-and-control organizational form. But, for brevity, throughout this book, I use the label "firm" to denote it.

Why are there firms? Why isn't every economic activity simply offered by individuals? We are so used to living in an economy organized into firms that questions like these don't occur to us. But they occurred to Ronald Coase, and his answers were part of the reason he was awarded the 1991 Nobel Prize in economics.

In the United States, Europe, and Japan, not only are firms common, but so are giant varieties of them, firms that employ many tens of thousand of employees. But outside of the military and parts of the government, giant organizations of this size are a recent phenomenon, dating back only to the end of the last century. Why have we only recently seen the emergence of such large hierarchical but nonmilitary organizations in a market economy? And why do we have large governmental organizations, such as the main departments in the U.S. government, some of which contain more than

100,000 employees? We consider questions like these in this chapter, starting with Coase's (1937) seminal work.

## 5.2   Ronald Coase on the Nature of the Firm

Coase's article, written in 1937, consists of a series of observations. The first observation, which is implicit and seemingly trivial, but crucial, is that a firm is itself an economy. Once one makes this observation, it is natural to compare this form of an economy with a market economy. This is essentially what Coase does in the remainder of his article, making six further observations:

1. Unlike in a market economy, the price mechanism does not coordinate the economy within a firm. Factors of production—labor, materials, cash flows—do not move in response to price changes. For example, in Tucson we have many freelance carpenters, who bid their services to get jobs on whatever construction projects are in progress or in the offing. The going prices for carpenters influence how much they bid, and, in turn, their bid influences these prices. At the University of Arizona we have carpenters who are University of Arizona employees, who do not bid their services job by job. Rather, they work on salary and are assigned work by their supervisors. In Coase's words, "a distinguishing mark of the firm is suppression of the price mechanism" (1937, 334).

2. Within a firm, coordination by the firm's managers replaces coordination by means of the price mechanism (Coase uses the term *entrepreneur* rather than manager).

3. There are costs to using the price mechanism. First is the cost of discovering what the prices are. Anyone who has recently done comparison shopping for a new computer readily understands that finding the lowest price for exactly the same quality computer with exactly the same features is no simple task. Then there is the cost of contracting. This cost may be high because of the large number of contracts that must be negotiated; it may also be high if the contract is of long duration and hence subject to uncertainty because unforseen events make it difficult for the supplier to perform.

4. A special type of contract is that between the employer and employee. Within limits, this is of the "master-servant" kind, wherein the servant agrees to do anything the employer asks of him or her. This differs from contracts in the marketplace, where the supplier has great freedom of action as long as he or she delivers the specified product or service on time at the agreed upon price.

5. Government actions may affect what is organized through the firm and through the market. Coase cites the sales tax as an example—this gives a firm an incentive to organize more activities internally in order to avoid having to pay the sales tax when purchasing the results of the same activity from the market. In recent times benefit packages offered by firms have increasingly had to conform to government regulations. In the United States, if the XYZ Corporation offers its employees a pension plan, the plan must conform to federal laws to ensure that it is fully funded; if XYZ offers a health insurance plan, state laws often require that the plan cover certain illnesses. There is of course a cost for the corporation to conform to all of these federal or state "mandates." To avoid these costs, large corporations have started to "outsource" to outside suppliers many activities that were formerly done within the corporation.

6. As a firm expands, it will find that its managers start to get in the way of each other. Eventually, the net—benefits less costs—of an additional manager will decrease to zero, and it will be more economical for the firm to buy goods and services directly from the market rather than to produce them internally. In other words, the firm will tend to expand until the cost of organizing an extra transaction within the firm equals the cost of organizing the same transaction in the market.

In a nutshell, a firm's size will be disciplined by the market. If it is more economical to organize activities through the market, the firm will do so. If it is more economical to organize them within the firm, the firm will do that. Put in other terms, the key to size determination is the *costs of transactions*. At the margin, we can expect that the costs of transactions for a given activity will be the same within a firm or through use of the market.

Why, then, at the end of the last century did the size of the largest firms in the United States suddenly jump from a few hundred to tens of thousands of employees? They did so because of massive technological advances that evolved during the last century. At least this is the prevailing theory among economic and business historians. The telegraph and then the telephone made communication almost instantaneous. The discovery of anthracite coal in Pennsylvania made cheap energy possible, which in turn made possible the Bessemer and open hearth processes for the production of cheap steel. Railroads provided cheap transportation, and so on. Each of these advances decreased the cost of some activity not by a factor of 2 or 3 but by a factor of 10 or 100 or even 1,000 or more. In keeping with astronomical terminology, where the term *order of magnitude* means "a factor of 10", these might be called "orders of magnitude" technological changes—they reduced the transactions costs of within-firm activities by orders of magnitude.

Together, these technological advances made economically feasible nationwide sales forces that could be managed and directed from central headquarters, production lines that could mass-produce things that could then be packaged by machines built of cheap steel. Products made in one part of the country could be cheaply transported to another part. And so on. The result was that it became economical to organize activities within the minieconomies of firms rather than through the market. In response, firms naturally grew in size; within a generation, some consisted of armies of employees mobilizing vast capital resources, and the economies of the developed countries suddenly saw the emergence of the modern large corporation.

## 5.3   Extensions of Coase's Basic Theory

Coase's 1937 article has spawned a large literature extending his basic thrust. For example, Alchian and Demsetz (1972) focus on team production —it may take three men working together to load a piano onto a truck; one person cannot do it by himself. In a society with many pianos to move, one expects piano moving firms to evolve that will have at least three members or employees. But teams also give rise to problems of obtaining information. How do we measure the input of each of the members of a team? How can we detect whether or not one of the piano movers is shirking, exerting less than a third of the force required to move the piano and letting his partners take up the slack? One way is to have a monitor who not only keeps track of inputs, but of outputs as well and who additionally assigns tasks and rewards or punishes adequate or inadequate performance. But then who monitors the monitors? Let monitors have claim to all of the revenue left after all expenses are paid, and as *residual claimants*, they will have an incentive to do their job well.

But as we go beyond simple teams to a more complex hierarchy, problems of information transmittal arise. In the Soviet system it was often said that orders were transmitted downward and lies sent upward. In Oliver Williamson's (1975) terminology, this is called "information impactedness". Likewise, a middle manager in a large organization may spend an inordinate amount of time and energy trying to outmaneuver rivals rather than tending to the firm's business, something that Williamson calls "opportunistic behavior".

The insights of Alchian and Demsetz and of Williamson concern the interactions between a firm's employees and its managers—the responsibilities of the firms' members, the risks and rewards they face, the information they have, their dependency on each other, and the incentives that all of these factors generate. These interactions are governed by *contracts*, contracts that are largely implicit and long-term. And this leads to the Jensen-Meckling (1976) view of the firm: a firm is a legal fiction that bundles together a collection of contracting relationships among individuals. Of course, the free market also consists of contracts, both implicit and explicit, among economic agents. In the Jensen-Meckling view, the difference is in the form of contracts within the firm and those in the market place, as typified by Coase's (1937) discussion of the special properties of the employer-employee contract.

## 5.4  More Differences between the Firm and the Marketplace

If we follow further Coase's (1937) idea that a firm is an economy in its own right, and consider the Alchian-Demsetz, Williamson, and Jensen-Meckling insights, we are led to a more complete contrast between a firm and a market economy.

For one thing, a firm's internal banking and financial system differs from that of a market economy; usually it is rudimentary—there are only limited ways, if any, that a unit within a firm can borrow money to be paid back over time. And the firm typically has no counterpart of money—a medium of exchange that is fully *fungible*, that is something that can be used to buy anything. For example, at the University of Arizona, we have State of Arizona moneys allocated to salaries and various operating expenses, money obtained from grants, from gifts, and from summer school; strict rules govern which sources of funds can be spent on which activities. For another, when disputes arise over the "bundle of contracts" that comprise a firm, there is typically no formal resolution mechanism like a court; rather, the resolution is informal, often worked out among the managers involved. Finally, within a firm, when a unit goes sour and its performance becomes inadequate, "bankruptcy" is handled differently. The failed unit does not go through a court-administered bankruptcy proceedings, but is typically eliminated, reorganized, sold, or absorbed elsewhere with the firm.

## 5.5  Organizational Failures within Firms

Parkinson's Law

In 1958 C. Northcote Parkinson, an obscure professor of management in Singapore, wrote a thin book, *Parkinson's Law*, on life within the large firm. The book is terse—only 122 pages long—and even today, very funny.

*Parkinson's Law* went through many editions, sold many copies, and "Parkinson's Law" became part of the English language. Nevertheless, perhaps because of its delightful tongue-in-cheek style, it never was taken all that seriously. My guess is that Parkinson actually meant his book to be a serious work on management. By choosing to write it in a light and entertaining style in order to get a wide readership, he may have dulled its impact.

The book's opening sentence, "Work expands so as to fill the time available for its completion," is often cited as *the* Parkinson's law. But the book contains many similar insights, and perhaps the sum of all of them should be considered as "Parkinson's law." At any rate, we can view *Parkinson's Law* as a compendium of common organizational or firm failures, of instances where the coordinating functions of managers that Coase envisions break down.

For instance, by the phrase "work expands to fill the time available for its completion," Parkinson means more than employees reading the newspaper, running personal errands, making endless personal phone calls, or sleeping on the job. More often than not, those expanding work are working hard, putting in long hours, and coming home at night thoroughly exhausted from having spent a stressful day at the office. Consider the following fanciful, made-up example to illustrate Parkinson's point.

The government mandates that paper clips must conform to new, complex standards. A firm decides that a new position must be created to ensure compliance; the person hired must be well trained, perhaps at least with an M.B.A., and have five years of experience. A search is undertaken and a high-powered person is brought on board. She immediately issues memos, calls meetings, gets management to require an annual report from each department on past clip usage and future clip needs, organizes workshops to teach employees how to improve their paper clip skills, and requests funds to attend national conferences with other paper clip administrators. At the end of a year, she reports that she is swamped with work and needs not one but at least two assistants. As Parkinson points out, she doesn't dare request only one assistant. Why? Because she would divide the work with her assistant, giving him or her the appearance of equal status, all the more so because the assistant would be her apparent successor.

Parkinson has similar insightful observations about hiring, committee meetings, the sizes of committees (they grow until they become unmanageable in size, at which point a small subcommittee does the real work and the remaining committee positions become honorific), financial management (the time boards of directors spend approving financial appropriations tends to vary inversely with the appropriation's size and importance), the opulence of corporate headquarters (the more opulent, the closer is the corporation to its demise), the effects of "injelitis" (the combination of incompetence and jealousy), and the problem of pushing chief executives out the door as they approach retirement age.

Parkinson does not stress or even mention two important points. First, the organizational failures that he describes tend to be hard for an outsider to identify. For example, an outsider will observe that our paper clip administrator and her assistants work very hard and that they write lengthy progress reports concretely documenting and extolling what they have accomplished. It won't occur to our outsider that they would not be missed if they were fired; because they are not fired, no one knows this. Second, the organizational failures will tend to be more frequent, the more monopoly power the organization has (we have more to say on this in chapter 14's discussion of monopoly rents). A firm that harbors organizational failures and that is in competition with other firms will have incentives to get rid of its failures. If it doesn't and its rivals do, the rivals' costs will go down, they will lower prices and business will flow to them. This will ultimately cause the firm to take stock and to take drastic measures. At some point, it will fire its paper clip administrator, or at least fire her assistants, and find that the firm's profits have increased.

So we can expect organizational failures to be most frequent in highly profitable firms—firms in the private sector that have a lot of monopoly power—and in regulated firms and governmental organizations that have no competitors. Both have monopoly power and without extraordinary measures will be prone to the operation of Parkinson's law.[1] We can also expect that it will be difficult to cut personnel in such organizations. Outside auditors looking for sloth will find none, and because they know far less than the insiders about the how the firm works, they will be hard pressed to come up with concrete proposals to trim "unnecessary" personnel.

## Rare-Event Scale Effect

An organizational failure that Parkinson does not discuss is what might be called the "rare-event scale effect," the tendency for large organizations to overreact to a specific instance by passing a general rule to be applied to all persons for all time. I illustrate this with another made-up example—a student cheating in a large university.

Assume that the university has a population of $n$ students, of which $b$ are "bad guys" and $g$ are "good guys," ($b + g = n$). Also assume that the bad guys will take every opportunity to cheat. For example, if hand calculators suddenly become available that provide alphabetic as well as numerical display, assume that every one of the bad guys will immediately buy one and will cheat by coding into it formulas, lists of significant dates and events that are required to be memorized, and so forth. Assume further that the cheating is certain to be detected. Thus, should a bad guy be an economics major, the result will be the Economics Department's banning forever the use of hand calculators in the class room.

If the Economics Department has $m$ students, what is the probability that it will have to deal with at least one bad guy? For a small department, a close approximation to this is simply $m(b/n)$—the number of students in the department times the fraction of the student population that represents bad guys. Suppose, then, that the "goodness-badness" of the student population follows a Gaussian distribution with a standard deviation of $\sigma$, and all of the bad guys fall at the $3\sigma$ point and beyond. This means that they constitute 0.13 percent of the population (see, for example, Johnston 1984, 547, table B-1), and thus, for small departments serving $m$ students, the probability of getting at least one bad guy will be approximately $0.0013m$.

But this approximation is not valid for large $m$ (for $m$ greater than 769, it yields a probability greater than unity, an impossibility), and we need the exact formula, which depends on the $n$, the number of students from which the $m$ students in the department are drawn. Fortunately, this is easy to derive.[2]

For example, if we consider the University of Arizona with 35,000 students, there will be 46 "bad guys" in the sense defined above, and 34,954 "good guys." The probability of a department of size $m$ getting at least one of the bad guys will then be given by table 5.1 and figure 5.1.

Table 5.1 and figure 5.1 illustrate the point: As the size, $m$, of the organization within the population of 35,000 grows, the higher is the probability that a cheating incident will befall the organization. When the organization reaches 3,500, the size of the student group served in a typical semester by the University of Arizona Economics Department, cheating has a 99.22 percent probability of occurring. On the other hand, in a department that serves only 100 students, its occurrence has only a 12 percent probability.

**Table 5.1**
Probability of at least one cheater in a department of $m$ students

| $m$ | $P(B^*)$ |
| --- | --- |
| 1 | 0.0013 |
| 10 | 0.0131 |
| 100 | 0.1234 |
| 1,000 | 0.7367 |
| 1,800 | 0.9120 |
| 3,500 | 0.9922 |

If we arbitrarily use 99 percent as the definition of "almost certain," then we can conveniently determine an upper bound on $m$ at which this occurs (say $m_{upper}$):[3]

$$m_{upper} = \ln(1 - 0.99)/\ln(g/n). \tag{5.1}$$

In the case at hand, with $g/n = 0.9987$, $m_{upper} = 3,540$, which is not far from the actual value of $m = 3,333$ at which $P(B^*)$ is 0.99. In any event, we see that for sufficiently large $m$, a critical size of organization will be reached.

Although we have made our calculations for the case of $n = 35,000$, the general conclusions hold for sufficiently large $n$—the probability of a rare, bad event first increases linearly, then it continues to increase with organizational size until a critical size is reached, after which the probability is close to unity.

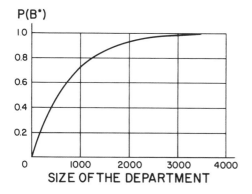

**Figure 5.1**
Probability of getting at least one cheater versus size of the department

The example is meant to be illustrative and I do not wish to make too much of it. However, if we think of organizations, say, large corporations, whose members are drawn from the population of the United States, we see that bigness in this case is not necessarily a blessing. A small organization of a handful of people may survive for decades without having to deal with a bad, rare event, while a large organization of many thousands may count on having to contend with them as a way of life. Clearly, the rare-event scale effect will be maximized in the largest organization of all—the federal government.

**Exercises**

1. When did the giant corporation emerge and what are the reasons for its emergence?

2. Describe the chain of observations made by Coase (1937) that comprise the heart of his theory of why firms exist.

3. Discuss the Alchian-Demsetz (1972), Williamson (1975), and Jensen-Meckling (1976) insights that extend Coase's (1937) basic theory of the reasons for the existence of firms.

4. Discuss other differences between a firm and market organization of economic activities.

5. Discuss Parkinson's basic law: "Work expands to fill the time available for its completion."

6. Describe the rare-event scale effect.

# 6

# Risk and Incentives; Principal-Agent Theory

*This total exemption from trouble and from risk, beyond a limited sum, encourages many people to become adventurers in joint stock companies, who would, upon no account, hazard their fortunes in any private copartnery.*

Adam Smith, *Wealth of Nations*

## 6.1 Importance of Principal-Agent Relationships

In the last two decades or so, economic theory has focused on a unit of analysis even more fundamental than the individual household or firm—the bargain or contract negotiated by two economic agents, say, a buyer and seller, a firm and a consumer, a landlord and tenant, or an employer and an employee. Of particular interest have been the bargains or contracts between a *principal* and the principal's *agent*. Here, the term *principal* means the person who is in control and has authority to act, while *agent* is someone who acts in place of the principal and by the principal's authority. Principal-agent bargains or contracts have been a subject of long-standing importance in the law, but only recently have been accorded comparable importance by economists.

What makes the principal-agent relationship so important? Although, in a perfect world of perfect information and no risk, it would not be, in the real world a principal can typically only very imperfectly monitor or police the agent's actions. The agent may have more information than the principal and may reveal only what is in the agent's self-interest; the information the principal receives may be inadequate to monitor the agent. In today's jargon, the agent may act "strategically". Also, the principal and the agent may have different attitudes toward risk. Perhaps the principal loves to take risks, while the agent prefers always to play it safe, or vice versa. All of these factors influence the types of bargains struck between principals and their agents and the bargains' outcomes. And principal-agent bargains pervade the economy.

For example, the regulated sector of the economy is replete with principal-agent relationships. In public utility regulation a regulatory commission can be viewed as the agent for a representative utility customer who is the principal; the public utility can be viewed as the agent for the regulatory commission, acting as principal; and of course the utility's management can be viewed as agents acting in behalf of the stockholders, their principals. Principal-agent theory holds the promise of bringing new insights to bear on public utility regulation, as well as on regulation in general, and much research on applying principal-agent theory to regulation has already been done. We consider this work in chapter 21.

An outcome of the recent focus on principal-agent relations has been to draw economists' attention to the importance of the risk, information, and incentive structures inherent in contractual arrangements. This chapter sketches some of the main themes in this relatively new development in economics research.

## 6.2   Risk

The starting point for the analysis of risk is an individual's satisfaction or "utility" for different amounts of money or wealth. For most of us, $2,000 does not bring twice as much satisfaction as $1,000, nor does $200,000 make us twice as happy as $100,000. As chapter 7 brings out, quantifying something like "satisfaction" is not trivial and runs the danger that we will use the same quantification scale for two or more separate persons. This is what the original utilitarians did, but economists now consider this to be unacceptable.

On the other hand, for a *particular* person, economists consider it perfectly acceptable to imagine a quantitative scale assigned to differing levels of satisfaction (also called "preference levels" or "levels of utility"). Furthermore, it doesn't matter what quantitative or numerical scale is used, as long as it is consistent—a larger value of utility should always correspond to a higher level of satisfaction.[1]

For most of us, such a numerical scale for the satisfaction or utility that money gives would result in a graph that looks like figure 6.1, where have used the modern economists' term *utility* to denote level of satisfaction. The graph will be a bowed-downwards or concave curve, as shown in figure 6.1, reflecting the fact that twice as much money gives us less than twice as much utility, or, in general, that $n$ (where $n > 1$) times as much

UTILITY

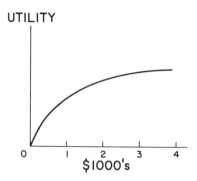

**Figure 6.1**
Utility derived from money

UTILITY

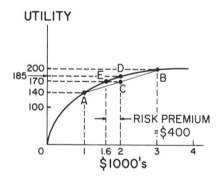

**Figure 6.2**
Diagrammatic representation of the risk premium

money gives less than *n* times as much utility. A curve of this shape typifies a *risk-averse* individual. Why is this so?

Consider such an individual facing a gamble. A coin is to be flipped; if it comes up heads, the individual gets $1,000, if tails, $3,000. If the individual faced this gamble repeatedly, over many coin flips, and the coin was unbiased, the individual's average return would be $2,000 per coin flip. In technical jargon, the *expected value* of the gamble would be $2,000. We can represent this diagrammatically, as shown in figure 6.2.

$1,000 yields a utility of 140 (point A), and $3,000 a utility of 200 (point B). The expected outcome is thus (1/2) × $1,000 + (1/2) × $3,000 = $2,000, while expected utility is (1/2) × 140 + (1/2) × 200 = 170. In figure 6.2 the expected result of the coin flip thus plots as point C, the midpoint of the line joining points A and B.

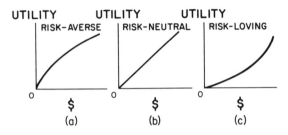

**Figure 6.3**
(a) Risk-averse, (b) risk-neutral, and (c) risk-loving utility curves

However, if someone simply gave our hypothetical individual $2,000, figure 6.2 shows that the individual would be at point D, and would have a utility of 185. Thus the utility of $2,000 with certainty is 15 greater than the utility of $2,000 in expectation (185 compared to 170). In fact, the downward-bowed curve of figures 6.1 and 6.2 shows that this individual would accept $1,600 with certainty in exchange for a gamble that returned $1,000 or $3,000 with equal probability (points C and E have the same utility of 170). We say that the individual would be willing to pay a *risk premium* of $2,000−$1,600 = $400 in order to replace the outcome of the gamble with a certain outcome.

More generally, we can classify individuals as *risk-averse, risk-neutral,* or *risk-loving,* depending on whether their utility curve for money is bowed downward (concave), a straight line, or bowed upward (convex), as shown in figures 6.3a,b, and c.

The classification of individuals according to their attitude or taste for risk may seem like an abstract exercise of no practical use in theorizing about economic activity. After all, few of us are gamblers and, should we go to Las Vegas, would gamble only a small amount for the pleasure of it. In fact, the theory of risk bearing has enormous applicability in economics.

Economic agents making decisions about how they will face the future drive the economy, and the future is, at best, known only in a probabilistic sense. The supplier of iron bars to my welding shop has been reliable and the soul of integrity, but he is retiring and his reprobate son is taking over his business. The probability is high that the son will be unreliable, but, then again, the new responsibility may be just the thing to finally straighten him out, and there is a small probability that he will suitably replace his father. My customers have come to depend on me, and my good reputation has been the heart of my business. But the rumor is that a new plastic will be a cheaper substitute for the welded assemblies that I make, and my operation and equipment may therefore become obsolete. I can count on customer loyalty only to a point, and I must consider the probabilities that substitutes will appear for the product that I make.

So the economy's agents routinely face risk in all aspects of their activity. Indeed, that different individuals have different attitudes toward risk—some avoid it at all costs, others love it—gives rise to the possibility of trades of assets or gambles of different risks, and such trades are an important part of the economy. We illustrate this with a highly idealized principal-agent example.

Assume that the principal, say, an owner of farm land, and the principal's agent, say the tenant farmer working the land, face two possible outcomes at the end of this growing season. If, during the growing season, the weather is good, the net yield—revenues minus expenses—will be $200/acre, while if the weather is bad, the net yield will be $100/acre. Let us further assume that the owner is risk-averse, while the tenant is risk-neutral. Further, assume that initially, the owner and tenant contemplate contract 1, wherein the tenant gets a payment of $50/acre with certainty, regardless of whether the weather should turn out to be bad or good. Finally, assume that there is an equal probability that the weather will be good or bad.

This means that, in the event of good weather, the owner will receive $200 − $50 = $150, and in the event of bad weather, $100 − $50 = $50. Thus, in the contract initially contemplated, the owner would receive an *expected value* of ($150 + $50)/2 = $100, while the tenant would receive $50 regardless of how the weather turns out. In other words, the risk-averse owner is absorbing all of the risk, even though the tenant, being risk-neutral, has more tolerance for it.

The differing tastes for risk give an opportunity for a Pareto-improving trade. For example, consider a new contract—contract 2—wherein the owner gets $100 with certainty and the tenant gets the remainder— $200 − $100 = $100 in the event of good weather and $100 − $100 = 0 in the event of bad weather. Because the owner gets more utility out of $100 with certainty than $100 in expectation, the owner is better off. On the other hand, the tenant now gets ($100 + $0)/2 = $50 in expectation and absorbs all the risk. However, because the tenant is indifferent between $50 with certainty and $50 in expectation, that is, equally well off, the new contract makes the owner better off without hurting the tenant.

As an alternative, consider contract 3, wherein the risk-averse owner forgoes the risk premium, say $30, in order to escape risk. Now the owner gets $100 − $30 = $70 with certainty and is equally well off as in the original contract. The tenant receives $200 − $70 = $130 in the event

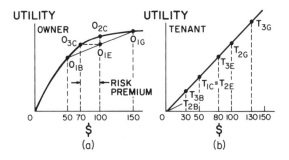

**Figure 6.4**
Diagrammatic representation of three contracts with different risk distributions

of good weather, $100 − $70 = $30 in the event of bad weather, and ($130 + $30)/2 = $80 in expectation. For absorbing all of the risk, the tenant has now increased expected return from $50 to $80 and is better off.

Figure 6.4 summarizes these three contracts. Here points $O_{1G}$, $O_{1B}$, and $O_{1E}$ denote contract 1 outcomes for the owner when the weather is good, bad, and in expectation, while point $T_{1C}$ indicates the certain contract 1 outcome for the tenant. Points $O_{2C}$ and $O_{3C}$ denote the certain contract 2 and 3 outcomes for the owner; points $T_{2G}$, $T_{2B}$, $T_{2E}$ denote the good weather, bad weather, and in expectation contract 2 outcomes for the tenant; and $T_{3G}$, $T_{3B}$, $T_{3E}$ denote the corresponding tenant outcomes for contract 3.

Contracts 2 and 3 are not the only Pareto improvements over contract 1. If the owner receives any payment, $x$, with certainty between $70 and $100, the owner will be somewhere on the arc between the points $O_{3C}$ and $O_{2C}$ in figure 6.4a. Correspondingly the tenant will receive a payment in expectation of $(200 − x)/2 + (100 − x)/2$, or $150 − x$, and will be somewhere on the line segment between points $T_{2E}$ and $T_{3E}$ in figure 6.4b. Every point pair consisting of a point on the arc in figure 6.4a and its corresponding point on the line segment in figure 6.4b will constitute a possible contract. Each of these possible contracts will be a Pareto improvement over contract 1.

### 6.3   Moral Hazard

Presumably, the outcome of the harvest will depend on the diligence and energy of the tenant in planting the crop, taking care not to waste seed and fertilizer, harvesting at the correct time, and so forth. Such effort is costly to the tenant, who could apply it to other pursuits to the tenant's benefit.

Suppose the owner and tenant stick to the original contemplated contract wherein the tenant gets $50, regardless of the growing season's weather. Suppose further that the principal has no way to monitor the tenant's performance. Then the tenant will have no particular incentive to farm efficiently and to bring in the most bountiful crop possible. In the jargon of economists, there will exist the *moral hazard* that the tenant will shirk, and thereby deliver less output than the owner expects.

Insurance contracts are premier examples of risk-sharing agreements, and insurers universally must concern themselves that they not make the terms of insurance so favorable to the insured as to generate moral hazard problems. Fire insurance that totally protects against fire loss runs the danger that the insured will not take elementary precautions to prevent fire; unemployment insurance that is overly generous dampens the initiatives among the unemployed to search for work; and fully insured depositors in savings and loan banks encourage the banks' presidents to invest in overly speculative ventures.

## 6.4   Incentive Compatibility

In our landowner-tenant farmer example, if the owner had no way to monitor the tenant, the owner could protect the owner's interests by negotiating provisions in the contract that would give the tenant an incentive not to shirk and to perform efficiently. Such provisions would embody the notion of "incentive compatibility."

Perhaps the simplest example of an incentive compatible contract is the well-known "cut and choose" procedure for fair division, usually illustrated by division of a cake. Mr. A and Ms. B are to share a cake and neither trusts the other. Should either of them be given the job of cutting the cake, the other is convinced that he or she will get less than half. They can solve the problem by entering into a contract wherein one of them, perhaps chosen by a coin flip, will be given responsibility for cutting the cake into two pieces, after which the other is free to choose the piece he or she wants. Clearly, if each desires as much cake as possible, whoever is chosen to cut the cake has an incentive to divide it into two exactly equal shares. Otherwise, he or she will end up with the smaller piece.

Incentive-compatible contracts abound—bonuses for salespersons tied to volume of orders obtained, piecework wages for production workers, and sharecropping arrangements for tenant farmers. The optimum design of such contracts depends on the taste for risk of the principal and agent. If either one is risk-averse while the other is risk-neutral or risk-loving, we can expect the risk-averse party to be willing to pay a risk premium in order to obtain a certain outcome and to have the other party bear the risk.

## 6.5   Information Asymmetries and Adverse Selection: The Market for Lemons

Moral hazard, as discussed above, involves *information asymmetries*—different parties to a contract have access to different information. It also involves strategic, that is, self-interested, behavior on the part of one of the parties to a contract. I have taken out flood insurance on my farm; nonetheless, I build a barn down by the river because it is in my interests to do so and I know that I can recover its cost should a flood wash it away.

Information asymmetries by themselves, in the absense of strategic behavior, can lead to important economic phenomena that go under the name of "adverse selection." For example, the landowner in our example may have inherited the land and may know nothing about farming. The tenant may be an expert farmer with a degree in agriculture who, by using the most scientific methods, can greatly increase the probability of a good harvest. Or, although well educated, the tenant may be someone who talks a good game but has bad judgment and, with the best of intentions, will employ methods detrimental to a good harvest. Having just acquired the land and needing to find a good tenant, the landowner may find it difficult to differentiate among the candidates' varying degrees of farming competency and may therefore run the risk of choosing poorly. Whenever one party to a contract has incomplete knowledge about the inherent characteristics of the choices available, there is generally the possibility of adverse selection and other bad economic consequences.

For example, suppose that you are the landowner. What would you do? You might hire the candidate who appears to be the most competent, but in negotiating the terms of the contract, you might assume the worst about that candidate. This might lead you to propose terms that are too severe for a prospective tenant to accept, or that might wreck your reputation in further negotiations with members of the pool of prospective tenant farmers, and so on.

We can get an idea of how economists model situations like these by considering the example made famous by Akerlof (1970), which led to a large literature on the adverse selection effects of information asymmetries. This is the example of the "market for lemons."

Suppose that 10 percent of this year's output of new DeSoto automobiles (a now extinct brand whose name I use so as not to give offense to existing brands) are "lemons," or defective, while the remaining 90 percent are "cream puffs," free of defects. Suppose further that you as a buyer have no way to determine whether you are buying a lemon or cream puff but that after you purchase your new DeSoto for $20,000, it quickly becomes apparent you have been lucky—you have in fact bought a cream puff.

Should a financial emergency force you to sell your cream puff almost immediately after you have bought it, you might put it up for sale in the used car market at essentially what you paid for it, say, $19,500. Will you succeed in selling it at this price? How will a prospective buyer react to your offer to sell your car? The buyer may in fact have read a consumers' magazine and discovered that 10 percent of new DeSotos are lemons. Will the buyer assume that your car is one of the 10 percent? Not having the resources to do a thorough investigation of the value of your car, very likely the buyer will assume the worst, that most of the new DeSotos the buyer looks at are lemons, irrespective of what the sellers say about them. In other words, the prospective buyer will simply discount all of your claims of what a marvelous cream puff you are offering for sale.

If you find that all buyers have the same view, you will eventually despair of recouping the full amount of what you paid for your car. In the extreme case, all buyers will assume that only lemons are on the market; they will make the assessment that the probability that an alleged cream puff is an actual cream puff is close to zero. No one will be willing to pay the price of a cream puff. You will then have the choice at selling your cream puff at the price of a lemon or withholding it from the market. If the price of lemons is sufficiently low, all cream puff owners will chose not to sell; cream puffs will be driven from the market by the lemons.

## 6.6   Reputations and Signaling

The theoretical work on information asymmetries and adverse selection in various markets has brought to the fore issues that were long well known to practical businessmen. The "market for lemons" example highlights the danger of inadequate information being conveyed to buyers about the quality of products. Of course, actual used car salesmen are aware of this danger and take measures to counteract it. One measure is to find ways to signal high quality. Many methods are used—prompt correction of defects that the buyer finds after purchase, selling cream puffs below cost when the used car business first opens in order to build a reputation that alleged cream puffs are real cream puffs but doing the opposite after the business is established, charging a high, though "fair", price and refusing to offer discounts but making certain that every car leaves the lot in perfect condition, and so on. There is now a sizable economic literature on the theory of signaling of quality and of reputation building.

## 6.7   Strategic Behavior and Game-Theoretic Models

Our discussion of risk bearing, asymmetry of information, and incentives highlights the importance in economic activity of the assumptions that each of us makes regarding the expected actions of others with whom we contract. And of course the parties with whom we contract must make similar assessments about us. The result is that, to understand the bargaining process, we must take into account the motivations and information available to both parties to the bargain. Theoretical models of such processes are called "game-theoretic models" because the processes have the characteristics of games with economic stakes. Further, when one of the players in such a game acts so as to turn the game's risk, information, and incentive structures to that player's advantage, we say that the player has acted "strategically."

A standard form of such a game that models not only strategic behavior but a wide and important class of bargaining activity is called the "prisoner's dilemma." A story like the following is usually used to illustrate it. Over several months there have been a string of convenience store robberies, always committed by two men. Finally, two men fitting the description of the convenience store robbers are caught red-handed. Each is told that he is sure to be convicted for the latest robbery and will receive a sentence of a year in jail. Each is also told, Squeal on your partner about the whole string of robberies and you will receive six months while your partner will receive ten years. However, should you both squeal on each other, you will each receive five years.

We can capture the alternatives facing the two robbers in a diagram, shown in figure 6.5. Here, the upper right-hand corner of each cell shows the sentence robber 1 faces and the lower left-hand corner that faced by robber 2.

Clearly, if each robber acts "strategically," that is, in his own best self-interest, the outcome will be that each will get a five-year sentence. In game-theoretic terms, the lower right-hand corner cell represents a *Nash equilibrium* of the game. It is an equilibrium in the sense that each player is doing as well as possible, assuming that the other player does not change his move. Thus, if robber 1 changes his mind and decides against squealing, while robber 2 holds fast and squeals, robber 1's sentence increases from

| | | ROBBER 1 | |
|---|---|---|---|
| | | Don't Squeal | Squeal |
| ROBBER 2 | Don't Squeal | 1 year<br>1 year | 6 months<br>10 years |
| | Squeal | 10 years<br>6 months | 5 years<br>5 years |

**Figure 6.5**
Prisoner's dilemma game

five to ten years. And the same is true if the roles are reversed; if either robber unilaterally changes his "squeal" strategy, he is worse off.

The reader should note that the notion of a game-theoretic or Nash equilibrium is different from that of Pareto optimality. For example, in this case, all remaining cells in figure 6.5—both upper cells and the lower left-hand corner cell—represent Pareto optima. In these cells neither player can be made better off without hurting the other player. But only the bottom right-hand corner is a Nash equilibrium. On the other hand, it is not a Pareto optimum; both players are better off by a move to the upper left-hand corner cell (from "squeal, squeal" to "don't squeal, don't squeal"). Hence, in the case of the prisoner's dilemma game, the Pareto optima and the Nash equilibrium are *disjoint*.

The prisoner's dilemma typifies a situation where circumstances have forced each party to a bargain to assume the worst behavior on the part of the other party. Unfortunately, it mirrors many real-life situations. It is the negotiator's nightmare. Instead of the parties negotiating to a win-win (Pareto optimum) outcome, they end up with a lose-lose (Pareto pessimum) outcome.

## Exercises

1. What is the assumed shape of the "utility of money" for risk-averse, risk-neutral, and risk-loving individuals?

2. By means of a graph, describe the concept of a risk premium.

3. By means of an example, illustrate the proposition that if two individuals have different tastes for risk, they may be able enter into Pareto-improving, risk-sharing contracts.

4. Discuss the concept of moral hazard.

5. What is the essential feature of an incentive-compatible contract or agreement?

6. In the "market for lemons" story based on Akerlof (1970), describe how cream puffs will be driven from the market.

7. What role does information asymmetry play in the "market for lemons" story?

8. In the standard "prisoner's dilemma" story, what does each party assume about the other's behavior? What is meant by a "Pareto pessimum"?

# II          Fairness Theory

# 7

## A Brief Intellectual History of the Economist's Current Ethical Outlook

*[W]elfare economics began with Pigou. Before that, we had happiness economics; and, before that, wealth economics.*

I. M. D. Little, *A Critique of Welfare Economics*

### 7.1 Economic Efficiency and Economic Justice

Chapter 2 introduced the reader to the economists' focus on economic efficiency, also known as "allocative efficiency", "economywide Pareto optimality", or, simply, "Pareto optimality". The goal of achieving Pareto optimality is very modest; there are usually numerous Pareto optima, many of which will be considered unfair by almost any ethical criteria. Thus, at best, economic efficiency is a necessary but far from sufficient condition for an economically just or fair economy. But the reality is worse, for without a means for winners to compensate losers, it may be very difficult if not politically impossible to get to a Pareto-optimal state—an issue that we discuss at length in chapter 15. To those who want to make the world a fairer and more just place, the goal of attaining economic efficiency may seem pitifully weak. For economists to have nothing stronger to say about justice and fairness would seem to be an abandonment of their responsibility.

In fact, this presents a dilemma to economists who are put into policy-advising positions. On the one hand, a strictly economic efficiency outlook is indeed unsatisfactory. On the other hand, their formal training probably included no moral philosophy or other subjects that would help deal with the ethical problems confronting any policy maker. Put in this position, economists sometimes adopt the view that fairness or economic justice is arbitrary. This in turn may lead them to espouse a simplistic utilitarian or maximize-societal-benefits-less-costs goal.

It was not always so. A century ago, many, perhaps most, American economists would have considered economic justice to be central to their subject. How the role of economic justice in the economics profession has evolved is an important history for anyone who wishes to understand the profession's current outlook.

To remain within the scope of this monograph, my summary of this history must be vastly oversimplified, at times, almost a caricature of the literature's treatment. I can only give a skeletal outline of the story; the full story is far richer and more subtle. Moreover, my characterization is impressionistic, not based on a scientific survey of the profession. Other economists will probably find something in it to quibble about and some might take violent exception to it. With these caveats in mind, let us proceed to the history.

## 7.2   A Brief History of "Economic Justice" in the Discipline of Economics

The ascendancy of Christianity in the Middle Ages brought with it the notion of the "just price." Sellers were supposed to be compensated for their costs and only a customary, "just" additional amount for their labor. A seller's extraction of the maximum price from a willing buyer was considered an immoral act, as was a buyer's extraction of an unfairly low price from an unsuspecting seller.[1] Just prices became official doctrine, backed by moral authority, throughout western Europe. Although the doctrine was often honored in the breach, it was the ethical norm until the end of the eighteenth century, when it was displaced through the efforts of Adam Smith and others.[2] According to economic historians (see, for example, Rosenberg 1979, 23), Smith lived in a highly regulated world that, among other things, placed restrictions on the movement of precious metals, on imported manufactured and luxury goods, and on the export of raw materials. At the same time, the government gave financial inducements to the export of certain goods and conferred numerous special rights and exclusive privileges on individuals and firms. In Smith's view, the whole "just price" apparatus had evolved into institutions that allowed monopolizing firms and merchants to manipulate government machinery to serve their own ends.

Seen from today's standpoint, perhaps most outrageous was the potential for the government's control of labor, based on the infamous Statute of Apprenticeship, adopted during Elizabeth's reign in 1562, and it successors. According to Hewitt (1912, 1:46–47), certain persons had to follow the craft in which they were brought up. Persons who did not own sufficient property had to work in agriculture. Others had to serve apprenticeships of seven years, the terms of which were strictly controlled; those who refused to be apprenticed were subject to imprisonment. The normal working hours were from 5 A.M. to 6 or 8 P.M. in the summer and from dawn to dusk in the winter; the government fixed wages.

Perhaps Hewitt's key observation is that wages fluctuated in spite of government control over them,thus indicating that market forces superseded regulation. Indeed, flouting the law seemed to have been common all throughout the "just price" period from St.Thomas Aquinas in the thirteenth century to Adam Smith in the eighteenth. Laws routinely prohibited practices like innovations in tools or techniques, selling below a fixed price, advertising, working into the evening, or employing one's wife or young children. Just as routinely, the laws were ignored; if caught violating them, businessmen simply paid their fines and carried on as before. It seems that the market is no more easily suppressed than are love and sex.[3]

This, then, was the sort of world in which Smith lived. As the occupant of the Chair of Moral Philosophy at Glasgow University, Smith had the opportunity to preach on how to reform it. From his most influential work, *An Inquiry into the Nature and Causes of the Wealth of Nations*, written in 1776, have come down the twin pillars of the economists' extremely simple behavioral model of economic man:

First pillar: the assumption that man will pursue self-interest;

Second pillar: the assumption that in the pursuit of self- interest man will, in Smith's words, "truck, barter, and exchange one thing for another" to mutual gain.

Students usually accept the first pillar without much question, but the second pillar is more subtle. To convey it to students and to convince them of its validity and importance requires time and energy.

As we saw in chapter 2, it asserts that economic transactions are not necessarily zero-sum or win-lose, where one person's gain is at the expense of another's equal loss. In fact, if the transaction is *voluntary*, all parties to it presumably will gain, or at least will not lose; voluntary transactions will be *win-win* rather than win-lose. Otherwise, the parties to the transaction would not have freely entered into it.

From Smith's ideas and his *Wealth of Nations* (1776) has evolved the discipline of economics. As Flubacher (1950) indicates in his synopsis of the ethical views of the important economists since Smith, an important issue in its evolution was whether economics should concern itself with how an economy actually *does* work or how it *ought* to work; in fancier terminology, whether it should be strictly a descriptive, analytical, *positive* activity, completely devoid of value judgments, or a prescriptive, *normative* one that espoused the proper ethical goals for an economy. In the two centuries since Smith there has been vigorous debate between the strict positivists and those who felt the economist had a moral responsibility to be both positive and normative.

The historical record makes clear that, as regards this debate, today's professional climate in economics differs from that of 1885, when the American Economic Association was founded. At that time, the historical school held sway in German economics departments; according to Flubacher (1950), this school felt that ethics and economic analysis were inextricably intertwined. Not only was it artificial to separate them, but it was the task of economists to integrate ethics and economics. Young Turk recent graduates of German universities brought this view with them to the founding meetings of the American Economics Association (AEA). They found allies in the ministers of the gospel who attended, and enemies among the Old Guard, mainly what few professors of economics there were in American universities. The debate was joined over the philosophical outlook the new society was to adopt on laissez-faire and free trade; the Old Guard espoused both in pure form, the Young Turks felt that both should be modified.

One of the Young Turks was Richard T. Ely, and in Ely's draft proposal for a prospectus for the AEA, we find the phrase "we hold that the doctrine of laissez-faire is unsafe in politics and unsound in morals" (Flubacher, 1950, 344), and in Ely's address to the founding meeting, the phrase "believing that our work lies in the direction of practical Christianity, we appeal to the church, the chief of the social forces in this country, to help us..." (Flubacher, 1950, 344). From today's vantage point, Ely's comments seem not only innocent, but value-laden. However, in Ely's 1936 reminiscences (Ely 1936) he stresses that the Young Turks wanted to do economic *science*; in particular, they wanted to apply the statistical techniques that they had learned in Germany. So, it is not clear what Ely felt was value-free.[4]

While it may not be clear what earlier economists considered to be value-free, less murky is what, in various periods, economists thought should be the goal of an economy. The quote from Little (1957, 79) at the beginning of this chapter succinctly summarizes this development from Smith until the early 1950s. In other words, primary to any discussion of how to increase the common good was the question of how to increase the wealth of an economy. But a natural follow-up question is how the wealth can best be spent. This question was vigorously pursued in the generation following Smith by Bentham, who is usually considered the founder of utilitarianism, or, in Little's words, "happiness economics."

Again, to appreciate where the utilitarians' were coming from, we must put ourselves in their places. The world of the "just price" was not only a highly regulated world, but a world of social stratification, ruled by an alliance of the Church and the Crown. One was born to a certain station in life, and one was not to question the rationale for being stuck in it. As the saying goes, "there was no reason, just policy." But if reasonable persons were suddenly to prevail, how would they decide to apportion a society's wealth? According to Schumpeter (1954, 131), the eighteenth-century "votaries of reason" assumed that each individual's pleasures and pains could be algebraically added together (pluses for pleasure and minuses for pain) to form a quantitative measure of happiness. Then the individual measures of happinesses could be added together, each with an equal weight, to get an overall societal measure of happiness. This notion in turn leads to the utilitarian's normative goal: the greatest happiness for the greatest number. As we shall see in what follows, this goal presents many problems, but we should keep in mind the times in which Bentham and the other early utilitarians lived. The goal may have seemed crude to them as well, but they felt it to be superior to "there is no reason, just policy" and "don't get ideas about escaping from your station in life."

The "happiness economics" of Bentham and other utilitarians prevailed until it began to be questioned in the 1930s. The utilitarian notion that "happiness" could be ranked on a *cardinal* scale that was the same for each individual in society was clearly a psychological leap of faith, without empirical foundation, and economists began to try to cope with the cardinal scale assumption.

Three leading economists—Hicks, Kaldor, and Hotelling—all suggested the same method of coping. If one had a consumer's demand schedule for a given good—what the consumer was willing to pay for different quantities of the good—one would have at least a cardinal scale for that consumer and for that good. If one had demand schedules for each good for a given consumer, then for that consumer, one would have a cardinal scale. Unfortunately, only *aggregate* demand schedules are usually available, that is, demand schedules that show demand summed over all consumers. Nonetheless, so the Hicks-Kaldor-Hotelling argument goes, aggregate demand schedules will tell the policy maker how much, in dollars, a class of consumers would be willing to pay in return for the benefit of enjoying the good, or, alternatively, how much they are willing to accept in compensation to forgo the enjoyment of the good.

Hicks, Kaldor, and Hotelling then argued that policy makers could avoid the cardinal scale problem by determining the benefit to society *on average*, where the average was taken either over all time for a given consumer or, at a given time, over all consumers. To do this, policy makers had only to determine whether or not, for a given policy move, winners could potentially compensate losers enough to get them to agree to the move. If policy makers effected all policy moves where *potential* compensation were possible, then, even though a particular individual might be a loser for a particular policy move, on average over all policy moves, that individual would be a winner.[5]

Obviously, hidden in the Hicks-Kaldor-Hotelling scheme is another empirical leap of faith. Suppose someone is ninety-five years old in the year that society decides to adopt the potential compensation principle. There is no guarantee that he or she will live long enough to be, on average, a winner from governmental policy moves. Nevertheless, in spite of flaws like this, the potential compensation scheme has not completely died and is still sometimes explicitly advocated as a basis of policy (nowadays, it is usually called "the Kaldor-Hicks compensation principle"). More important, my guess is that if one queries policy makers carefully, one will find that something like the potential compensation principle is routinely invoked as a justification for policy initiatives, even though the policy maker never thought of explicitly articulating the justification by appeal to the Hicks-Kaldor-Hotelling argument.[6]

The modern view that evolved from Robbins's (1938) critical attack on utilitarianism once and for all, scrapped "pleasure and pain" as the fundamental unit of analysis and replaced it by choice or trade-off. Furthermore, it abandoned as hopeless the quest for a universal cardinal scale or measuring rod for measuring societal happiness.

Thus, rather than imagining the individual seeking pleasure and avoiding pain, the modern view imagines the individual making choices and trade-offs. For example, the individual might get equal satisfaction from owning a Ford and traveling to Europe for a vacation or from owning a Cadillac and visiting in-laws for a vacation. Although indifferent in choosing between these "commodity bundles," our individual would prefer owning a Rolls-Royce and vacationing on the Riviera to either. More generally, the analysis imagines an infinite number of "bundles" like the (Ford, European vacation), (Cadillac, vacation with in-laws), (Rolls-Royce, Riviera) bundles. Among all such possible "commodity bundles," there will be a set of equivalent bundles—every bundle in the set will give equal satisfaction, and the individual will be indifferent as to which bundle in the set he or she consumes. Presented with a second set also containing bundles that give equal satisfaction, however, our individual will be able to rank bundles from the two sets and state whether he or she prefers a bundle from the first set over one from the second, or vice versa. In this way, the individual will be able to make a complete and consistent ranking of all sets of bundles that give equal satisfaction.

In this process it is again an empirical leap of faith that the process will yield a consistent ranking. The individual makes no attempt to find a way to measure the absolute degree of satisfaction received from each bundle but simply constructs a personal *relative* ranking of satisfactions or utilities —and this relative ranking forms an *ordinal* rather than a cardinal scale. Most important, and this is the major deviation from utilitarianism or "happiness economics," modern economics assumes that there is no way to compare these individualistic ordinal scales *across persons*. Of course, the new use of *ordinal* scales means that there is no universal measuring rod to measure total societal happiness, and, thus, the economic analyst would seem to be left with a much more formidable problem than he had in the utilitarian framework.

Nevertheless, economists observed that in the modern framework, the idea of trading to mutual gain still had validity. To tell whether or not a transaction was win-win, all that was required was that all parties to it know whether or not it will make them better off. No measurement of the degree of "better off" is required; analysis can be carried out by imagining that each individual has formed an ordinal scale of satisfactions or "utilities" and that these ordinal scales are not comparable across individuals. Thus modern economics avoids what Samuelson (1957) calls the "a-scientific interpersonal comparison of utility."

The result is that, since the 1950s, economists have elevated to center stage Adam Smith's observations about the importance of man's predisposition to "truck, barter or exchange one thing for another" for mutual gain. During the probing of the 1930s to find an alternative to utilitarianism, several economists pushed the central role of this idea. However, it came to be identified with Pareto's treatment (Pareto, 1909), and to be called "Pareto optimality".[7] In a nutshell, as discussed in chapter 2, the idea is that all gains from exchange (win-win transactions) should be exploited; and conversely, if all win-win transactions have occurred, then it is sensible to declare that optimality has been achieved.

The work of 1930s and 1940s led to an intense reexamination of the foundations of economic methodology and to a search for the proper goals for an economy. From an ethical viewpoint, it seemed obvious that Pareto optimality was a necessary condition for economic justice, for if unattained gains from exchange exist and are not allowed to occur, some will be denied benefits that result in harm to no one. This denial clearly seems unjust.

But the elevation of Pareto optimality to the status of a central, if not *the* central goal of an economy, did not completely solve the economic justice problem. There are typically many possible Pareto optima, and, obviously, Pareto optimality is not a sufficient condition for economic justice. To most persons, some of the Pareto optimal states may seem more just than others. A textbook example is the Pareto optimum where I own everything in the world and the rest of you own nothing. This is a Pareto optimum because we have nothing to exchange to our mutual advantage. However, few (except, possibly, me) would consider this to be a just state of affairs.

The economists' eventual resolution of the multiple Pareto optima dilemma was to embrace a strictly positive methodology with a vengeance.In the extreme view of this methodology, the economic world was to be neatly divided into two parts—analysis and prescription, or in economists' jargon, efficiency and equity. Economists were to be in charge of the first part—analysis or "efficiency," and were to identify possible "Pareto improvements," possible instances where win-win transactions were not being realized. In Little's imagery, we might say that "happiness economics" was followed by today's win-win economics. Prescription, deciding which of many possible Pareto-optimal states should be society's final goal, was to be left to unspecified others.

Although not embraced by all economists, this dichotomy was, by and large, accepted and was extremely productive. It focused economists' attention and energy squarely on analysis that was guided by a mathematically expressible paradigm and led to an outpouring of research results that have enormously increased our understanding of how a market economy works. But the productivity came at a cost. It led not only to the abandonment of the "happiness economics" of previous generations of economists. It also led to a view that, aside from the self-evident, self-valid "pursuit of self interest" ethic of Adam Smith's economic man, ethics was not a proper subject for economists to interject into economic research, nor even a proper subject to study.

Thus, with the exception of a small minority who do research in economic or "distributive" justice, economists today generally do not professionally concern themselves with economic justice, beyond their concern for the advancement of Pareto optimality or "economic efficiency." Economists are, of course, human beings, who have the normal range of compassion and who may feel strongly about social issues. Although their strong views on how to right societal wrongs may be fair game for cocktail parties, economists are careful to keep them out of their professional lives. This is reasonable; however, this mind-set also keeps economists from treating fairness and economic justice as a topic to be analyzed, objectively and dispassionately, with a view toward improving conventional economic analyses.

## 7.3 The Economist's Ethical Role in Policy Making

So, the economics profession has gone from the wealth economics of Adam Smith to the happiness economics of Bentham and the nineteenth-century utilitarians to the win-win economics of today, and has evolved to a neat ethical mind-set—efficiency to be analyzed by the professional economist, ethical norms to be prescribed by society. In fact, in my experience, the very mention of fairness or justice can be cause for an economist's methodological attack that fairness arguments are simply a smoke screen for self interest, something to be exposed for the fraud that they really are.

However, in the complex world of actual policy making, the economists' neat division into efficiency and equity has serious ethical problems of at least three sorts. First, strict Pareto-improving moves rarely exist. Almost every policy change generates *some* losers, and the losers don't like it. Ethically, a policy change where there is only one loser may be miles away from a change where there are no losers. Secondly, even if a Pareto-improving or win-win move exists, there is the ethical issue of how the gains from exchange should be divided. Is it ethically tenable for one party to get a minuscule fraction of the gain while the other party gets virtually all of it? These are important problems, yet they are small compared to a third problem, hinted at in chapter 6. In a risky, dynamic world of imperfect information, pinning down Pareto-improving moves and finding Pareto optima becomes immensely more difficult than in a static, riskless, deterministic world of perfect information; economists are just beginning to characterize Pareto optimum states in such an imperfect world.

Unfortunately, the real policy world will not stand still until economists complete their work. The real world is filled with risk and rarely are we completely informed. None of us knows what fate may befall us. We may be struck by a dreaded disease or be in an airplane catastrophe or be hit by a truck. And governments are not spared the consequences of uncontrollable, random events—natural disasters, bad weather wiping our harvests over large areas, technological change making industries obsolete, and the like, all of which can dramatically impact the effects of governmental action and make former sensible policies seem silly. In a risky and imperfectly informed world, to insist that government policy should generate only guaranteed winners is to insist on policy paralysis. None of us can expect a societal guarantee against a personal loss as a consequence of governmental action.

Perhaps most importantly, an "only winners" policy would not only result in governmental paralysis but would generate outrage. Potential winners would feel their justly deserved winnings were being thwarted by those who justly deserve to lose. The potential winners would then become frustrated and mad. So the economists' clever escape from having to face ethical issues is no escape at all, at least not in the real world of policy making. In the final analysis, some poor policy maker still has to bite the ethical bullet as to who will win and who will lose.[8]

**Exercises**

1. Did the "just price" doctrine serve to justify the Crown's imposition of (a) a market economy, or (b) a regulated economy? Explain your answer. During the time it was in force, was the "just price" doctrine strictly adhered to?

2. What are the two pillars of economists' behavioral model of human beings?

3. Discuss the origins of what Little (1957) calls "happiness economics" or utilitarianism.

4. Discuss the Kaldor-Hicks-Hotelling compensation principle, including its justification.

5. Discuss the sentence, "Thus, modern economics avoids what Samuelson calls the 'a-scientific interpersonal comparison of utility.'"

6. The quote from Little (1957) at the beginning of the chapter states that before Pigou, we had "happiness economics" and, before that, "wealth economics." The text extends Little's characterization, claiming that, today, we have "win-win economics." What does the text mean?

7. What is meant by the equity (income-distribution)-efficiency dichotomy?

8. Discuss the failings of Pareto optimality and Pareto improvements as goals of economic policy.

# 8

# Normative Theories I: John Rawls

*The classical demand is that the state ought to treat all people equally in spite of the fact that they are very unequal. You can't deduce from this the rule that because people are unequal you ought to treat them unequally in order to make them equal, and that's what social justice amounts to.*

F. R. Hayek (on the TV program "Firing Line," 11 November 1977)

## 8.1  Fairness's Role in Regulation

Regulation, which can be a highly public affair, often extensively reported on by the media, is unlike the common law, which has developed over centuries of argument and counterargument and which is administered by judges trained to approach their decisions from a common legal framework. Regulators need not be and often are not lawyers and may come from various occupational backgrounds. They are also afforded wide scope in their decision making. As Breyer (1982, 3) puts it:

At one time, students of the administrative process believed that the congressional statues themselves would control administrative discretion. If administrators strayed outside their statutory authority, the courts would reverse their action. This hope proved ill founded, however, for Congress began to delegate authority in very broad terms. At the same time, the courts exercised restraint, hesitating to set aside administrators' action on review. It proved equally illusory to look to regulators as "scientists," professionals, or technical experts, whose discretion would be held in check by the tenets of their discipline. It has become apparent that there is no scientific discipline of regulation, nor are those persons appointed to regulatory offices necessarily experts. Indeed, some of the most successful—as well as some of the least successful—regulators have had political backgrounds and have lacked experience in regulatory fields.

The actions of regulators are controlled primarily by administrative law. Breyer points out that, initially, administrative law was concerned with protecting individual liberties and property against government incursions. Judges focused on "control," that is, on ensuring that a regulatory agency's decisions conformed to the agency's legislative mandate. But an evolution away from this viewpoint toward a "fairness" viewpoint culminated in the Administrative Procedures Act (APA). Breyer explains (1982, 378):

Between 1945 and 1965, by way of reaction to excessive agency freedom, Congress passed, and the courts enforced, the federal Administrative Procedures Act (APA). This act imposed certain procedural constraints upon federal administrative bodies—whether located in the executive branch or in independent agencies. Its basic object was to achieve "fairness" rather than "control." It forms the basis of current federal administrative law.

The APA puts only limited constraints on the regulatory process and still significantly differs from other judicial processes; for example, judicial rules of evidence do not necessarily apply (see Gellhorn and Levin 1990, 265). These factors—regulators' lack of a common background, the flexibility that the Administrative Procedures Act gives regulators in their adjudicatory role, the act's stress on fairness, and wide media exposure of regulatory decisions—mean that regulatory hearings often center around intuitive, primitive notions of fairness and justice. (Needless to say, other forms of government intervention—for example, the levying of taxes are also driven mainly by intuitive, primitive ideas of fairness.)

In order to develop an understanding of fairness, this chapter and the next consider normative ethical theories of economic justice or fairness; chapters 10 and 11 consider positive theories. In so doing, I have embraced the "normative-positive" dichotomy, something many social scientists refuse to do on the grounds that the dichotomy is simplistic, nonproductive, and misleading. After all, any normative theory of economic justice must be based on models of human behavior, and thus, on some positive theory. At the same time, it is difficult if not impossible for the analyst to remove his own value judgments from a positive analysis. A claim that the analysis is objective and value-free misleads the reader and may simply indicate that the analyst has misled himself. These are valid objections. Nevertheless, I find the normative-positive dichotomy useful, both as a starting point of analysis and as a way of organizing a summary of fairness research, and have used it throughout this book.

We start our study of normative theories with the theory outlined in John Rawls's *Theory of Justice* (1971) and his *Political Liberalism* (1993). The theory presented in these books is perhaps one of the most ambitious and comprehensive of modern theories of economic justice—it is no less than an attempt at a theory for the economically just design of a society. Because my space is limited, I must drastically truncate Rawls's presentation, only outlining the main ideas and omitting major topics that Rawls addresses. *A Theory of Justice* is nearly six hundred pages long, and, in various publications, Rawls has modified the views expressed in it, culminating with his *Political Liberalism* (371 pages). Nevertheless, even the truncated version of Rawls that follows should give the reader an idea of the enormous difficulty of constructing a comprehensive normative theory of economic justice.[1]

Rawls's work is fundamental and has generated an enormous literature. My philosopher colleagues tell me that, prior to Rawls, "political philosophy" had become a backwater in their discipline. Rawls resurrected it, in the process gaining the attention and acclaim not only of philosophers but of economists, political scientists, sociologists, and social scientists generally. For example, one of Rawls's severest critics, and to some extent, one of his rivals, is the political and moral philosopher, Robert Nozick. Yet Nozick (1974, 183) writes glowingly of what Rawls has accomplished:

*A Theory of Justice* is a powerful, deep, subtle, wide-ranging systematic work in political and moral philosophy which has not seen its like since the writings of John Stuart Mill, . . . it is impossible to finish his book without a new and inspiring vision of what a moral theory may attempt to do and unite; of how *beautiful* a whole theory can be.

Rawls does not draw a distinction between positive and normative theory; strictly speaking, he does not claim his theory to be a normative theory of justice, asserting rather that his aim is to elaborate on social contract theory and to develop a theory that is superior to utilitarianism yet accords with our life experiences (Rawls 1971, vii–viii). However one interprets the goal of *A Theory of Justice*, *Political Liberalism*, and Rawls's other writings, it is clear that Rawls hopes his theory will be applicable to the design of social institutions; it is also clear that the literature his work has generated concerns itself primarily with normative issues. For these reasons, I feel it appropriate to make Rawls's theory the centerpiece of a chapter on normative, rather than positive, theories of economic justice.

## 8.2 Rawls's *Theory of Justice*

It is useful to discuss Rawls's work in the order in which he wrote it, starting with *A Theory of Justice* and finishing with the modification of it contained in *Political Liberalism*.

In reading Rawls's *Theory of Justice*, I was struck by how strongly Rawls has been influenced by economists' concepts and methods. Nonetheless, it is also apparent that Rawls's mind-set and goals are fundamentally different from those of most contemporary economists; he sets out on a different journey, traveling in different conveyances, using different lenses with which to view the landscape, and having a different terminus in mind.

For example, Rawls (1971, 7) starts at the level of a social institution, not at the level of economic man "For us the primary subject of justice is the basic structure of society, or more exactly, the way in which the major social institutions distribute fundamental rights and duties and determine the division of advantages from social cooperation." And further (1971, 11):

> [T]he guiding idea is that the principles of justice for the basic structure of society are the object of the original agreement. They are the principles that free and rational persons concerned to further their own interests would accept in an initial position of equality as defining the fundamental terms of their association. These principles are to regulate all further agreements; they specify the kinds of social cooperation that can be entered into and the forms of government that can be established. This way of regarding the principles of justice I shall call *justice as fairness*. (emphasis added)

In his analysis, Rawls thinks of society as being divided into groups or "classes," each of which is characterized by a "representative man," discussing Pareto efficiency not in terms of whether or not one person can be made better off without making another worse off but in terms of "representative men": "Thus we can say that an arrangement of rights and duties in the basic structure is efficient if and only if it is impossible to change the rules, to redefine the scheme of rights and duties, so as to raise the expectations of any representative man (at least one) without at the same time lowering the expectations of some (at least one) other representative man" (1971, 70).

But even with this alternative definition of Pareto efficiency, the familiar arguments against it as a conceptual basis for justice remain. Using the example of serfdom, Rawls points out that there will be generally many Pareto-efficient states, and some will be prima facia unjust: "[I]t may be that under certain conditions serfdom cannot be significantly reformed without lowering the expectations of some representative man, say, [those] that of landowners, in which case serfdom is efficient" (1971, 71). If his alternative version of Pareto efficiency won't do, what will? How does Rawls even begin to formulate an adequate conception of justice?

Rawls begins by resorting to the artifice of the following thought experiment. Suppose you were not even born, and yet you were able to enter into a social contract with all other members of society, also not yet born. Further suppose none of us knew whether, upon being born, we were to be blessed with marvelous talents, energy, and health, so that we could become a world leader in politics, science, or the arts, or whether we were to be a hopeless cripple, with the IQ of a moron, and unable even to care for our basic bodily needs. Upon due reflection, how would we contract with our fellow about-to-be-born members of society in this "original position" behind a "veil of ignorance" as to what fate will befall us?[2]

In formulating such a contract would we start like a conventional economics course? That is, would we think in terms of bundles of all possible commodities to be consumed, bundles made up of physical items like food, clothing, transportation, and so forth, or the services that provide them? Rawls does not do so; rather, he puts great importance on what he calls "primary goods." These are defined to be (1971, 62)

things that every rational man is presumed to want. These goods normally have a use whatever a person's rational plan of life. For simplicity, assume that the chief primary goods at the disposition of society are rights and liberties, powers and opportunities, income and wealth. (Later on ... the primary good of self-respect has a central place). These are the primary social goods. Other primary goods such as health and vigor, intelligence and imagination, are natural goods....

Self-respect looms large in Rawls (1971, 440):

On several occasions I have mentioned that perhaps the most important primary good is that of self-respect.... It is clear then why self-respect is a primary good. Without it nothing may seem worth doing, or if some things have value for us, we lack the will to strive for them. All desire and activity becomes empty and vain, and we sink into apathy and cynicism.

(I challenge the reader to find a mention, must less a discussion, of self-respect in a contemporary elementary economics text!)

Another point of departure from modern economics is Rawls's introduction of a lexicographic ordering of an economic agent's desires and needs. He argues that, in the "original position" behind a "veil of ignorance," the social contract that society would agree on would start with a first principle (1971, 302):[3]

*First Principle*

I. Each person is to have an equal right to the most extensive total system of equal basic liberties compatible with a similar system of liberty for all.

Rawls describes "basic liberties" as follows (1971, 61):

The basic liberties of citizens are, roughly speaking, political liberty (the right to vote and to be eligible for public office) together with freedom of speech and assembly; liberty of conscience and freedom of thought; freedom of the person along with the right to hold (personal) property; and freedom from arbitrary arrest and seizure as defined by the concept of the rule of law. These liberties are all required to be equal by the first principle, since citizens of a just society are to have the same basic rights.

In a "First Priority Rule (The Priority of Liberty)," Rawls further argues that liberty can be restricted only for the sake of liberty; there are two cases (1971, 302):

(a) a less extensive liberty must strengthen the total system of liberty shared by all;
(b) a less than equal liberty must be acceptable to those with the lesser liberty.

Coming lexicographically after the first principle is Rawls's second principle (1971, 302):

*Second Principle*

II. Social and economic inequalities are to be arranged so that they are both:
(a) to the greatest benefit of the least advantaged, consistent with the just savings principle, and
(b) attached to offices and positions open to all under conditions of fair equality of opportunity.

The "just savings principle" in IIa refers to Rawls's discussion of the intergenerational problem of the manner and extent that one generation is to bequeath resources to future generations. The key to arriving at just savings from generation to generation is to include representatives of all generations in the original position. Because no one in the original position knows which generation he or she will be a member of, all will want to contract to prevent one generation from squandering resources to the detriment of future generations.

Rawls calls principle II(a) "the difference principle." With this terminology in mind, we can understand Rawls's elaboration of the second principle as given in a "Second Priority Rule (The Priority of Justice over Efficiency and Welfare)" (1971, 302):

The second principle of justice is lexically [lexicographically] prior to the principle of efficiency and to that of maximizing the sum of advantages; and fair opportunity is prior to the difference principle. There are two cases:

(a) an inequality of opportunity must enhance the opportunities of those with lesser opportunity;

(b) an excessive rate of saving must on balance mitigate the burden of those bearing this hardship.

## 8.3   Rawls's Difference Principle

Rawls's difference principle has generated much discussion and has also been trivialized and misinterpreted. One must go beyond the words of the principle into the body of *A Theory of Justice* to understand how Rawls arrives at the principle and what meanings he attaches to the words in it.

The difference principle is not drawn out of thin air but is a result of an optimization-under-uncertainty argument. In the original position Rawls imagines "representative men" drawn from all future classes of society *in all future generations* considering the social contract to be drawn up. They have limited knowledge[4] of what fate will have in store, and thus have to make decisions under uncertainty. Rawls argues that rational persons in this situation would adopt what decision theorists call a "least worst," or "maximin," rule.

Rawls argues that, in the original position, members of society would apply the maximin rule only to the *primary social* goods of rights and liberties, powers and opportunities, and wealth and income. This proposal is of course vague and has been attacked as such. Rawls makes various suggestions as to how it might be implemented. One is to form an index, that is, some weighted combination of the primary social goods, and to calculate the index for the representative man of the least advantaged group, but even if this suggestion could be implemented, Rawls (1971, 98) notes, "The serious difficulty is how to define the least fortunate group," and goes on, perhaps even more vaguely:

Here it seems impossible to avoid a certain arbitrariness. One possibility is to choose a particular social position, say that of the unskilled worker, and then to count as the least advantaged all those with the average income and wealth of this group, or less. The expectation of the lowest representative man is defined as the average taken over this whole class. Another alternative is a definition solely in terms of relative income and wealth with no reference to social position. Thus all persons with less than half of the median income and wealth may be taken as the least advantaged segment.

In spite of its vagueness, Rawls feels that the difference principle is key to his aim of improving on utilitarianism. This is clearly brought out in a subsequent paper (Rawls 1974), where he defends the superiority of the difference principle over utilitarianism at length.

There is much more in *A Theory of Justice* than the argument that, in the original position and behind a veil of ignorance, members of society would contract for the first and second principles to be their guide. After stating these principles, Rawls (1971) elaborates on them and what persons in the original position would do, arguing that they would go further in three subsequent stages—a constitutional convention stage, a legislative stage, and a judicial/administrative stage—which would enable them to think through and sort out in more detail how the basic structure of a just society would be designed. Here, Rawls admits that his four-stage sequence was suggested by the United States Constitution and its history (1971, 196). He also takes up the problem of distribution in more detail, saying at the outset that the market needs to play a central role (1971, 274): "The ideal scheme sketched in the next several sections makes considerable use of market arrangements. It is only in this way, I believe, that the problem of distribution can be handled as a case of pure procedural justice."

The sketch of the "ideal scheme" starts with the "four-branch" public finance model pioneered by Musgrave (1959). That is, the government is assumed to comprise (1) an allocation branch consisting of the free market but with taxes and subsidies and changes in property rights designed to correct the "more obvious departures from efficiency caused by the failure of prices to measure accurately social benefits and costs" (Rawls 1971, 276); (2) a stabilization branch to ensure full employment; (3) a transfer branch to guarantee a social minimum of resources; and (4) a distribution branch "to preserve an approximate justice in distributive shares by means of taxation and the necessary adjustments in the rights of property" (1971, 276).

Rawls follows his discussion of the branches of government with a discussion of a wide range of other issues having to do with proper institutional design, including how to deal with time preferences, duties, the status of majority rule, civil disobedience, and conscientious refusal. Finally, in a concluding part of *A Theory of Justice*, Rawls takes up "Goodness as Rationality," "The Sense of Justice," and "The Good of Justice."

### 8.4  Rawls's *Political Liberalism*

As discussed below, many philosophers and social scientists faulted various aspects of Rawls's *Theory of Justice*, and after its publication, Rawls wrote several articles rebutting his critics. One of the most extensive criticisms of *A Theory of Justice* was spelled out by Rawls himself in his *Political Liberalism* (1993).

What did Rawls find lacking in *A Theory of Justice*? Upon reflection, Rawls realized that it did not sufficiently accord with the way that modern democratic societies function; in a word, *A Theory of Justice* was inadequate as positive theory, which, in turn, undermined its value as normative theory.

Specifically, in part III of *A Theory of Justice* Rawls envisions a "well-ordered," stable society wherein all of the members hold a common view of the social good. All of this is the result of society's members having entered into a social contract arrived at by means of the thought experiment of the initial position behind a veil of ignorance. But, in democratic societies, one doesn't find the cohesiveness of view that Rawls's "well-ordered" society envisions; instead, one finds a diversity of outlooks based on different comprehensive moral doctrines. What is more, some of these comprehensive doctrines are profoundly incompatible on fundamental issues. How is it that democratic societies exist in relative tranquility, somehow accommodating these basic differences?

The task of *Political Liberalism* is to explain this phenomenon and to modify *A Theory of Justice* to take it into account. The explanation rests on two fundamental ideas. First is the idea of an "overlapping consensus." That is, in democratic societies, although there are differing comprehensive moral doctrines, they overlap to form a set of commonly held moral beliefs. The second is the idea of "reasonableness." Rawls considers persons to be *reasonable* when, in social interactions, they are willing to abide by rules or norms, given the knowledge that others will so abide (1993, 49). By the same token, those who violate the rules, while others are abiding by them, are *un*reasonable. Reasonableness is required if a society is to evolve a system of fair cooperation.

The result of Rawls's reexamination is a revision of his notion of a well-ordered society. Unlike *A Theory of Justice*, which envisioned a single comprehensive moral doctrine, *Political Liberalism* envisions a number of comprehensive doctrines coexisting because of a common core and because reasonable members of society have evolved a system of fair cooperation.

Nevertheless, the basic edifice of *A Theory of Justice* remains. Perhaps most fundamental is the notion that there is such a thing as the common or social good, that it can be found, and that reasonable persons can enter into a social contract to construct a well-ordered society. The thought experiment of the original position behind a veil of ignorance keeps its central place, as do the lexicographic ordering of principles of justice, the difference principle, and the notion of primary goods.

## 8.5   Attacks

Rawls has been attacked by theorists who span the political spectrum from Marxism to libertarianism, as well as by theorists who represent probably all disciplines within the social sciences. For example, Buchanan (1982, 122–161) lists no less than ten fundamental Marxist objections to Rawls and discusses each in detail.

The sweeping comprehensiveness of Rawls's theory is at once its strength and its weakness, for it makes Rawls vulnerable to being skewered by the telling concrete example. For instance, the difference principle would suggest that money earmarked for a National Merit Scholarship should be diverted to improve the lot of accident victims who are in hopelessly terminal, vegetative states, even if the diverted money brings only minuscule improvement. Rawls (1974) rejects such examples on the grounds that they are "micro" examples and the difference principle is meant to apply to "macro" policy matters, such as the determination of income tax policy. But this defense simply invites critics to find less extreme concrete examples, including ones in the present income tax code, that still skewer, and so on.

Offering no evidence to support his claims of what individuals in the original position would do, Rawls makes empirical leaps of faith throughout *A Theory of Justice*. In chapter 10 we consider laboratory experiments by Frohlich, Oppenheimer, and Eavey (1987), as well as successor experiments extensively reported on by Frohlich and Oppenheimer (1992). These indicate that members of society, American and others, would not necessarily use the difference principle as a distributive justice starting point.

Then, there is the issue of how universal Rawls's scheme really is. At bottom, Rawls's theory is a secular moral construct, one that tries to replace the notion of a Supreme Being by reasoning, starting with the idea of the original position behind a veil of ignorance and evolving by means of the application of logic. It is hard to imagine that such a secular theory would be accepted by all religious groups within the Western world, much less by all cultures.

However easy it is to list serious infirmities with Rawls's theory, one cannot deny its successes. *A Theory of Justice* is perhaps *the* most cited work in the social sciences within recent memory; it has stimulated new research in economic justice and political philosophy and has gotten scholars in disparate disciplines to talk to each other. Moreover, as I argue in chapter 11, Rawls's introspection has in fact revealed principles that are routinely invoked by members of society as they strive "fairly" to interact with each other, with businesses, and with governmental agencies.

## Exercises

1. Describe the evolution of administrative law to its present-day view.

2. What thought experiment does Rawls use to come up with the main elements of the social contract? What are the "primary goods" that are central to the social contract that Rawls envisions?

3. Rawls's first and second principles are *lexicographic*. What is meant by this term? Describe how it applies in the case of the two principles.

4. Discuss Rawls's difference principle.

5. Discuss some of the criticisms of Rawls's theory of justice.

6. Contrast and compare Rawls's *Theory of Justice* (1972) with his *Political Liberalism* (1993).

# 9

**Normative Theories II: Robert Nozick, Utilitarianism, and Superfairness**

*Taxes are about more than money and about more than economics. They are about fairness, and this bill is fair.*

Senator Robert Packwood (*New York Times*, 27 September 1986)

## 9.1  Introduction

The theoretical economic justice world does not begin and end with Rawls; there are other, contending normative theories. This chapter considers three of them: (1) Nozick's procedural justice approach, (2) utilitarianism, and (3) superfairness.

## 9.2  Nozick's Procedural Approach to Justice

Historically, one of the objections to the social contract philosophy has been the artificiality of the notion of society's agreeing on how to go from some primitive state to a new, "just" state. In the social contract view, history does not matter—at any time society can start over again with a proper organization.

In reality, however, history does matter. Intuitive notions of justice generally take into account how the present state of affairs has come about; theories of justice that depend only on a "current time slice" or "end state" must by their nature be deficient. Although Rawls addresses the question of procedural justice, at bottom, his theory is contractarian; its thrust is to find a basic structure of society that will lead to a just end state. Thus Rawls's theory is subject to the general criticism leveled at social contract theories.

Where history and procedures matter a great deal is how and under what circumstances property rights are assigned and transferred. Coase's

(1937) work on externalities discussed in chapter 4 is a excellent illustration of the importance of property rights. Rawls (1971), however, aside from listing the right to hold property as one of the basic liberties (p. 61), has little to say; he has no theory of property rights, and what he has to say reads like a brief for condemning the free market (p. 308):

Accepting the marginal productivity theory of distribution, each factor of production receives an income according to how much it adds to output ... In this sense, a worker is paid the full value of the results of his labor, no more no less. Offhand this strikes us as fair. It appeals to a traditional idea of the natural right of property in the fruits of our labor. Therefore to some writers the precept of contribution has seemed satisfactory as a principle of justice.

It is easy to see, however, that this is not the case. The marginal product of labor depends upon supply and demand. What an individual contributes by his work varies with the demand of firms for his skills, and this in turn varies with the demand for the products of firms. An individual's contribution is also affected by how many offer similar talents. There is no presumption, then, that following the precept of contribution leads to a just outcome unless the underlying market forces, and the availability of opportunities which they reflect, are appropriately regulated.

This, of course, immediately brings up what Rawls means by "appropriately regulated"; in particular, to what extent will government interference, in Rawls's scheme, encroach on market allocations of resources. Without further elaboration, Rawls's statement would appear to be a glaring contradiction to his earlier espousal of relying on the market as the "allocation branch" of his basic structure.

In contrast to Rawls, Nozick focuses on procedural justice and developing a theory of the just assignment and transfer of property rights. Instead of starting with a collective of persons negotiating a social contract for the social good, Nozick (1974, 32–33) rejects the very notion of "social good" and focuses on the individual:

[T]here is no *social entity* with a good that undergoes some sacrifice for its own good. There are only individual people, with their own individual lives. Using one of these people for the benefit of others, uses him and benefits the others. Nothing more.... Talk of an overall social good covers this up.... To use a person in this way does not sufficiently respect and take account of the fact that he is a separate person.

Like Rawls, Nozick (1974) uses the thought experiment—in fact, two main thought experiments—to formulate his theory or model of how society should function. In the first thought experiment, Nozick considers how a society would spontaneously form associations to protect individuals from harm inflicted by others. He concludes that the result would be a minimal state, that is, a state that maintains a monopoly over all use of force except that necessary in immediate self-defense and which limits redistribution of resources to that necessary to protect everyone: "Out of anarchy, pressed by spontaneous groupings, mutual-protection associations, division of labor, market pressures, economies of scale, rational self-interest—there arises something very much resembling a minimal state or a group of geographically distinct minimal states" (pp. 16–17). In the second thought experiment, Nozick considers the other extreme—utopia. That is, suppose members of society were completely free to join together with other members to form a coalition, which, in turn, they could leave should that benefit them. Nozick argues that, again, the result would be a minimal state.

The bulk of *Anarchy, State, and Utopia* is devoted to spelling out these two thought experiments in detail. What has gotten the most attention, and what is of most interest to us, are Nozick's relatively brief discussions of the acquisition and transfer of property. Nozick argues that the justice of a given distribution of wealth or income in society should depend only on the historical evolution that leads to it. In Nozick's (1974) schema "a distribution is just if it arises from another (just) distribution by legitimate means" (p. 151). Deviation from this notion in the name of achieving a desired end state will require unjust state interference.

Nozick (1974) cites what has now become known as the "Wilt Chamberlain example" to illustrate this. The example is dated because Wilt Chamberlain is no longer playing professional basketball and because inflation and skyrocketing salaries of professional athletes make Nozick's illustrative dollar amounts seem inconsequential. However, we do not need the particulars of Wilt Chamberlain's situation when he was an active player.

Nozick's (1974) argument is straightforward. Suppose we agree that a given, initial societal income distribution is just. Now, a superstar basketball player emerges, and he negotiates a contract to receive a small fraction of the price of every ticket for each of his games, a fraction that fans are delighted to pay. The result is that he collects an exorbitant salary, which markedly skews society's income distribution. This, now apparently unjust income distribution or end state can only be corrected by government intervention. Nozick argues that the Wilt Chamberlain example illustrates the procedural fairness difficulties of end-state principles of justice: such principles can be realized only by continual government interference in peoples lives (p. 163).

More generally, Nozick (1974) argues that justice revolves around the principles that determine the justice of one's holdings. These are three: (1) the principle of acquisition of holdings, (2) the principle of transfer of holdings, and (3) the principle of rectification of violation of the first two principles. As an economy functions, redistributions of holdings constantly take place, and as long as the transfers and acquisitions are just, the end states are acceptable. However, some transfers and acquisitions may occur through theft, treachery, fraud, unjust use of force, or through other unjust means, and we cannot be sure that all the redistributions will be just. The principle of rectification allows us to accommodate unjust distributions and to correct them. Nozick suggests that if an injustice has occurred, we base rectification on what the expected outcome would have been if the injustice had not occurred. In cases of ties, we can perhaps use end-state principles to resolve which of the expected outcomes to choose.

One of the Nozick's (1974) principal aims is to argue against state involvement on matters of justice; his theory is an explicit attempt to formulate an "invisible hand" scheme of justice that essentially operates at the individual level and avoids the involvement of society. In Nozick's words: "Our main conclusions about the state are that a minimal state, limited to the narrow functions of protection against force, theft, fraud, enforcement of contracts, and so on, is justified; that any more extensive state will violate persons' rights not to be forced to do certain things, and is unjustified; and that the minimal state is inspiring as well as right" (p. ix).

Nozick's (1974) theory has been faulted on a number of grounds. For example, how can society implement the principle of rectification without some rules? These rules must come from someplace. This, in turn, leads to the issue of a just starting position of the just historical evolution that Nozick envisions—the heart of the distributional problem. Likewise, suppose through a series of just transfers, perhaps over many generations, a handful of individuals acquire control over most of society's assets, leaving the rest of society in abject poverty, below a subsistence level? This, of course, is not far from the situation in some Third World countries, and has resulted in societies that most observers do not consider just.

### 9.3   Utilitarianism

Utilitarianism is far from dead, in spite of Rawls's devoting a good part of *A Theory of Justice* to attacking it. As I argue in the next chapter, policy makers routinely act on utilitarian principles without giving their actions a second's thought. And what they do is buttressed by a modern literature that defends various versions of utilitarianism.

Ironically, Harsanyi (1976), an ardent defender of utilitarianism, independently of Rawls and prior to him conceived of the same starting point for a theory of economic justice—members of society in an original position behind a veil of ignorance. However, Harsanyi argues that, in this situation, decision theorists (he is a decision theorist) have rejected the use of the maximin decision rule because of the bizarre results it leads to. In particular, if you were to take the maximin rule to its logical conclusion, you would not venture outdoors (after all, you might be shot by a drive-by shooter), nor would you drive a car (you might be involved in an accident or a car-jacking). That is, according to the maximin principle, your decisions— venture or don't venture outdoors, drive or don't drive a car—are independent of how large or small a probability you attach to the possible outcomes. In applying the maximin rule, your goal is simply to avoid the worst of possible outcomes (Harsanyi 1976, 40).

In contrast to Rawls, Harsanyi (1976, 45) argues that in an original position with $n$ members of society, the rational person would assign a probability of $1/n$ of becoming the best-off individual, or the second-best-off individual, and so forth, up to the worst-off individual. This would lead the rational individual to choose the social structure that maximized the individual's *average* level of feeling "best-off". Of course, in determining "best off," each individual would use his or her own measuring rod of "happiness," or, in modern jargon, "utility," and thus would maximize the average utility level for each possible social structure. But the average utility level is a sum of utilities, each weighted by equal probability of $1/n$, and Harsanyi's argument is, in effect, an argument for the rational person in the original position to opt for utilitarianism as the basis of the design of society. If accepted, Harsanyi's argument undermines Rawls's difference principle, and thus Rawls's main theoretical tool for constructing an alternative to utilitarianism.[1] But what about the standard objection to utilitarianism, that it disregards individual rights, usually illustrated by a patently outrageous example?

For instance, suppose that, with the completion of a few more experiments, medical science is guaranteed to produce a cure for cancer. The experiments require subjects who are healthy twenty-year-olds and who have a rare combination of genetic heritage and blood chemistry. Only ten such persons exist, but all have been identified. Unfortunately, the experiments require that the lives of all of them be sacrificed; utilitarianism would seem to say that the sacrifices are morally acceptable because they will enhance the greater good. Modern utilitarians, however, would reject examples like these, rebutting the general proposition that utilitarianism ignores individual rights. One such rebuttal argument is sketched by Murphy and Coleman (1990, 73–74):

[T]he kind of utilitarian theory that we will now consider will depend upon two important distinctions: (1) a distinction between things that are valuable for their own sake (intrinsically valuable) and things that are instrumentally valuable because they lead to things that are intrinsically valuable; and (2) a distinction between applying the Principle of Utility ("the greatest good for the greatest number") in choosing each particular *act* that one performs and applying that principle in choosing various social *rules* or *practices*. . . . We might, as utilitarians, approve of certain general rules or practices that assign certain rights to persons—e.g., the right not to be experimented on without one's consent. . . . The reason we adopt this rule or practice, however, is because of our belief that the majority of people will be happier in the long run living in a society having a rule (conferring a right) of this nature. . . . It is a mistake, indeed a caricature, to claim, as some critics have, that utilitarians can make no place for such important moral concepts as justice, fairness, rights, merit, or desert. . . . What the utilitarian cannot do (does not *want* to do, indeed) is regard rights as having ultimate or primary or fundamental value; only utility (the promotion of general welfare) can have that. Rights thus have only instrumental value. . . .

Nevertheless, Murphy and Coleman (1990) also caution that, at bottom, the differences between utilitarianism and theories based on fundamental human rights are profound. They use Kant as an example, remarking that in many ways, both Rawls and Nozick are modern attempts at formulating a Kantian moral theory. For, utilitarianism is based on *"sentience*, the capacity to feel pleasure and pain," and assumes that (1990, 76):

[e]thics is about preference satisfaction, and the basic requirement is that preference satisfaction be maximized.

By contrast, for Kant, as well as for Christianity generally, the starting point is the special status of human beings (p. 78):

A core claim of Christian ethics—a claim accepted by Kant—is that there is something uniquely precious about human beings from the moral point of view. There are, for example, certain special moral requirements (rights) that attach to human beings that do not attach to any other animal—e.g., the requirement that we not kill and eat them for food, or hunt them for sport, or experiment on them without their consent for medical science.

These different starting points lead to different ethical outlooks (p. 77):

According to Kantianism, ethics is not primarily about preference satisfaction ... it is rather about how to respect the freedom of rational beings ... to control their destinies by their own choices even if this tends to produce social and individual unhappiness.

Furthermore (p. 78),

Thus, utilitarianism fails in large measure because it cannot capture the special respect that, according to Christianity and Kant, is owed to human beings because of their special moral status.

Put another way, every theory or model must start *somewhere*. Otherwise, we would need a "metatheory" to explain the theory, and a "meta-metatheory" to explain the "metatheory," and so on, ad infinitum. Whether the starting point is the original position of Rawls and Harsanyi, Nozick's thought experiments about protective associations, or the revelations of a religion's Superior Being makes a difference, and different starting points can ultimately lead to deep contradictions. For a modern discussion and critique of utilitarianism by moral philosophers and economists, the reader is referred to Sen and Williams (1982).

## 9.4   Envy-Free and Superfairness Theory

The last decade or so has seen a burst of activity in economics on what is variously called "envy," "equity," or "superfairness" theory. In its present state, the theory would seem to have limited applications to policy making, and it has attracted little attention from other disciplines. It remains to be seen whether it can it can be extended to become a more practical tool.

The theory is simplest to understand in the context of a pure exchange economy, that is, a situation where one is concerned with a just or fair distribution of goods among the members of society, without regard to how the goods were produced. The theory's starting point is the technical notion of envy; if each member of society is allotted some "consumption bundle" of the total goods available to society, then individual 1 is said to "envy" individual 2 if 1 prefers 2's bundle to 1's own. If no individual prefers the bundle of anyone else to his or her own, then the economy is said to have an "equitable" distribution (Baumol 1986 calls this a "super-fair" distribution).

An obvious equitable distribution is an equal division of the available goods, so that each person in the economy has an identical bundle of goods. However, as we saw in chapter 2, if the individuals comprising the economy have different tastes, this equitable division may not be economically efficient. You and I may be initially given equal amounts of coffee and tea, but if you prefer coffee and abhor tea and the reverse is true for me, then we can mutually benefit by an exchange of coffee for tea. Following previous writers, Varian (1975) reserves the term *fair* for those allocations that are simultaneously equitable and economically efficient. An appealing feature of this fairness notion is that in a perfectly competitive, pure exchange economy, at least one fair allocation will always exist. The proof of its existence follows essentially from an extension of the process alluded to above: first divide the goods into equal consumption bundles for each of the members of the economy, and then allow mutually beneficial exchanges to take place through the market mechanism.

Matters become more complicated when one introduces production into the economy. For one thing, one must now take explicit account of labor, a key element in production. But in Varian's (1975) words: "What do we mean by equal division when labor is present? Should we correct for ability? Should we give one agent some of the other agent's labor? Or what?" The matter is even more serious than the quotes indicate. As Pazner and Schmeidler (1974) have demonstrated, if we simply append hours of labor and leisure to the list of commodities and proceed as before, it can be shown that a fair allocation does not necessarily exist.

To get around these difficulties, Varian (1975) introduces the notion of comparisons of *complete* positions of the agents in the economy. One considers not only what each agent consumes but also what he produces— that is, the consumption-*output* bundle of each agent. An agent is said to prefer the *"complete* position" of the other agent if the agent would rather consume what the other agent consumes *and* produce what the other agent produces. The notions of equitable and fair are then extended. An allocation is *wealth-equitable* if each agent prefers his or her consumption-output bundle to that of every other agent; it is considered *wealth-fair* if it is also efficient. Varian then shows that a wealth-fair allocation will always exist.

Finally, Varian (1975), arguing that his theory incorporates the elements of both Nozick's and Rawls's theories, proposes that at birth each agent in society be given an initial endowment of an equal share of society's resources, and upon death that the agent's property revert to the state to be distributed equally to new generations. Further, agents are to transfer ownership of goods and services only through the market mechanism. Such a scheme accords with the notions of both Rawls and Nozick, but leads to a wealth-fair allocation.

Because Varian's (1975) scheme has agents transfer ownership through the market mechanism, it is in effect an invisible hand scheme that operates at the level of the individual. In a perfectly competitive economy Varian's scheme thus fits economic justice into the action of the market and, except for the initial endowment at birth and transfer at death, avoids society's being brought in to administer economic justice. Unfortunately, the regulated sector is a case, at least in theory, where markets fail, and one does not expect perfect competition to be efficient; one therefore does not expect Varian's ideas to carry through without modification.[2]

Like all of the other normative theories we have considered, envy-free theory is open to more fundamental attacks. For example, when one thinks of Rawls's great concern for individual self-respect and the primary goods of rights and liberties, power and opportunities, and income and wealth, or of Nozick's concern with the individual's being protected from harm inflicted by others, envy-free theory seems sterile, abstract, and unworldly. According to the media, Ralph Nader lives a spartan existence, with a minimal income and number of possessions. Many who own much more than he envy him his power, yet do not envy his "consumption bundle"— nor he theirs.

In a word, envy-free theory starts with the notion of exchange of material things as the self-evident beginning and end of human behavior, and attempts no construction of a deeper foundation for the theoretical edifice that follows. At the same time, the theory has given us a framework of analysis for a whole class of economic fairness issues, and has laid the groundwork for further applications.

## 9.5   Discussion

The outrageous example of sacrificing a few human beings for the greater good is perhaps not completely far-fetched. At least three presidents of the United States have had to make soul-searching decisions as to whether or not hostages should be sacrificed to prevent more widespread hostage taking. Likewise, in approving new drugs, the Food and Drug Administration (FDA) faces the trade-off between the rights of citizens to be protected from unexpected serious side effects, sometimes fatal ones, and conferring the drug's benefits on the vast numbers who will suffer only minor side effects, if any.

The balancing of individual rights and the common good is a problem that policy makers cannot escape. It is also an ancient problem in moral and political philosophy, which, as the above literature review indicates, does not have an easy, universally accepted solution. The debate over this and other fundamental matters in distributive justice and moral theory goes back to antiquity and continues to this day. Our review has only scratched the surface and, because of limited space, has had to omit the review of such contributions as the writings of economists who have taken moral philosophy seriously, for example, Gordon (1980), LeGrand (1991), Schotter (1985), Silver (1989), and Sugden (1986). Nor did we have space to discuss the enormous Marxist-oriented literature on social justice or some of the recent Catholic Church writings, for example, the Catholic Bishops' Letter (National Conference of Catholic Bishops 1986) and the recent papal encyclical on distributive justice, *Centesimus Annus* (Pope John Paul II 1991).[3] That the debate continues encourages the notion that distributive justice is relative, merely "a matter of opinion," and thus something not to be taken seriously.

However, this is a view that is both too pessimistic and, for the policy maker, dangerous. Even though the foundations of a moral theory will always be open to debate, this does not mean that there are no standards of rational discourse about moral issues and standards as to what it is admissible to discuss. More to the point, that attempts at a comprehensive moral theory, such as Rawls's, will probably always be subject to attack, does not mean that there is a total lack of consensus about distributive justice. On the contrary, in our daily functions in society we routinely make moral judgments and decisions and routinely base economic transactions on mutual trust; this would be impossible if there were not a strong consensus view as to what is morally acceptable. This is, in fact, Rawls's notion of "overlapping consensus" that is a basis of the reformulation of his theory contained in *Political Liberalism* (Rawls 1993). Indeed, there is now a considerable literature of empirical work that tries to delineate this consensus; we examine it in the next two chapters.

## Exercises

1. What are Nozick's three principles for the determination of the justice of one's property holdings?

2. Contrast and compare Rawls's and Nozick's theories of justice.

3. Describe Nozick's "Wilt Chamberlain example." What point does the example make?

4. What is Harsanyi's objection to the use of the maximin principle as a decision rule?

5. What is Harsanyi's (1976) argument for utilitarianism?

6. Distinguish between "act" and "rule" utilitarianism.

7. Why are utilitarianism and Kantianism fundamentally different?

Positive Theories I:
The Formal Principle of
Distributive Justice and
Institutional Framing

*What is fairness? Well, unless you are going to take the position that everyone should earn the same thing, fairness is going to be arbitrary.*

William F. Buckley (*Tucson Citizen*, 17 March 1992)

## 10.1 Legitimacy of Fairness Principles

A common view, reflected in the above quote, is that fairness is ill defined and arbitrary, "a matter of opinion." Some economists push this observation further: because fairness is arbitrary, when it appears in a policy debate, it is simply a smoke screen for self-interest. A skilled economic analyst of this mind-set will brush aside fairness arguments to get to the underlying self-interest agenda, much as the archaeologist brushes aside surface dirt to get to the underlying artifacts.

However, if fairness is such a charade, how does one explain the importance attached to it? For example, chapter 8 cited authorities to the effect that administrative law—the law that governs the procedures of regulation—has evolved to the point that fairness is its centerpiece. How do we explain this? In the administration of regulation and in other parts of the polity, how do we explain which fairness arguments will be effective and which not?

Clearly, if perceived fairness is important for policy making, and to my mind the evidence is overwhelming that this is the case, then we cannot dismiss or ignore fairness. Instead, we have to accept that "perceptions are realities" and deal with fairness. If we decide to deal with perceived fairness and still adhere to the notion that fairness arguments are insincere, then we have the task of constructing a theory of insincere fairness argumentation.

As it happens, the notion that fairness is arbitrary and simply a smoke screen for self-interest is simplistic and contradicts not only the evolution of fairness in the administrative law, but common experience. For example, suppose faculty salaries were determined by the color of shirt that each faculty member wore last Tuesday. There would undoubtedly be a cry of outrage from faculty members, including of course the members of the economics department faculty. Instead, we observe that faculty salaries, and salaries in society generally, are determined by accepted principles, chosen from a class of principles that are considered to be legitimate bases for salary determination. The range of principles in the legitimate class may be wide, but it will not be infinite, and there may be much disagreement about the particular principle that is chosen. Indeed, self-interest will undoubtedly arise, and those who can benefit from the adoption of some alternative principle will lobby to have it adopted. But, again, the alternative will also belong to a class of principles that meet standards of legitimacy.

How are the standards of legitimacy described? How in fact does society act "fairly," and can we characterize its actions succinctly in a theory that can forecast fairness outcomes? These are some of the questions addressed in this chapter and the next in a survey of positive theories of economic fairness, justice, and equity.

Our survey of positive theory is divided into several parts. First we contrast the different goals of positive and normative fairness theory. Then we consider the deep-seated notion that fairness requires like treatment of like cases, something which in moral philosophy is captured by what is variously called the "Aristotelian" or "Formal Principle of Distributive Justice." We follow this by a discussion of institutions and group formation, and of some of the factors that give society stability—trust, order, conventions, and coordination. Finally, in the next chapter, we consider other general principles of perceived economic justice.

## 10.2   Goals of a Positive Theory

The structural engineers who designed the building in which I work did not use atomic physics to do their job. In their training they probably studied little atomic physics. Instead, they used highly idealized theories of stresses and strains and structural stability that have evolved over several hundred years—theories that can be easily implemented and that have proved themselves through the building of thousands upon thousands of successful structures.[1]

The theories make big abstractions from complex realities, but they are simple enough to be implemented by hand or computer calculations. These theories are typically based on research done many years ago by some academic, who either derived them theoretically from more basic theories or proved them through laboratory experimentation, and they are continually refined and improved by basic researchers in departments of materials science and engineering, some of whom in fact use physical theories at the level of the atom or molecule. The engineers directly responsible for building design, however, have neither the time nor the training to delve into details at the atomic level. They need grosser methods that they know "work," in the sense that they lead to buildings that do not fall down. Similarly, when we compare the normative theories of economic justice discussed in chapters 8 and 9 with the economists' views of ethical issues in the design of economic institutions discussed in chapter 7, the economists' views seem crude and simplistic. Yet, they "work" to the satisfaction of many economists.

On the other hand, the society in which we function is highly interconnected and depends to a large extent on trust and complex moral codes that we pay little conscious attention to and may not even realize we are following and that, in turn, are the result of childhood training in the home, church, school, and schoolyard, as well as accumulated life experiences. We are all "programmed from birth" to act in ways that are considered morally acceptable, and, for that matter, preprogrammed genetically before birth. When one reflects on the economists' present ethical mind-set in approaching policy issues, there clearly seems much room for theories of fairness that can complement and strengthen present economic theory to the benefit of policy makers.

Our review in chapters 8 and 9 of professional moral philosophers' attempts to construct a comprehensive, normative ethical theory that accords with common experience and yet is free of internal contradictions shows that theirs is a formidable job, akin to that of the physicist trying to understand the physical world from the level of the atom upwards. Likewise, an equally formidable job is that of constructing an economic theory based on rational, self-seeking economic agents that again accords with common experience and explains all economic phenomena consistently and without internal contradictions.

As is the case in moral philosophy, advances in economic theory continue apace. For example, in the last few decades we have seen an outpouring of economic theorizing that explicitly takes into account the information, risk, and incentive structures of the economic environment in which the economic agents find themselves. Self-interest typically implies conflicting goals, with the result that the actions of the agents can be modeled as an economic game. The goal of this strand of research is to characterize the game's equilibrium, that is, a state in which all agents are acting optimally, given the economic environment. Modern economic methodology is powerful, and the skilled theorist can often explain, especially after the fact, what appear to be "fairness" phenomena purely in terms of pursuit of self-interest and without recourse to fairness notions, thus giving a "rational choice" explanation that is competitive with a "fairness theory" explanation.

The scope of such "rational choice" explanations of fairness phenomena is, however, limited at best; basic research in economic theory only indirectly addresses the constellation of phenomena we generally associate with fairness issues that arise in policy making. Fortunately, in parallel with advances in basic ethical and economic theory have recently come advances in the construction of *positive* theories of economic justice and fairness, theories about how economic justice and fairness actually *is*, rather than *ought to be*, perceived and dealt with.

The advances are interdisciplinary. The earliest work, going back over thirty years, has been done by social psychologists and sociologists and is known by them as "equity theory"; more recently, a smaller but still substantial "fairness theory" literature has grown out of game theory and economics, based primarily on laboratory experiments and anecdotal evidence.

In my view, the research on positive theories holds the most short-run promise of giving policy makers tools to cope with fairness issues. What they need is a theory whose benefits—in particular, its ability to predict—outweighs its costs. Ideally, they would like a theory that, confronted with a given fairness situation, will predict the outcome of a proposed course of action much better than "common sense" or some competing theory, and that will take fewer resources to implement. In analogy with structural engineering, they need a simple theory that will successfully lead to the robust, low-cost design of regulatory and governmental institutions.

I accept at the outset that, to the moral philosopher, the theory we are looking for may appear very crude, with gaping holes and internal contradictions.[2] I also accept that, to the economic theorist, our theory may seem ad hoc and "irrational" because it does not fit the economists' standard theories and methodologies.

In summary, in reviewing the research on positive theories of fairness and justice, the reader should keep in mind that the goal of a positive theory is fundamentally different from that of a normative theory. A normative theory seeks comprehensiveness and internal consistency. But the main goal of a positive theory is for it to "work." It should be able not only to explain; it should be both cheaper and have more predictive power than alternative theories, including modern economic theory.

## 10.3   The Formal Principle of Distributive Justice

We typically learn to share early in life, both in the home and in nursery school or kindergarten. Thus candy or fruit is apt to be divided equally among a group of children. Of course, if there is some "fair" basis for unequal division—perhaps one of the children has won a spelling bee that entitles him or her to a larger share (desert), or perhaps a child must ingest sugar for health reasons (need)—the division may be unequal.

The notion that fairness requires like treatment of like cases is deeply ingrained in American society and perhaps in most societies. As a normative principle, it can be traced at least as far back as Aristotle's writings. Nowadays, it is often called the "Formal Principle of Distributive Justice"; a modern formulation, due to Feinberg (1973), is

Equals should be treated equally, and unequals unequally, in proportion to relevant similarities and differences.

As stated, the Formal Principle is vague, containing the terms *equally*, *unequally*, and *relative similarities and differences*, which require further delineation. Nevertheless, even at this level, the Formal Principle has normative content; it tells us that "unequal" treatment should be based on "relevant" similarities and differences. Thus American society no longer accepts color of skin as a morally relevant basis for unequal treatment, nor religious belief as a relevant basis for the unequal provision of public education. However, the Formal Principle is otherwise silent, and we must turn to *material* principles of distributive justice such as need, desert, merit, productivity, supply and demand, and the like, to get a more specific basis for resource distribution.[3]

But even if we accept the notion of material principles of justice, there remains the question of which of them is applied in which circumstances. To answer this question, in recent research, Mark Isaac, Deborah Mathieu, and I (Isaac, Mathieu, and Zajac 1991) have focused on the notions of an institution and institutional framing. According to North (1990, 3), "Institutions are the rules of the game in a society or, more formally, are the humanly devised constraints that shape human interaction." Stated still more formally, following Smith (1982), North's idea defines an institution as a system of economic agents' property rights in communication and exchange, given an economic environment characterized by the agents' preferences, knowledge, and initial endowments of resources. By *framing* we (Isaac, Mathieu, and Zajac 1991) simply mean the shaping of perceptions of fairness. As a result of a survey of the existing literature consisting of anecdotal, survey and laboratory evidence, my coauthors and I concluded that the economic environment, operative institutions, and history "frame" or give specific meanings to the terms in the Formal Principle. More loosely, *institutional* framing is the key to understanding how and under what circumstances the Formal Principle will be applied.

Put in other terms, all of us function in a number of institutions—the family, our place of employment, the church, civic organizations, the town in which we live, and so forth. Within each of these institutions there typically exist well-defined notions, sometimes formally codified in a set of rules or bylaws and sometimes simply a matter of common understanding, of who is equal and who is unequal, and of the relevant similarities and differences that are to be used to implement the formal principle. These notions in turn cause us, in each of our roles as members of the various institutions to which we belong, to form expectations about the "like treatment of like cases." In effect, the expectations form an explicit, or more often an implicit, contract among the members of a given institution. We feel outraged when we conclude that the contract has been broken; we have been treated "unfairly."

Thus you and I may feel equal on the tennis court, but if you are the CEO of a large corporation in which I am a middle manager, then we will accept as fair the corporation's assignment to me of less office space and fewer secretarial services than to you. On other hand, if I sense that you expect favorable treatment from me on the tennis court, say, that I am required to give you the benefit of the doubt on out-of-bounds calls, I will feel that your behavior is unfair.

Next, we consider some of the evidence that has led my coauthors and me to our point of view.

### 10.4   Evidence for Institutional Framing

Equity Theory of Social Psychology

The most intense empirical work on how economic justice is actually perceived has been done by social psychologists. The work started in the early 1960s, and, in 1979, Walster, Walster, and Berscheid reported that over 400 empirical studies had been done; by now, the number is much larger.

The typical study involves a few subjects who are asked to divide some economic pie, given a particular set of circumstances.

Walster, Walster, and Berscheid (1979, 6) summarize what in their words is the "heart of equity theory" by four propositions:

*Proposition I:* Individuals will try to maximize their outcomes (where outcomes equal rewards minus costs).

*Proposition IIA:* Groups can maximize collective reward by evolving accepted systems for equitably apportioning resources among members. Thus, groups will evolve such systems of equity and will attempt to induce members to accept and adhere to these systems.

*Proposition IIB:* Groups will generally reward members who treat others equitably, and generally punish (increase the costs for) members who treat others inequitably.

*Proposition III:* When individuals find themselves participating in inequitable relationships, they will become distressed. The more inequitable the relationship, the more distress individuals will feel.

*Proposition IV:* Individuals who discover they are in an inequitable relationship will attempt to eliminate their distress by restoring equity. The greater the inequity that exists, the more distress they will feel, and the harder they will try to restore equity.

Walster, Walster, and Bersheid (1979) further formulate the basis of what is considered an equitable relationship by a "definitional formula," which says essentially that the ratio of rewards must be equal to the ratio of contribution if two parties are to view an economic interaction as just. This is, of course, a particular example of the Formal Principle, where "relevant similarities and differences" are formulated in terms of rewards and contributions. Or put another way, equity theory experiments give an institutional context that frames the division of an economic pie into a question of just desert, based on contributions to solving the problem at hand.[4]

## Bargaining Experiments and the Tendency toward Equal-Split Outcomes

A striking finding from laboratory experiments by game theorists and economists is the tendency for small group experiments to result in equal-split outcomes. The tendency is most profound when the number of subjects is small, say fewer than six, and the experimental setting does not single out any subjects for special treatment. One form of experiment, come to be known as an "ultimatum game," typically consists of two subjects, one of whom, picked at random, proposes, while the other accepts or rejects, with rejection resulting in zero payoff to both. For example, the experimenter may state that $10 is available, and if you have been chosen to be the proposer, you are to make a once-and-for-all offer of an amount of it to me, the remainder going to you. If I accept the offer, the game concludes; if I reject it, neither you nor I get anything, and the game also concludes. For example, if you offer me $3 and I accept, you keep the $7 and the game concludes. Should I reject the $3 offer, we each get nothing, and the game also concludes.

Game theorists and economists initially assumed a "rational" outcome of this game, consisting of the smallest possible offer (one cent) by the subject who proposed, followed by acceptance by the other subject. After all, this outcome was a Pareto or win-win improvement over each subject's getting nothing. However, in ultimatum game experiments conducted in the United States, England, and Germany, the results have clustered around the 50-50 split; the subject who is given the advantage of the proposer's position has typically offered one-half the amount at stake, and the other subject has accepted.

Forsythe et al. (1988) have taken the ultimatum game a step further to the "dictator" game, in which the proposer, also picked at random, is given unilateral authority to divide an economic pie, say, $10. The "rational" solution would have the proposer giving away nothing and keeping the entire $10. Forsythe et al. find that the results of the dictator game depend on whether the game is hypothetical, where the proposer is asked how much he or she would give away, but is not offered the chance to actually give the amount away, or real, where the proposer actually parts with some fraction of the $10. In the hypothetical form of the dictator game, there is again a clustering about a 50-50 split, but in the real form, fewer than 20 percent give away half of the money and 35 percent keep everything.

Still another set of bargaining experiments, by Hoffman and Spitzer (HS) (1982, 1985), initially focused on how two subjects might share an "extra" amount of money that becomes available. The intent was to model synergistic situations which produce added benefits ("externalities") by virtue of mutual interaction of two or more parties or effects. In the initial HS experiments, one of the two subjects was chosen by a coin flip and told that he or she was the "controller" of $12, but that a total of $14 was available if the "controller" and the other subject could agree on how to split it among themselves. If no agreement was possible, the "controller" would get $12, and the other subject nothing. A game-theoretic, "rational" prediction, called the "Nash bargaining solution," says that the two subjects will split the "extra" $2 equally, with the "controller" receiving $12 + $1 = $13, while the other subject gets $1. Again, the ($13,$1) split is a Pareto or win-win improvement over ($12,0). HS's first set of experiments involving forty-four pairs of subjects. In each case the controller and the other subject tried to agree on how to divide a total amount of money, but with the controller having the power to take almost the entire amount for himself or herself (the $14 total available amount and the $12 maximum for the controller were varied slightly in some of the experiments). The modal result was again an equal split, with twenty-nine of forty-four pairs choosing it or within $1 of it (Hoffman and Spitzer, 1982, Table 2, p. 92).

As a result of their first set of experiments, HS (1985) made two changes in the experimental design and conducted a second set. One change was to add to the written instructions an exhortation, designed to convince the subjects that the controller had a moral entitlement to $12 (or whatever maximum amount he or she could take by simply ignoring the wishes of the other subject). The second change was to replace the coin flip by a simple parlor game (the game of nim or "pick up sticks"), thereby creating a "game trigger" rather than a "coin flip trigger" for choosing the controller. Although both the moral exhortation and the game trigger by themselves each had some effect in reducing the frequency of equal splits, most dramatic was their combined effect. When the written instructions conferred moral authority on the controller *and* the game trigger was used to choose the controller, only seven out of twenty-two pairs chose an equal split or within $1 of it, while in fifteen cases the controller received his or her maximum or the Nash's bargaining solution amount (Hoffman and Spitzer, 1985, Table 1, p. 276). HS (1985) attribute the dramatic change to a Lockean notion of just desert, that when individuals "mix their labor" with resources it gives them a property entitlement in the resources. In this case, the winning of a parlor game required an investment in labor that, when combined with the authority of the written instructions, justified an entitlement to the Nash bargaining solution or close to it. On the other hand, winning a coin flip required no investment of labor and, without some exogenous moral authority, earned the controller no greater entitlement than that earned by the loser of the coin flip. The Lockean notion of just desert is, of course, a particular "materialization" of the Formal Principle.[5]

## 10.5 Lack of Fairness Considerations in Marketlike Experiments

As the above brief summary indicates, in bargaining experiments with a small group of persons (six or fewer) in a personal setting, fairness considerations typically loom large (see Isaac, Mathieu, and Zajac 1991 for a more extensive discussion of the literature on bargaining experiments). At the other extreme—marketlike experiments in an impersonal setting,

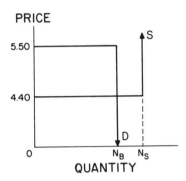

**Figure 10.1**
Smith and Williams's "swastika" supply and demand with more sellers than buyers

especially involving large numbers of persons (twenty or more)—fairness considerations tend *not* to influence outcomes.

An example of a marketlike experiment is that of Smith and Williams (1990), based on a "swastika" design of supply and demand, as shown in figure 10.1.

A number, $N_B$, of buyers and a number, $N_S$ of sellers have the opportunity to strike bargains with each other in a computerized "double auction" setting. That is, from a computer terminal, any buyer can make an offer for an hypothetical item to all of the sellers, also seated at computer terminals, and vice versa. A bargain is struck when one of the offers is accepted. In the design depicted, the buyers are given the opportunity to resell the hypothetical item at $5.50; any purchase price below $5.50 gives them a profit, which is paid to them in cash at the conclusion of the experiment. Likewise, all sellers are told that the item cost them $4.40, and if they sell at more then $4.40, they are paid the difference as their profit.

In the design of figure 10.1, where $N_B < N_S$, there are more sellers than buyers. Because the buyers and sellers are arbitrarily chosen and there is no notion of Lockean desert, one might expect that the buyers and sellers would split the difference between $5.50 and $4.40 and strike bargains at $4.95. In initial trials of the experiment, they do indeed typically strike bargains near the "equal split" price of $4.95. But when the same group of subjects repeats the trials many times, the price quickly converges to slightly above the crossing of the supply and demand schedules at $4.40. The buyers get almost all of the profit, and the sellers get almost none.

On the other hand, if $N_S < N_B$, so that there are more buyers than sellers and the swastika is reversed, the results are also reversed. After repeated trials with the same group of subjects, prices converge to an equilibrium price near $5.50, and the sellers get almost all of the profit.

The work of Coursey, Hovis, and Schulze (1987) and Knez and Smith (1987) on "willingness-to-pay" versus "willingness-to-accept" offers more evidence of the effect framing has in creating the perception of a marketlike institution. On questionnaires Coursey Hovis, and Schulze (1987) found that subjects typically demanded much more than they were willing to pay for the same item (I want $150,000 for my house, but I am willing to pay only $100,000 for the identical house down the street). However, when the same situation was presented to subjects in the laboratory in a marketlike setting, where subjects made or lost money as a result of their decisions, the divergence between "willingness-to-pay" and "willingness-to-accept" markedly decreased. A similar experimental result was reported by Knez and Smith.

## 10.6   Status Quo Property Rights and the Importance of History

Another interpretation of the Hoffman-Spitzer result described above is that history influences perceptions of fairness; the game of nim gave an historical context or institutional frame for legitimating a ($13,$1) split of $14. As we discuss in chapter 11 on perceptions of fairness, historical establishment of property rights plays a important role in regulation and governmental policy formation. Indeed, the notion of a "status quo property right,"—that one is entitled to continue to enjoy a beneficial status quo—is a cornerstone of Owen and Braeutigam's (1978) economic theory of regulation. Thus, as discussed in chapter 22, the Tucson City Council has recently passed an ordinance requiring swimming pools to be fenced in order to "child-proof" them; it applies only to new pools, existing pools are exempt, even though they presumably present equal dangers to children. When a profession is first licensed, it is commonplace for existing practitioners to be "grandfathered" and exempt from educational requirements and having to pass a rigorous examination. In the face of having to reduce pilot's salaries to meet competition, major airlines set up a two-tier system, keeping old pilots on their old salaries, while drastically reducing the salaries of new pilots.

In this section we describe only the survey work of Kahneman, Knetsch, and Thaler (KKT) (1986) on this effect; in chapter 11, we take up the issue of status quo property rights in greater detail. KKT and their assistants conducted extensive telephone surveys of more than 17,000 respondents in Canada. Two examples of their questions are the following (pp. 730, 732):

Example I: A small photocopying shop has one employee who has worked in the shop for six months and earns $9 per hour. Business continues to be satisfactory, but a factory in the area has closed and unemployment has increased. Other small shops have now hired reliable workers at $7 an hour to perform jobs similar to those done by the photocopy shop employee. The owner of the photocopying shop reduces the employee's wage to $7.

Acceptable 17%          Unfair 83%

Example II: Suppose that, due to a transportation mixup, there is a local shortage of lettuce and the wholesale price has increased. A local grocer has bought the usual quantity of lettuce at a price that is 30 cents higher than normal. The grocer raises the price of lettuce to customers by 30 cents per head

Acceptable 79%          Unfair 21%

Each of the many questions on the KKT surveys involved a "firm" (merchant, landlord, or employer) making pricing or wage decisions whose "outcomes" affected "transactors" (customers, tenants, or employees).

KKT (1986) summarize their findings in a theory, centered around the concept of a "reference transaction". This is defined as a relevant precedent that is characterized by a reference price or wage, and by a positive reference profit to the firm. The main theoretical result is called the "principle of dual entitlement": Transactors have an entitlement to the terms of the reference transaction and firms are entitled to a reference profit.

In terms of institutional framing of the Formal Principle and status quo property rights, a characterization of the KKT principle of dual entitlements is the following. Respondents to the KKT surveys perceive that the persons in the scenarios described to them are functioning in familiar institutions. Within these institutions, history has identified "equals" and "unequals" and "relevant similarities and differences" and, as a result, has established status quo property rights both in transactions at a "fair" price or wage and in "fair" profits.

## 10.7   Experimental Tests of Rawls and Harsanyi

Chapters 9 and 10 discuss the contrasting theories of Rawls and Harsanyi regarding what rational persons would do in the original position behind a veil of ignorance. Rawls argues that rational persons would opt to maximize the lot of the worst-off member of society (in terms of primary social goods) because, after all, any one us could end up being the worst off after the veil lifts. Harsanyi argues that the "maximin" strategy leads to bizarre outcomes, and rational persons would choose to be utilitarians.

In a set of ingenious experiments, Frohlich and Oppenheimer (1992) created an original position behind a veil of ignorance in order to test Rawls's and Harsanyi's theories. Subjects first read a description of the contending theories; they also learn that the outcome of the experiment will be to randomly assign them to one of five income classes ranging from high to low, and that they will receive $1 for every $10,000 of annual income received by the income class. In the original position, subjects are then asked to choose a *principle of distributive justice*, operationalized to mean a choice of *distribution of income classes*. In the choice set, Frohlich and Oppenheimer place not only the Rawls choice (the distribution that maximizes the income of the lowest or *floor* class) and the Harsanyi choice (the distribution with the highest average income) but two additional choices: the distribution with the highest average income subject to (1) a constraint on the floor and (2) a constraint on the range of incomes. Frohlich and Oppenheimer artfully arrange the income distributions so that none of the choices subsumes another. That is, subjects face trade-offs; the distribution with the maximum floor income has the lowest average, and the average increases as the floor income increases, and so on. Thus subjects confront four principles of distributive justice; (1) maximize floor income, (2) maximize average income, (3) maximize average income with a floor constraint and (4) maximize average income with a range constraint; each of the income distributions uniquely corresponds to one of the four.

The subjects were college students in the United States, Canada, Australia, and Poland. In the experiments, they were formed into groups and were required to deliberate with the goal of reaching a unanimous group decision in the original position as to which principle of distributive justice should be chosen. The results were as follows: (1) In the original position, the groups unanimously chose a principle in all but 8 percent of the experiments. (2) The strong consensus choice in all countries was *maximize average income with a floor constraint*. Neither Rawls nor Harsanyi got much support. (3) Although 78 percent of all groups chose this principle, the strength of the choice varied geographically, receiving the most support in Manitoba, at the time the home of the only socialist government in North America, and the least in Florida.

Because Frohlich and Oppenheimer (1992) use money rather than utility or Rawls's "primary social goods" as the subjects' reward functions, their results can be criticized as testing neither Rawls nor Harsanyi. Nonetheless, these results cast doubt on both Rawls's and Harsanyi's theories as positive theories of human behavior; most important, they open up a new avenue of research on ethical questions.

## 10.8   Theoretical Research on Institutions

The theory of institutional framing of perceptions of justice that has been presented here is ad hoc; it assumes that institutions exist and says nothing about how they originate, change over time, and react to outside forces, or why and how different types of institutions function differently. Nor does it attempt to classify institutions into types and categories. Although these are important considerations if the theory of institutional framing of perceptions of justice is to progress further, there is already a considerable body of literature on them and related matters, which bears at least brief mention.

A central question in sociology is, How and why do groups and institutions form? An enormous literature on this question exists (see, for example, Hechter 1987; Coleman 1990). On the other hand, to my knowledge, comparatively little has been done on constructing a detailed typology of institutions, especially as it relates to fairness issues. The most extensive work is that of Elster (1989, 1992) and coworkers, whose approach is similar to that outlined in this chapter and who also focus on institutions, calling justice at the institutional level, "local justice," to contrast it to "global justice" at the level of a national government.

In Elster's 1989 paper, a goal was to construct a taxonomy of "the main criteria used in selecting recipients of scarce goods and necessary burdens" (p. 3). Examples of criteria are lotteries, rotation (taking turns), queuing, waiting lists, seniority, age, and sex. Elster (1989) follows his taxonomy of criteria with a taxonomy of the main causal mechanisms that go into the choice of a selection mechanism, including administrators' having to take into account (1) their desire to achieve main goals like giving jobs to the best qualified or admitting the most able students; (2) exogenous forces, including public opinion; (3) the incentive effects of their decisions; (4) the costs of their decisions; (5) the fear of complaints, including litigation; (6) their need to strike bargains with other administrators; (7) their desire to capture resources; and (8) their need to cope with the internal bureaucracy of their institutions.

The combination of Elster's two taxonomies gives a start on the problem of classification and characterization of institutions. Elster is pessimistic regarding the construction of a general theory of local justice (1992, 15):

I do not think the study of local justice will ever yield much by way of robust generalizations . . . local justice is above all a very messy business. To a large extent it is made up of compromises, exceptions, and idiosyncratic feature that can be understood only by reference to historical accidents.

On the other hand, Elster argues that local justice theory offers promise of more than mere description and that the key is to combine description with "mechanisms" (1992, 16):

Between theory and description...there exists the intermediary category of a *mechanism*—an identifiable causal pattern that comes into play under certain, generally unknown, conditions.... In the present context it suggests that we try to establish a list of allocative principles together with a repertoire of mechanisms that can lead to their adoption.

Elster's suggestion can be rephrased in the terminology of this book. Elster's "mechanism," seems to me to correspond to Smith's (1982) definition of an "institution." Thus Elster's suggestion that we search for "mechanisms" and their corresponding allocative methods would appear to support this book's premise that "institutional framing" is a key to developing a positive theory of fairness.

## 10.9   Societal Stability: Trust, Order, Conventions, Norms, and Coordination

On several occasions I have mentioned both the importance of trust in society and how much it is taken for granted. Trust is one aspect of a number of factors that make for stability in society, among which are order, conventions and norms, and implicit coordination mechanisms: they are related to fairness in that they form understandings or implicit contracts among members of society. When these contracts are broken, members of society are apt to feel that they have been treated unfairly and react by seeking redress or retribution.

Although in my view much remains to be said about these issues, again there is already a considerable literature about them. An early and still seminal work is David Lewis's *Convention* (1969); other important works include Ullmann-Margalit's *Emergence of Norms* (1977), Sugden's *Economics of Rights, Co-Operation, and Welfare* (1986), and Coleman's massive *Foundations of Social Theory* (1990).

### Exercises

1. What does the text have to say about the notion that "fairness is arbitrary, merely a matter of opinion"?

2. Contrast and compare the goals of normative and positive theories of fairness or justice.

3. State the "Formal Principle of Distributive Justice," as formulated by Feinberg (1973).

4. What does the text mean by institutional framing of the Formal Principle?

5. Summarize the results of bargaining experiments with small numbers of subjects in face-to-face situations.

6. Summarize the results of marketlike experiments with large numbers of subjects in non-face-to-face-situations.

7. What is meant by "status quo property rights"? Give an example.

8. Discuss the surveys of Kahneman, Knetsch, and Thaler (1986).

# 11

## Positive Theories II: Perceived Economic Justice in Public Utility Regulation

*I have heard sworn testimony from people who watched their house or barn burn down because of unreliable telephone service. I also heard a woman testify that a baby is alive today because the telephone system at St. Mary's Village, Alaska, had been installed the week before the child became ill, and it was possible to summon the bush pilot and fly the child to a hospital.*

Katherine Sasseville (former Chair, Minnesota Public Service Commission)

## 11.1  Overview of Public Utility Fairness Propositions

The fairness notion that like cases should be treated in a like manner does not of course exhaust all notions of fairness. In regulation and government policy formation, one sees additional fairness principles at work; these are summarized in this chapter, based on my own experience in public utility regulation. Before launching into the summary, I'd like to make two points. First, the summary concentrates on *unfairness* rather than fairness. This seems to me to be more a fruitful way to develop a theory that is parsimonious and has predictive power. Except for professional moral philosophers, few persons give much thought to what is fair. But they know when they have been treated *unfairly*; perceived unfair treatment is what makes people shout, "I have been had (screwed, taken to the cleaners, etc.)!" As we discuss further in the next chapter, the sense of unfair treatment typically comes from a perception that a contract, explicit or implicit, has been broken. Second, my thesis is that in formulating economic policy, legislators and regulators take into account six principles of economic justice, which I formulate as propositions. These propositions, in effect, form an unwritten constitution or "metalaws" of economic justice for public utility regulators (see chapter 14 for more on the concept of a constitution), or are at least part of such a constitution. Part of this unwritten constitution is a direct outgrowth of the Fifth, Tenth, and Fourteenth Amendments to the United States Constitution. Other parts have their roots in the law on limited liability and bankruptcy. I summarize these principles in six "propositions."

The noneconomist public, uneducated in the importance of Pareto optimality and gains through exchange, tends to see life as a struggle for a just share of an economic pie of fixed size. One member of society's getting a share of the pie is viewed as denying that share to other members. The public recognizes life to be unfair, but still, in the struggle for a share of the economic pie, no one should receive less than a minimum amount. This is proposition 1. Proposition 2 is the application of the Formal Principle to government policy; the public routinely expects regulatory and governmental agencies to apply the Formal Principle and gets upset at apparent violations of it. Proposition 3 states that if one has fairly acquired a share of the pie, it should not be confiscated; proposition 4, that the share should not be lost because of circumstances beyond one's control. Proposition 5 deals with the perceived injustice of economic inefficiency. Individuals will balk at market impediments when the impediments cause them to lose potential gains through exchange, but, at the collective level, the public requires substantial evidence to form the perception that some rearrangement of resources can result in a larger pie. This is because the public has little conception of what constitutes a Pareto improvement; thus the public perceives the injustice of economic inefficiency not as a denial of gains through exchange, but as the work of a small group thwarting potential large-scale benefits for society. This is especially the case if the public perceives the thwarters as merely resisting the loss of some unfair advantage they already enjoy. Proposition 6, the last proposition, relates to the public's desire for due process mechanisms to prevent the unjust exercise of monopoly power.

The six propositions overlap, and, as in the case of the U.S. Constitution's articles and amendments, we can expect the overlaps to generate conflicts between them. The Constitutional guarantee of freedom of the press suggests that a reporter's sources should be protected; the right of the accused to confront his or her accusers suggests that they be divulged.

As will be apparent, in a fairness controversy more than one concept of economic justice may apply and different groups may be winners or losers depending on which concept society thinks is paramount. The resolution of the resulting conflict may be difficult, requiring lengthy legislative, judicial, or regulatory proceedings. And, of course, as in the case of the Formal Principle, the possibility of conflict means the possibility of strategic behavior to maneuver a fairness issue into a context favorable to the maneuverer.

## 11.2   Six Propositions

Economic Rights

Every developed nation now recognizes the notion that every individual somehow has a right, or an entitlement, to a minimum level of economic "necessities" such as food, shelter, clothing, a job, health care, and education. Perhaps the most dramatic example of this has been the 1948 United Nations's unanimous adoption (but with abstentions) of its Universal Declaration of Human Rights. Of the thirty articles of the declaration, five pertain to economic rights, twenty-three to civil rights, and two to administrative matters (see Green 1956).

In the United States, this notion has been extended to utilities. An explicit example is New York State's 1981 Utility Bill of Rights passed in 1981 and focused on the rights of consumers in dealing with gas and electric utilities.[1] The bill specified that customers

• must receive service within five days after their application for service has been approved;

• cannot be required to pay a security deposit;

• must receive service if they are on welfare, even if they cannot pay for it. Upon passage of the bill, the New York State Department of Social Services was required to pay for up to four months of welfare consumers' bills in arrears and to guarantee future payment for no more than two years.

The bill also requires that gas and electric utilities must

• follow specific procedures in shutting off service;

• not turn off service during cold weather without giving an adult in the household at least 72 hours notice;

• maintain service if a doctor has certified that a person in the household is experiencing a medical emergency;

• annually inform consumers of their rights in writing.

In the case of both electricity and telephone service, state public utility commissions have typically mandated "lifeline" rates, targeted at low-income and/or elderly households. In the case of telephone service, the Federal Communications Commission (FCC) has extended lifeline rates to a federal program, partly to offset its 1984 imposition of a "subscriber line charge"—an explicit charge to cover the cost of the line from a household to the central office.[2]

The evidence leads me to the first and perhaps most important perceived economic injustice proposition:

*Proposition 1*
It is now accepted that every individual has basic economic rights to adequate food, shelter, heat, clothing, health care, education, and in the United States, to basic utility services. Deprivation of basic economic rights is considered unjust.

Equality of Gain and Pain; The Formal Principle Applied to Regulation and Government Policy

As it does in most walks of life, the Formal Principle plays a large role in public utility regulation and in governmental policy making in general. For that matter, it generally played a large role in economic theorizing in the last century and, to a lesser extent, still plays an important role in economics in the literature on taxation ("public finance"), a subject that we take up in more detail in chapters 13 and 16.

One version of the Formal Principle requires "equal sacrifice" by each member of society, a notion that was emphasized by Ross Perot in the 1992 presidential campaign. In the economic theory of taxation, this is embodied in the notion of "vertical equity," which in turn is made operational through progressive taxation (higher percentage income tax rates for higher incomes). At the same time, "vertical equity" is accompanied by the notion of "horizontal equity"-—that those in an "equal position" should carry the same tax burden. Vertical and horizontal equity are, of course, a specific "materialization" of the Formal Principle in the context of taxation.

Rate-of-return regulation of public utilities rests on the horizontal notion that investors in a natural monopoly should get a return equal to that of other investors who bear comparable risk. Utilities that would price discriminate among like-appearing consumers, say residential users within a given state, generally bear the burden of proof that price differentials are based on cost differentials; appeals to economic efficiency as a basis of price discrimination are difficult to sustain. For example, time-of-day pricing for telephone long distance services was not introduced until after World War II; in hindsight, the loss in economic efficiency because of the refusal to lower rates during off-peak evening hours seems appalling.

On the other hand, vertical equity notions are also prevalent. Telephone business rates for local service have historically been higher than residential rates, based on the notions that businesses were somehow richer than residences and also that businesses derived more value from the service than did residential costumers. A justification sometimes given for long-distance subsidization of local service was that richer people made the bulk of long-distance calls, although empirical studies later showed that the justification had no basis in fact (see Brandon 1981).

This brings us to

*Proposition 2*
The Formal Principle is seen as a just basis for pricing or taxation policy, especially when common measurements, such as dollars or time, of individual gain or sacrifice are at hand. Treatment that violates the Formal Principle is considered unjust.

Rights in the Status Quo

People normally voluntarily form queues in front of ticket windows, bank tellers, to enter a bus, or generally when many are served by a few. Those holding a place in the queue feel they own it, a fact that sometimes led to bloodshed in the 1974 and 1979 gasoline crises in the United States.

The sense of ownership in the status quo is a commonplace phenomenon. Feelings about the justness of such ownership rights may swamp feelings that equality should prevail. For example, long-standing rent control in New York City has evidently established the notion that status quo rents should be raised only to cover "fairly" incurred costs (e.g., due to inflation) and not merely to respond to market forces. Tenants occupying rent-controlled apartments strongly resist attempts to raise rents—even attempts carried out by regulatory officials—sometimes violently (Zajac 1985, 140).

A striking example of status quo property or equity rights is the attempt to "vintage" utility rates, that is, to charge "old" customers a different, usually lower rate than "new" ones. For example, as western U.S. cities develop, successive rings of new developments generate successively increasing water costs. Residents and businesses often feel it is only fair that they should continue to pay the rates that prevailed before more recent development, on the grounds that the new developments caused the higher water costs. The classic economic efficiency counterargument is put forth by J. T. Wenders (1981):[3]

Both old and new customers are equally responsible for the capacity and operating costs of the LVVWD [Las Vegas Valley Water District]. An old customer, by occupying facilities which could otherwise be transferred to new customers and save the LVVWD the cost of building new facilities at current cost, is just as responsible for the growth in the size of the LVVWD deliver system as is the new customer.

Put another way, suppose Las Vegas is allowed to grow, but that, each year, it is completely repopulated by new residents. Should they be charged other than uniformly for water? If the answer is no—and here we consider that Las Vegas grows by normal means—why should length of residence suddenly become a criterion for lower water rates? For that matter, why should length of residence take precedence over such traditional criteria as need and affordability as the basis of charging water users different rates?

Arguments like these may carry great weight in the court of economists, but not much with the noneconomists, as the Kahneman, Knetsch, Thaler (1986) surveys of the last chapter indicate. I formulate the feeling as

*Proposition 3*
The beneficial retention of a status quo is considered a right whose removal is considered unjust.

Society as an Insurer

Protection against all contingencies is impossible. No matter what disaster or misfortune we provide for, something worse is possible, and it is common in almost all societies to provide shelter and food when natural disasters destroy homes, or medical care when an unexpected grave illness strikes. Institutions that do so are common. The idea that such protection is only fair is behind the notion of economic rights; it is also behind the notion of society protecting the individual against the fickleness of the marketplace.

Historically, American society seems to have evolved away from the idea of individual responsibility to insure for unexpected events to the idea that the government should be responsible for such insurance. In Adam Smith's day, the limited-liability, joint stock company was still a relatively new institutional innovation, and Smith took a dim view of the idea that a group of persons should be allowed to escape full responsibility for their actions simply by declaring that they were doing so (Smith 1776, 2:264). Likewise, debtors' prisons were common in Dickens's day and bankruptcy has a similar history to corporate limited liability, with an evolution of the law that has generally made it easier to escape the full consequences of one's economic acts (Zajac 1985, 141–144). In more recent times, we have seen the "bail-outs" of Lockheed and Chrysler.

The idea that regulations and regulatory bodies should protect against the volatility of the market is pervasive. This is especially the case when the government, through the action of its regulators, is partially or completely the cause of the sudden changes in economic fortunes. Thus Bell's development of the cellular telephone threatened to destabilize the mobile radio telephone industry, an industry that was basically divided into Bell and non-Bell interests. When the revolutionary potential of the cellular telephone became apparent, it was natural for the affected parties to fight to obtain advantage and, at a minimum, to demand a preservation of status quo property rights to the markets they already had. The result was protracted litigation before the Federal Communications Commission, which held up Bell's cellular trials and delayed the introduction of the cellular telephone for an estimated ten years (Rohlfs, Jackson, and Kelly 1991).

As Owen and Braeutigam (1978, 23–24) point out, such delay in the name of due process is akin to unemployment insurance or agricultural price supports. Like these, regulatory due process is a societal mechanism for protecting both financial and human interests from the shocks and blows of market forces; also like these, it cloaks regulatory action in the mantel of "fair" governmental adjudication.

"Society as an insurer" works more subtly in regulation than it does in the case of natural disasters or catastrophic illness, but it works effectively nevertheless. Public utilities may incur excessive cost overruns because of bad management, bad forecasts of demand, or technological developments, but the utilities are not allowed to fail to the point that their subscribers are left without service. Instead, the cost consequences are usually spread over the rate payers and stockholders. I summarize this discussion by

*Proposition 4*
Society is expected to insure individuals against economic loss because of economic changes. Failure to insure is considered unfair.

Economic Efficiency

As Adam Smith wrote in the *Wealth of Nations* (1776, 1:17), "the propensity to truck, barter, and exchange one thing another . . . is common to all men. . . ." As mentioned in chapter 7, attempts to suppress this propensity by government authority are apt to meet with as much success as attempts to suppress love, sex, or original sin. And, of course, we have recently seen the collapse of the "command and control" economies of Eastern Europe, together with descriptions of how they functioned with a large underground or black market economy.

Regulation in the United States is a form of a "command and control" economy applied to a particular sector. When the opportunities for economic gain by circumvention of its controls become sufficiently great, we can expect initiatives to circumvent; indeed, this has led to the massive wave of deregulation that in the last few decades has swept over trucking, agriculture, financial institutions and markets, and telecommunications.

In the telecommunications industry the movement began with the FCC's 1960 "above-890" decision to allow private parties to build their own microwave carrier systems. By the 1960s Bell's long distance rates had evolved through a series of agreements between the FCC and state regulators. Each in the series had increased the amount of joint and common costs attributed to long distance service and decreased the amount attributed to local service. Because regulators adjust revenues to cover costs, the effect was to raise the share of total costs covered by long distance revenues. Long-distance prices were higher than they would be if regulation were absent. In addition, Bell provided long-distance service by means of a variety of technologies of different vintages, most of which were insufficiently depreciated, and regulators mandated uniform rates throughout the United States, dependent only on the distance of the call.

The result were regulated rates that restricted Bell's freedom to price in response to market forces. This created opportunities for many private parties to provide service by themselves at a fraction of the cost of renting it from Bell. What was true for private parties was obviously also true for public carriage, and in 1970 the FCC allowed Microwave Communications, Inc., to provide public service, initially to interconnect different branches of a single firm with service of lower quality but also lower price than Bell's. This process continued until the FCC allowed full-blown, switched service to be provided by firms other than Bell. Similarly, Bell's "foreign attachments" doctrine allowed only Bell terminal equipment to be used on the Bell network. This was attacked in the early 1970s, as new technology made a plethora of new terminal equipment offerings possible.

The result of all these forces was the breakup of the Bell System on 1 January 1984. However, the breakup occurred only after twenty years of dramatic examples where competitors to Bell could offer services like Bell's at lower prices, or could offer new services that were not available from Bell, while Bell sat frustrated, looking on in its regulatory straitjacket.

Offsetting the current deregulatory climate are the many years of motion toward more regulation rather than less, as described by Hughes (1977) and in chapter 22. Evidently, the examples of waste and inefficiency because of regulatory impediments to the market must be numerous and flagrant in order to evoke popular sentiment for unfettering market action. Hence, I postulate

*Proposition 5*
The existence of numerous and significant economic inefficiencies is considered unjust, especially if their existence is seen as conferring benefits on special interest groups who oppose their removal.

Resentment of Abuse of Monopoly Power

Since 1877, the United States Supreme Court has struggled with the problem of defining the boundaries of regulation. To a large extent, the struggle has been a conflict between individual and corporate rights to control property and the police powers of individual states. The battles have centered on the Fifth Amendment to the Constitution ("No person...shall be deprived of...property without due process of law"), the Tenth ("The powers not delegated to the United States by the Constitution, nor prohibited by it to the States, are reserved to the States respectively, or to the people"), and the Fourteenth ("No State shall make or enforce any law which shall abridge the privileges or immunities of citizens of the United States; nor shall any State deprive any person of...property without due process of law"). A typical history of a dispute is the following: the citizens of a state become sufficiently outraged over some perceived abuse of economic power to cause the state legislature to pass a law curbing the power; those curbed sue on the grounds that their constitutional rights have been violated.

The first landmark decision was *Munn v. Illinois* in 1877. At the time, virtually all of midwestern grain flowed through Chicago; nine firms owned all of Chicago's grain elevators and met periodically to fix storage rates. In 1871 the Illinois legislature passed a law fixing the rates the firms could charge. Munn and Scott, owners of one of the firms, ignored the law and were sued for failing to comply. Upholding Illinois, chief Justice Waite argued for the majority in a famous passage:

[W]e find that when private property is "affected with a public interest, it ceases to be *juris private* only." This was said by Lord Chief Justice Hale more than two hundred years ago...and has been accepted without objection as an essential element in the law of property ever since. Property does become clothed with a public interest when used in a manner to make it of public consequence, and affect the community at large. When, therefore, one devotes his property to a use in which the public has an interest, he, in effect, grants to the public an interest in that use, and must submit to be controlled by the public for the common good, to the extent of the interest he has thus created.... (*Munn v. Illinois*, 1877, 125–126)

*Munn v. Illinois* was followed by two cases that expanded the states' power to regulate grain and how it was loaded and stored from ships (*Budd v. New York*, 1892) and to the fixing of storage rates within an entire state (North Dakota) (*Brass v. Stoeser*, 1894). The grain cases were followed by a case that permitted Kansas to regulate the fire insurance business (*German Alliance Insurance Co. v. Lewis*, 1914). Then the trend to granting the states broad regulatory powers was halted in a series of decisions in the twenties. In *Wolff Packing Co. v. Court of Industrial Relations* (1923) Kansas was not allowed to fix prices and wages in a variety of industries; in *New Ice v. Liebmann* (1925), Oklahoma was prevented from regulating the ice business; in *Tyson and Brother v. Banton* (1927) New York was not allowed to fix prices of theater tickets; Tennessee was not allowed to fix the price of gasoline in *Williams v. Standard Oil Co.* (1929); and New Jersey was not allowed to fix employment agency fees in *Ribnik v. McBride* (1928).

These cases were generally not unanimous, but the decisions handed down eventually evolved to the conferring of broad powers to the states, with the last landmark case being *Nebbia v. New York* (1934), in which the Court allowed New York to regulate the milk industry and to fix milk prices. Justice Roberts wrote:

It is clear that there is no closed class or category of business affected with a public interest, and the functions of courts in application of the Fifth and Fourteenth Amendments is to determine in each case whether circumstances vindicate the challenged regulation as a reasonable exertion of governmental authority or condemn it as arbitrary or discriminatory

. . .

So far as the requirement of due process is concerned, and in the absence of other constitutional restriction, a state is free to adopt whatever economic policy may reasonably be deemed to promote public welfare, and to enforce that policy by legislation adapted to its purpose. The courts are without authority either to declare such policy, or, when it is declared by the legislature, to override it. (*Nebbia v. New York*, 1934, 536–537)

Thus, except where Congress says otherwise and except for the vague mandate to "promote public welfare," *Nebbia* would seem to allow the states to regulate anything.[4] To stay beyond the long regulatory reach of

*Nebbia*, firms, especially large public utilities that are in the public eye, have a strong incentive to walk extra miles to act in the public interest, both in fact and in appearance. Public utility executives soon learn the importance of this fact of life; their constantly affirmed dedication to serve the public is not idle rhetoric, but grounded in years of experience of incurring the public's wrath if service quality falls below the public's expectation, or if prices appear exorbitant or exploitative.

Generally speaking, the fewer the close substitutes for a regulated firm's products and services that are available, the more intense the public's feeling that it has an interest in the use of the firm's property. The remedy for poor service or high prices at a shoe store is easy; shop at another shoe store down the street. But there is generally no alternative local telephone, electricity, gas, or water company down the street. Further, as already remarked, basic utilities are now generally considered necessities that should be provided by society as an economic right. If a complaint against a utility providing a "necessity" is not satisfactorily resolved, one can be left with a profound feeling of frustration, with no place to turn, like a prisoner despairing of freedom.

The history of public utilities is replete with disputes between the state's police powers and corporate freedom to deploy property, not only on such matters as service quality and rates, but on matters affecting the basic management of the utility, with regulators asserting a near ownership say in the utility's activities.

This brings me to my last proposition of perceived economic injustice:

*Proposition 6*
The fewer the substitutes for a regulated or monopoly firm's output, and the more the output is considered an economic right, the more the public expects to exert control over the firm. Denial of control is considered unjust.

## 11.3   Discussion

In reflecting on the above six propositions, I am struck with the similarities with much of Rawls's *Theory of Justice*. Proposition 6 (resentment of abuse of monopoly power) relates to Rawls's first principle on liberty; proposition 2 (equality of gain and pain—the Formal Principle) relates to Rawls's second principle on social and economic equalities and inequalities; proposition 1 (economic rights) and proposition 4 (society as an insurer) both relate to Rawls's difference principle; and the stress in proposition 5 (economic efficiency) on inefficiencies having to be significant and seen to confer benefits on special interest groups accords with Rawls's giving justice priority over efficiency in his second priority rule. Finally, although Rawls does not explicitly discuss status quo property rights, he does pay considerable attention to the importance of stability and trust, and thus proposition 3 (rights in the status quo), as well as Proposition 4 (society as an insurer) relate to this discussion.

Of course, to a libertarian the quest for "fairness" in regulation gives unwarranted justification for government interference to construct an apparatus to administer it. Administration is done by people, to whom the police power of the state must be entrusted, but people have incentives to set agendas that further self-interest at the expense of the public interest, and we have the familiar debate on the proper limits of governmental activity.

Nevertheless, the libertarian argument may slight the fear the public has of facing the economic risks associated with an unfettered free market. Owen and Braeutigam (1978, 25) argue that, because the public is risk-averse, it is willing to pay something to reduce the risks; furthermore, they demonstrate the validity of this assertion by means of a mathematical model (pp. 36–42). In effect, Owen and Braeutigam are arguing that, from a broader view of economic efficiency, taking risk into account, regulators who pay serious attention to "fairness" are not necessarily acting to undermine economic efficiency; they may in fact be helping to attain it.[5]

**Exercises**

1. Why does the text stress "unfairness" rather than "fairness"?

2. What are the text's six unfairness propositions? Give an example of each.

3. Contrast and compare the text's six propositions with Rawls's *Theory of Justice* (1971).

# 12             Strategic Uses of Fairness

*During the [1971 wage-price] freeze, we sadly observed that every exception to the regulations created one ingrate and two enemies. Economic policies must meet the test of "fairness," illusive as that standard may be.*

Arnold Weber (*New York Times*, 16 August 1981)

## 12.1   Legitimacy of Fairness Principles

In previous chapters I have repeatedly argued that fairness is not arbitrary and that, generally speaking, an institution will choose fairness principles its members consider legitimate. The class of principles it considers legitimate depends on the economic environment and history, and differs from institution to institution. As an illustration, consider the practice of airlines "buying out" passengers on oversold flights—a ticketed passenger who is willing to switch to an undersold flight later that day is offered a voucher worth several hundred dollars for a future flight. Julian Simon proposed this procedure in 1966,[1] but without effect until an economist, Alfred E. Kahn, became chairman of the Civil Aeronautics Board (CAB) in 1978. Kahn immediately ordered that "buying out" be tried, and the CAB found that the public readily accepted what is now standard practice on U.S. airlines.

On the other hand, I suggest that the reader try "buying out" someone in a line at the checkout counter at a supermarket. That is, approach a customer who has a full basket of groceries and who is at the head of a line, preferably the longest; make sure that your basket contains fewer items than that of the customer whom you propose to buy out. Then offer the customer, say, ten dollars, to replace him or her in the line, requiring the customer to go to the back of the line. If someone objects, point out that you are offering a Pareto improvement. Those in back of the customer whom you wish to buy out will get faster service because your basket has fewer items; by accepting your offer, the customer shows that the $10 is sufficient compensation for the extra wait; you are better off because your time savings exceeds $10. At a minimum, you will trigger off a lively discussion. To my knowledge, unlike in air travel, the "buying out" of customers is not seen as acceptable in supermarkets. The institution of airline travel accepts the practice, while the institution of supermarket shopping does not.[2]

The older the institution and the more ingrained its mode of operation, the more likely there will be a strong consensus within the institution about what the legitimate fairness principles are. Indeed, all of us operate daily in numerous institutions in orderly, stable interactions with colleagues, neighbors, family members, waiters, store clerks, and so on; we apply fairness principles that are considered legitimate without giving the matter a moment's thought.

Nevertheless, circumstances change. Until recently in the United States, society treated persons of color differently and tolerated practices that today are considered outrageously unjust. In a budget crisis institutions may have to furlough employees, reduce salaries, merge groups that have different modes of operation, or otherwise face personnel decisions that are nonroutine and for which there are few precedents. Also, technological change can change modes of operation, or even create totally new institutions. When an institution faces change, the range of legitimate fairness principles that are applicable to the new situation may be quite wide and leave much room for fairness strategizing. And, of course, change may cause rock-bottom ethical differences to surface (see the discussion in chapter 9 of the Kantian versus utilitarian views on individual rights).

In any event, strategic uses of fairness to advance self-interest is commonplace. However, to develop a theory of fairness strategizing, it seems to me that we will have to incorporate two features of human behavior: (1) people are not usually energized by a sense of duty to take fair action out of regard for others, but rather by a feeling that some contract, explicit or implicit, has been *unfairly* broken, with the result that they have been *unfairly* treated; and (2) people (all of us, really) have a marvelous ability to deny, or in more technical terms, to be subject to cognitive dissonance. Before we consider strategic uses of fairness, we discuss each of these in turn.

## 12.2   Satisfying, Other-Regarding Fairness versus Infuriating, Contract-Breaking Unfairness

Altruism and charity can be thought of as examples of a more general phenomenon—sacrificing some of one's resources out of regard for the welfare of others. I found your wallet with the winning lottery ticket and decided that it was only fair that you should claim the jackpot when I could just as easily have claimed it for myself. Such "other-regarding" behavior is satisfying and gives us a good feeling. Unfortunately, "fair" behavior is sometimes exclusively interpreted to imply what might be called "satisfying, other-regarding" fair behavior.

Nevertheless, when we think of how considerations of fairness affect the formation of economic policy, "satisfying, other-regarding" fair behavior seems to play a relatively minor role. As already pointed out in chapter 11, more important may be policy acts that infuriate us. Again, at work is a general phenomenon—the feeling that some understanding or contract, explicit or implicit, has been broken. We might classify this as "infuriating, contract-breaking" unfair behavior.

All six of the unfairness propositions of chapter 11 can be so characterized. We have come to feel that we have a contract with society at large to guarantee us basic economic rights, that we have a contract with our elected representatives and government officials that they will appropriately and competently apply the Formal Principle in the formation of government policy, and so on. Should we judge that one of these contracts has been broken through no fault of our own, we are apt to become infuriated and driven to protest, unite with others in the same boat, or even retain an attorney to file a formal action. We rarely will take such measures in order to accomplish "satisfying, other-regarding fair" actions.

## 12.3   Denial or Cognitive Dissonance

During the creation of the 1986 and 1993 tax acts, the media interviewed many congressmen who had inserted special provisions in the act to benefit individual constituents. The congressmen reacted with outrage to the suggestion that they had succumbed to special interest lobbyists; instead, most pointed out heatedly that they had merely introduced legislation to correct an obvious egregious injustice in the then-current tax code.

Persons who felt themselves aggrieved by the pre-1993 tax code seemed to be sincere and to be pleading for the righting of what they perceived to be genuine wrongs; however, to the disinterested outside observer, their arguments often seemed to be transparent pleas for special treatment, seemingly based on the flimsiest of fairness pretexts. In watching some of the congressmen arguing constituents' cases, I was sometimes reminded of the old joke about the young boy who murders his parents and then pleads for clemency on the grounds that he is an orphan.

The joke is far-fetched, but it highlights a common psychological phenomenon that we are all prone to and that economists have almost completely ignored—denial or "cognitive dissonance" (but see also Akerlof and Dickens 1982; Schlicht 1984). That is, our minds deal with simplified versions or models of reality, and internal contradictions make us feel ill at ease. Given evidence that contradicts the internal order we have created, we tend to dismiss it. On the other hand, we readily accept evidence that reinforces the order in our heads. In our thought processes or cognition, we like and accept consonance, while we dislike and suppress dissonance; we tend especially to accept evidence and arguments that further our self-interest and deny reality when it is at odds with it.[3]

Thus, until the 1940s, the American Medical Association (AMA) official policy was to be against prepaid group medical practice (what today are called "health maintenance organizations," or HMOs); the policy was reversed only after a group of doctors in Washington, D.C., won an antitrust suit to force the AMA to reverse it.[4] More recently, a chiropractor has prevailed in an antitrust suit (*Wilk v. American Medical Association*, 1990) in which Doctors of Chiropractic accused Doctors of Medicine of restraint of trade—that M.D.s had conspired to keep patients from seeking chiropractic cures for their ailments. Undoubtedly, both in the case of group medical practice fifty years ago and chiropractic in recent times, M.D.s felt totally sincere in their beliefs. My guess is that M.D.s would be shocked and outraged by accusations that they were acting in their self-interest and not for the benefit of society at large. Similar examples could be cited from across the spectrum of interest groups.

In citing the two M.D. examples, I claim no moral superiority nor immunity from the phenomenon of denial or cognitive dissonance. Economists like to think that their discipline is at the top of the pecking order in the social sciences. They sometimes say that "economics is the physics of the social sciences." In discussions with colleagues in sociology or political science, economists may patronizingly claim that "economic imperialism" is on the ascent and that soon there will only be economics, all other social sciences becoming mere subdisciplines. Economists, and I include myself, do not like to hear evidence to the contrary and rarely are in a mood to accept it.

The obvious point is that we all have a proclivity toward self-serving behavior; it may even be a coping mechanism that we need to survive in a stressful world. As a result, it is not always easy to separate cynical, self-serving arguments from sincere ones. This proclivity explains a common observation that economists make: regardless of their basis, justice or fairness arguments seem always to end up favoring those presenting them. It is no accident that economists automatically look beyond fairness arguments to the underlying self-interest, as cynical as this point of view often seems.

## 12.4 Policy Implications: Special Interests versus Aggrieved Persons

Fairness research helps explain the power of interest group theories of regulation and holds promise of strengthening and deepening these theories, but it is also important to understand what seems to me an obvious psychological aspect of interest groups—that they are motivated by noble goals. In the heat of political campaigns, one hears much rhetoric about political officeholders caving in to special interests, but often in general terms and without specific identification of who the special interests are. If much of government action is controlled by special interests, why are not the special interests' motives exposed, their actions thwarted, and any ill-gotten gains confiscated?

The above discussion shows that matters are not that simple. A group is also prone to denial and cognitive dissonance, to minimizing the importance of evidence that undermines the group's self interest, and to inflating the importance of evidence that supports it. Thus a group that pressures legislators and hires lobbyists to plead its case may not look on itself as a "special interest," at least not in the pejorative sense of that term. Rather, it is likely to look upon itself as an aggrieved group; its plea is that some "unfair" government policy be reversed or modified. Indeed, my perception is that there exist almost no "special interests" in the pejorative sense, only seekers of simple fairness and justice. Whether in some objective sense the claim of "unfairness" is justified is beside the point; the pleaders will typically have convinced themselves that it is and will deny any evidence to the contrary.

And, of course, the best defense against an attack of "unfairness" is an "unfairness" counterattack. Thus the environmental movement was born because special interests were felt to be destroying nature in pursuit of material gain, which was unfair to the rest of us and to future generations, who wish to enjoy nature. Recently, we have seen the movement resisted because the preservation of nature requires the sacrificing of jobs—something unfair to those who felt that they had a status quo property right to their jobs.

Thus the "regulation game" is apt to be fought in terms of fairness arguments or, more precisely, in terms of "unfairness" charges and counter-charges, with all affected parties holding their beliefs sincerely and firmly. For instance, even a cursory reading of the history of the Bell System shows it to be replete with examples of such fairness games, with accompanying strategic maneuvering by the game's players. Almost from the outset, legislators, regulators, and consumers levied the charge that Bell was abusing its monopoly power. Garnett (1985, 58–59), in his history of the early evolution of Bell's horizontal structure, describes how in 1880, only four years after Bell had acquired his fundamental telephone patents, the Massachusetts state legislature was already objecting to Bell's perceived unfair exercise of monopoly power:

[T]he company had been warned that as a monopoly it had a less favorable public image than it had once enjoyed as a struggling, competitive enterprise. J. J. Storrow, Bell's leading attorney and legislative representative had alerted officials to the considerable concern that the emerging telephone monopoly had produced within the [Massachusetts] state legislature... the lawmakers appeared determined to limit through regulation Bell's capacity to charge what they considered exorbitant rates.

Bell's patents expired in 1894, which led to an era or fierce competition in which Bell at times dealt with rivals with no mercy. This, plus the turn-of-the-century's "trust-busting" climate, helped further arouse the public's ire over Bell's unfair wielding of monopoly power and led in 1913 to the first federal antitrust suit filed against AT&T. The suit's aim was to make Bell divest itself of its recent acquisition of properties in Oregon (Garnett 1985, 153). Bell's counterargument was that it was unfair to society to have wasteful duplication of facilities. After settlement of this suit, in its famous 1913 "Kingsbury Commitment", Bell strove to subject itself to regulation in order that the public might benefit from "one policy, one system, universal service."

The strategy was a master stroke of turning adversity into opportunity, for Bell shrewdly focused on being regulated at the state rather than the federal or town level (Garnett 1985, 130–131), thus seizing the opportunity to form a powerful coalition with officials at the state level. This effectively eliminated town-level regulatory fairness games and gave Bell powerful allies in dealing with the federal government in federal regulatory games. The coalition was effective and created an institution that lasted in calm and stability until the early sixties, in spite of the creation of the Federal Communications Commission (FCC) during the New Deal.

The opening salvo in what was to prove to be the unraveling of the coalition was the FCC's 1960 "above-890" decision to allow private microwave carriage of telephone messages. As briefly recounted in chapter 11, the motivating force for the decision was again charges of "unfairness." Not only was Bell perceived to be unfairly wielding its monopoly power, but the FCC was perceived to be unfairly thwarting the introduction of a technology that would lessen the cost of telephone service. This is only a smattering of Bell's experiences in regulatory fairness games; the full story is much more complex, far richer, and would take a book to treat. Needless to say, the Bell experience is not unique, and we consider several other examples of fairness strategizing in the case studies of part IV.

## 12.5   How to Level the Playing Field

The above suggests that we should not be surprised to see fairness arguments used strategically in order to advance someone's self-interest. Indeed, we can expect fairness strategizing to be the norm, not the exception. Political campaigns now routinely spend vast amounts of money on focus groups, much of it spent to find which fairness arguments are effective and which are not.

The anecdotal evidence illustrating the propositions of the previous chapter provides examples of fairness strategizing, but it is useful to summarize how the fairness theory developed in this part of the book might be purposefully used as part of a strategic plan. A graphic method of summarizing is to list a set of maxims that contain within them the main points that have been made, just as the Ten Commandments summarize a moral code. In this spirit, I borrow a leaf from the self-help literature which generates countless how to manuals on all sorts of subjects. Of course, such a manual runs the risk of oversimplification; in the present instance, it also runs the risk of appearing to be cynical and to deride morality and stongly held ethical beliefs. This is furthest from my intent, as the discussion of normative theories of fairness in chapters 7, 8, and 9 shows. Nonetheless, such a manual has the appeal of being succinct and to the point.

So, as a means of summary, I offer a set of ten maxims on "How to Level the Playing Field":

*1. Frame your initiative as a concrete unfairness issue.* As a strategist who can frame your point as an "unfairness story", with vivid imagery and in concrete terms, you are apt to prevail over an opponent presenting an abstract argument not explicitly pegged to unfairness. During the 1992 elections, the Clinton campaign effectively used the image of the greedy rich reaping "more than their fair share" during the 1980s, and the Republicans were also effective with their image of "tax-and-spend Democrats" unfairly squandering your tax contributions, whereas the Republican initiative for lowering the capital gains tax got nowhere. Yet there are many graphic "unfairness stories" associated with the capital gains tax on businesses. For example, thirty years ago "Ma and Pa" borrowed every cent they could to raise $100,000 to open a dry cleaning store, which through hard work they have repaid over the years. Adjusting for inflation, their investment should be worth $450,000 today, but the market price of their store is only $350,000, which is their retirement nest egg. However, if they sell, they will receive even less, because they must "unfairly" pay the government almost a third of their $250,000 capital gain "profit." Although this is a hypothetical example, countless real-life stories similar to this could have been brought out, but they weren't. Instead, the Republicans advanced the abstract argument that a lowering of the capital gains tax would stimulate economic growth.

2. *Fight unfairness charges with other unfairness charges.* Public utilites are routinely accused of charging exorbitant rates. Over the years they have developed a countercharge that high-quality electric and telephone service is essential to job creation and that their rates must be high enough to enable them to offer high-quality service. Thus they have countered the charge "your rates are unfairly high" with "overregulation will mean the unfair loss of jobs."

3. *Convince yourself of the righteousness of your position.* Your opponents will undoubtedly have gone into denial; they will reflexively tune out any challenge to the validity of their position and will simply respond to challenges by offering supporting arguments for what they espouse. The emotional intensity of their arguments is likely to convince voters. If you don't do likewise, you are likely to lose out.

4. *Exploit the Formal Principle.* If you are now in an *unequal* position, argue that you should be in an *equal* position, if this should be to your advantage. This is the principal argument of the "comparable worth" movement that seeks to raise the pay of women.

Likewise, if you are now in an *equal* position, argue you should be in an *unequal* position, if *that* is to your advantage. Large corporations that have a compensation system based on rank rather than discipline often find themselves having to cope with this argument. For example, when computer programmers suddenly came into great demand and their salaries rose dramatically, they naturally demanded higher pay than colleagues in the jobs of the same rank.

5. *Try to convert a non–status quo institution into a status quo institution.* For example, if you rent an apartment, lobby for rent control. Rent control that favors tenants seems to become a status quo institution almost instantly everywhere in the world.

6. *Try to convert a status quo institution into a non–status quo institution.* This is difficult. Nonetheless it has been accomplished to the advantage of those advocating it, for example, in the deregulation of airlines, trucking, telephone, financial services, and agriculture.

7. *To avoid fairness fights, deregulate.* Deregulation to create a market not only removes status quo property rights, but it eliminates other fairness fights over such things as "fair" rates of return, "fair" values of assets, and "fair" wages. Deregulation of the airlines has eliminated the costly and lengthy hearings, sometimes extending over years, over the "fair" assignment of routes.

8. *Exploit the principle "Society should be the insurer of last resort."* The notion that society should protect its members who are victims of adversity born of matters beyond their control runs deep. As many commentators have pointed out, the list of categories of protected victims continues to grow. This notion is also behind most of social (health, safety, and environmental) regulation discussed in chapter 22. An obvious strategy is to get yourself included in one of the victim categories—or, as a politician, to become the champion of as many categories as practical.

9. *Exploit "basic economic rights."* Try to get "economic rights" defined so that you are included. Or if you are a politician, try to get as much of your voter constituency as possible swept into those who will be awarded economic rights. This is the principal fairness strategy being used at the time of this writing in the fight over health care.

10. *Exploit the vulnerability of holders of apparent monopoly power.* Again, at present writing, this strategy is also being used in the health care debate with regard to pharmaceutical companies. Various initiatives would control drug prices in order to curb the perceived drug companies' monopoly power.

## Exercises

1. Give an example wherein two different institutions treat the same fairness situation differently.

2. Discuss the text's distinction between "satisfying, other-regarding fairness" and "infuriating, contract-breaking unfairness."

3. What role does denial or "cognitive dissonance" play in fairness strategizing, that is, the use of fairness to advance self-interest?

4. Why is it hard to find evil "special interest" groups?

5. What is a typical defense against a charge of unfairness?

# III

**Normative and Positive Economic Theories of Regulation**

Public Interest
(Normative) Economic
Theories of Regulation

*Don't kill the patient with improvement.*

Old physician's saying

## 13.1  Reasons for Regulation and Government Intervention

Rawls and Nozick present us with two different philosophies about the role of government. As the quoted in chapter 9 indicates, Rawls advocates "appropriate regulation" to ensure that the wage outcomes of a market economy are "just." On the other hand, Nozick finds abhorrent any government interference beyond that necessary to protect individuals from harms inflicted by others.

Most societies in developed countries eschew Nozick's extreme, and we find governments routinely interfering with the working of the free market to achieve a variety of goals. Since the Great Depression, a major goal of most governments has been to "stabilize the economy" by using fiscal and monetary policy to control inflation and to stimulate the economy when perceived to be necessary. Another goal has been to redistribute income to achieve a social purpose. For example, in chapter 11, we discussed the notion of "economic rights", or "entitlements", as something members of society now take for granted and expect government to provide. A problem for every administration is how to formulate a policy for economic rights, either explicitly or implicitly specified. Upon taking office, even the "conservative" Reagan administration promptly announced its goal of constructing adequate "safety nets" for all members of society.

Chapter 11 also discussed the notion of government insurance against natural disasters or other financially disastrous events beyond an individual's control. We have seen, in 1992, the Bush administration dealing with

Hurricane Andrew; in 1993, the Clinton administration dealing with extensive flooding of the Mississippi River and its tributaries and, in 1994, with
a disastrous earthquake in California. In all of these cases, government
policy was to act expeditiously to bail out the distressed persons, in spite
of the formidable cost. Arguments that the damage could have been miti-
gated with more attention paid to hurricane-proofing, earthquake-proofing,
or to floodplain avoidance were downplayed.

Another standard role of government is to rectify the economy's inability to achieve static economic efficiency, for example, in the provision
of public goods—police and fire protection, national defense, education,
libraries, parks, and so on. Other reasons advanced for government interference in the marketplace are to rectify

• market imperfections resulting from monopoly power
• harms caused by externalities
• the failure of the market to provide economic agents sufficient information on which to base rational decisions

To achieve these various goals, the government has two main instruments—taxes and direct control of actions. That is, the government either
taxes its citizens, the monies then being used to finance its programs, or it
controls their behavior directly through regulation. Only those who have
the necessary education and have passed the required examinations are
allowed to practice medicine, factories are not allowed to dump toxic
wastes into rivers, and the rates that public utilities can charge are set by
regulatory commissions.

But how can government best achieve these social goals and rectify
these market failures? An obvious approach is to (1) work out the theory
of the most economically efficient way for government to accomplish these
ends and (2) appoint disinterested, expert public servants to apply the
theory. This approach is called the "public interest" or "normative" theory
of government intervention and regulation. In the next chapter, we consider the problems with this approach and subsequent research into *interest
group* or *positive* theories of government intervention and regulation.

In this chapter we discuss economically efficient ways of raising funds
through taxation and then economically efficient ways of dealing with the
some of the market failures listed above. The discussion will by no means
be exhaustive, but should give the reader an idea of how economists
approach these issues.[1]

## 13.2   Economically Efficient Taxation

The search for economically efficient taxes is so important that it has evolved into a subdiscipline within economics—public finance. The next sections summarize two elementary models from this field: lump-sum taxation as a "first-best" solution to the problem of finding efficient taxes and Ramsey taxes as a "second-best" solution.

Lump-Sum Taxes as "First Best"

A lump-sum tax is one that does not depend on an individual's actions. It deprives all individuals of a certain amount of their income, regardless of the size of that income, what they have for breakfast, how much they drink, or what clothes they buy. The theory usual considers the simplest form a *lump-sum tax*—the same amount of tax levied on every individual or household in society. For example, if the United States decided that it needed to raise $1 billion by taxing its 250 million citizens, it could do so by a lump-sum tax of $4/individual, regardless of the individual's income, occupation, status in life, and so forth.

From an economic efficiency point of view, a lump-sum tax is *nondistortionary* or *first best*—it doesn't distort relative choices. Of course, a lump-sum tax leaves consumers with less money to buy things. But the lump-sum tax doesn't interfere with how they spend whatever money they have.

Consider, for example, a sales tax of $1 per pack of cigarettes. The effect is the same as the cigarette company's raising its price by $1 per pack. Suppose you smoke a pack a day and thus pay $7 a week in sales taxes. The government could tax your income by $7 per week instead. You would thereby be better off. Why? Because you could continue to buy a pack of cigarettes a day and pay the same amount of tax as before. But if the government removes the $1/pack sales tax on cigarettes, it makes them cheaper relative to the other things that you consume. You might want to consume more of them relative to the other things, and might find consuming only a pack a day unsatisfactory. So, the switch to a lump-sum income tax can't make you worse off, but it may make you better off. Put in other terms, for the pack-a-day smoker, a lump-sum tax of $7 per week is a Pareto improvement from a sales tax of $1 per pack of cigarettes, and no Pareto improvement from the lump-sum tax is possible.

As simple as this economic reasoning is, we don't find the lump-sum tax accepted by the public. A problem is to decide the magnitude of a lump-sum tax. If we decide to make it different for different individuals, we need some basis for differentiating. If, for example, we differentiate by income, we no longer have a lump-sum tax but an income tax; if we don't differentiate, we end up levying the same lump-sum tax on everyone, rich or poor, something that most societies will not tolerate.

Ramsey Taxes as Second Best

An alternative approach is to design a tax system that attains Pareto optimality, given as a constraint that a certain amount of money must be raised for the government's treasury. This is in fact what Ramsey taxes do. Because they yield Pareto optimality only under a constraint and are Pareto-inferior compared to an unconstrained Pareto optimum, they are often called a "second best" solution to the taxation problem.

It is simplest to assume that the constrained Pareto-optimal taxes are to be levied in a perfectly competitive economy, as described in chapter 2. Few economies are perfectly competitive, but to extend the analysis to nonperfectly competitive economies complicates it and obscures the gist of the theory.

In equilibrium in a perfectly competitive economy, the price of each commodity will equal its marginal cost and the economy will be at an economically efficient state. The task of the policy maker is then to levy taxes on some set of commodities in order to raise the money necessary for the various purposes described above. We consider the case of two commodities, commodity 1 and commodity 2, although the derivation will apply to the general case of n commodities.

Assume that, for each commodity, the tax is a small fraction of marginal cost, and that price changes in one market do not influence demands in other markets, that is, assume independent demand schedules. Consider first that the government has decided how much tax revenue, $T$, it needs and that all commodities have been taxed in order to raise this amount. Perhaps in the perfectly competitive baseline that we are assuming, commodity 1 was priced at $9/unit, reflecting a like marginal cost, and a tax of $1/unit is imposed to bring to $10 the total amount per unit the consumer must pay. Now suppose the tax is increased such that it that reduces demand for a commodity 1 by one unit. Perhaps at $10/unit, 10,000 units are consumed, and a tax increase of $0.02 results in a demand of 9,999 units, as shown in figure 13.1a (not drawn to scale in order to illustrate the effects).

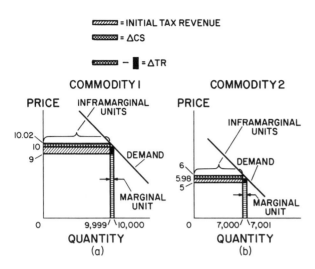

**Figure 13.1**
Effects of small tax changes

It is important to distinguish two effects. First is the effect on the *marginal* consumer, that is, the consumer who decides to forgo the consumption of one unit when the $0.02 tax increase is levied. For this person, the tax rise results in a standoff: the consumer doesn't get the satisfaction of consuming the unit but also doesn't part with $10.02. Put in other terms, the refusal of the marginal consumer to buy the commodity when it was taxed $0.02 indicates that the consumer was willing to pay somewhere between $10 and $10.02, but not as much as $10.02. Our marginal consumer refused to buy at $10.02 because the purchase wouldn't have resulted in any consumer's surplus. In the extreme, knife-edge case, if the marginal consumer refuses to buy the additional unit for *any* tax that is levied, no matter how slight, the consumer's value of one unit is exactly $10. A tax in addition to the $10 price then means an exact trade of forgone consumption for retained income (see figure 13.1a).

The second effect of the price rise is felt by the *inframarginal* consumers, that is, those who continue to consume the 9,999 units. Because they consume exactly the same number of units they did at the $10 price, the aggregate effect of the $0.02 tax is a loss in consumer's surplus of 9,999 × $0.02 or $199.98, as shown in figure 13.1a.

Clearly, a tax reduction evokes symmetric effects, as figure 13.1b shows. Say, in the market for commodity 2, there was also an initial tax of $1/unit on a price of $5/unit, resulting in a total amount per unit of $6.00. Suppose then that a tax decrease of $0.02 reduced the amount per unit to $5.98 and increased demand from 7,000 to 7,001 units (figure 13.1b, again, is not drawn to scale in order to illustrate the effects). In this case, the marginal demander values the additional unit somewhere between $6.00 and $5.98, and in the knife-edge case, the marginal demander has a value of exactly $6/unit. For the inframarginal consumers, the tax decrease represents an aggregate gain in consumer's surplus of 7,000 × $0.02 or $140.

Now imagine that, in order to compensate for the tax rise of $0.02 on commodity 1, the policy maker slightly lowers the tax on commodity 2 so as to keep the tax revenue constant at the level of $T$. The amounts by which the taxes must be adjusted depend of course on the economy's cost structure and the sensitivities of demands in the first and second markets to these markets' prices, including the taxes appended to them. In particular, whereas the tax rise of $0.02 on commodity 1 decreased demand for it by one unit, the policy maker may find that the tax has to be lowered on commodity 2 so that demand for it increases by several units. However, whatever the relation between commodity 1's tax increase rise and commodity 2's compensating tax decrease and the consequent output adjustments, the inframarginal customers of commodity 1 will lose the consumer's surplus and those of commodity 2 will gain it, while the marginal customers of both services will break even.

If the consumer's surplus gains to customers of commodity 2 exceed the losses to customers of commodity 1, then, in principle, the commodity 2 customers could compensate the commodity 1 customers for accepting the tax adjustment and there would be money left over to be shared by both. Likewise, if commodity 1's losses in consumer's surplus exceeded commodity 2's gains, the directions of the tax changes could simply be reversed, and again the winners could compensate the losers with money left over to be mutually shared. In either case, the tax collector would presumably be indifferent between the initial taxes and the adjusted taxes because both sets of taxes would yield the needed revenue. However, from the standpoint of the consumers of commodities 1 and 2, the adjusted taxes are potentially preferable since, in principle, they allow both sets of consumers to be better off.

For any two taxed commodities, we can imagine such an exploration for a "Pareto-improving" tax adjustment, given any initial set of taxes that raises the necessary tax revenue and given that prices throughout the rest of the economy are maintained at marginal costs. The *Ramsey taxes* are the taxes that raise the required revenue and from which there is *no* Pareto-improving adjustment. That is, at the Ramsey taxes, the economy raises that tax revenue that it needs and, further, any slight price adjustment that maintains tax revenue at a constant level will result in aggregate gains in consumer's surplus being *just equal* to aggregate losses. Ramsey taxes are thus economically efficient in the sense that there is no way that they can be adjusted to benefit some without harm to others.

We can summarize the above discussion as follows. For commodities 1 and 2, let $\Delta CS_1$ and $\Delta CS_2$ be the changes in consumer's surplus corresponding to a small tax change, and let $\Delta TR_1$ and $\Delta TR_2$ be the corresponding changes in tax revenues. Then we have the balancing conditions:

$$\Delta CS_1 + \Delta CS_2 = 0, \tag{13.1a}$$

$$\Delta TR_1 + \Delta TR_2 = 0, \tag{13.1b}$$

which give

$$\Delta CS_1 / \Delta TR_1 = CS_2 / \Delta TR_2. \tag{13.2}$$

That is, in figure 13.1, in each market the ratios of the areas indicated by 'CS and 'TR must be the same, while the sum of the $\Delta TR$'s must be zero. Because Commodities 1 and 2 can be *any* two commodities, this result extends to the case of $n$ markets. When expressed in terms of prices and taxes, equation (13.2) becomes the Ramsey formula.

In particular, if the prices of commodities 1 and 2 are $p_1$ and $p_2$, the Ramsey taxes turn out to satisfy the formula,[2]

$$e_1 t_1^R / p_1 = e_2 t_2^R / p_2, \tag{13.3}$$

and the condition

$$\text{Total tax revenue} = \text{Fixed amount} = T, \tag{13.4}$$

where, $t_1^R$, $t_2^R$ = Ramsey taxes in the first and second markets, and $e_1$, $e_2$ = elasticities of demand in the first and second markets (elasticity of demand = percent change in output for a one percent change in price).

The above formulas lead to a simple diagrammatic apparatus for interpreting Ramsey taxes. Figure 13.2 illustrates it for the case of two markets, 1 and 2, but the construction applies to any finite number of markets. When taxes are set at their Ramsey levels, the ratio $DA/AD'$ is the same in all markets. In addition, the sum of tax revenues in all markets—the sum of the shaded areas in figure 13.2—is equal to the required tax revenue, $T$.[3]

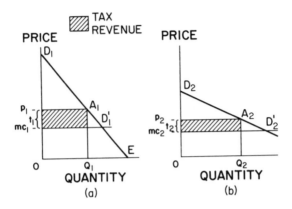

**Figure 13.2**
For Ramsey taxes, $D_1 A_1 / A_1 D_1' = D_2 A_2 / A_2 D_2'$, and the sum of tax revenues in all markets equals the required tax revenue, $T$

## 13.3   Economically Efficient Regulation to Cure Market Failures

The previous section considered the problem of raising taxes in order to pay for government programs. In other terms, the section dealt with the revenue-raising side of the problem of economically efficient methods of redistributing income—a standard reason for government intervention into the marketplace. Another standard reason for government intervention is to rectify or cure perceived market failures. This is the basis for most regulation; the next section considers some economically efficient approaches to it.

Monopoly

A classic argument, going back at least to John Stuart Mill in the mid-nineteenth century, is that certain industries will exhibit economies of scale even when the complete market is served.[4] That is, the more the industry produces, the lower will be the cost per unit of its output. To suppress such a "natural monopoly" is to deny the public the benefits of economies of scale. Thus, if the government divides a natural monopoly market between two or more firms, each will produce at a higher unit cost than if there were only one provider, and the cost of service will be higher than it needs be. On the other hand, if a natural monopoly market is left open to competition, it will be taken over by a single firm, which will charge monopoly prices rather than price at marginal cost, thereby denying service to customers who are willing to pay marginal costs but are unwilling to pay the monopoly price. So, for example, while it makes little sense to have two water companies tearing up streets to install their pipes, if the market is left to only one of them, it will gouge the public and not everyone who is willing to pay the marginal cost of water service will get it.

By and large, European countries have dealt with this problem by government ownership of single, "natural monopoly" companies; in the United States this has also been the approach for the provision of water in major cities. But for other natural monopolies—gas, electricity, telephone, and water service in small communities—the solution has been for the government in each case to grant a franchise to a single, privately owned, natural monopoly firm. The firm, called a "public utility", typically must serve all those who request the service, and its prices are controlled by a special regulatory commission.

How then should the regulatory commission set the firm's prices? From the standpoint of economic efficiency, the "first-best" solution would be to have the firm's rates set at marginal costs. But because of economies of scale, the cost of serving the last customer will be below average cost, and setting the firm's rates at marginal cost means that the firm will earn a negative profit—it will incur a yearly deficit. If the firm is state-owned, the deficit can simply be absorbed by the state, but if the firm is privately owned, the deficit must be financed by other means.

As discussed in chapter 19, in the United States, the legal precept is that the firm's rates should be adjusted above marginal costs so as to reward the firm's stockholders "fairly," interpreted to mean that stockholders' return on their investment should equal what they would in an alternative investment of comparable risk. It turns out that under this arrangement, the problem of fixing rates for the regulated public utility is exactly the same as the Ramsey problem for calculating economically efficient taxes.

To see this, consider the simplest cost structure that exhibits economies of scale. In each market, marginal costs, including the cost of raising capital, are constant, but in addition, the structure includes a fixed overhead cost, $F$, that must be recouped through prices. If we think of the amount above marginal cost that the firm must charge as a tax, with the proceeds of the tax being used to cover overhead, we have a complete correspondence with the Ramsey taxation problem.

Mathematically, we substitute $(p - mc)$ for $t$ in equations 13.1 and 13.2 to get

$$e_1[p_1^R - mc_1]/p_1^R = e_2[p_2^R - mc_2]/p_2^R \tag{13.5}$$

and the condition

Total tax revenue = Fixed amount = $F$,                                    (13.6)

where $p_1^R, p_2^R$ = Ramsey prices in the first and second markets, $mc_1, mc_2$ = marginal cost in the first and second markets, and $e_1, e_2$ = elasticities of demand in the first and second markets.

Likewise, the diagrammatic interpretation of figure 13.2 carries over to the case of Ramsey prices rather than taxes. We can interpret the shaded areas in figure 13.2 as *overhead coverages*, the amount of money that each market contributes to covering the firm's fixed cost or overhead. Then, the sum of the overhead coverages must equal the fixed cost, $F$. At the same time, the ratio $DA/AD'$ must be the same in each market.

For an alternative derivation of Ramsey prices for the regulated firm, as well as for a survey of public utility pricing literature prior to 1970, the reader is refereed at Baumol and Bradford (1970).

Externalities

Coase's research shows us how to think about externalities from an economic efficiency standpoint. As the reader will recall from chapter 6, when externalities or spillover effects exist, the trick is to think "one owner," or in economists' jargon, to imagine what would happen if the property rights that enter were all held by a single economic agent.

For example, suppose you live in a small town whose only business is a copper smelter that employs every person in the town. Suppose that there is a trade-off in copper production: the higher the copper production, the larger the volume of foul smoke from the smelter, smoke that dirties the town's housing, kills some of the trees, and so forth. Suppose further that the smelter is owned by out-of-town shareholders, but the smoke damage is suffered entirely by the town residents. We can expect a battle, with the town fathers passing smoke control ordinances and the smelter company responding by threatening to pull out of town.

On the other hand, suppose the smelter is entirely owned by the town. This would "internalize" the smoke externality. The town fathers would then be faced not with fighting "them," the evil out-of-town smelter owners, but with choosing the optimum level of copper production. Presumably, they would balance the benefits of having more wealth in the town as a result of higher copper production with the cost of more pollution, which would result in expanding production until the marginal benefit of copper production was just equal to its marginal cost.

Similar reasoning applies to the economy as whole. The production of steel, copper, semiconductor chips, lumber—almost anything—requires energy. But the production of energy, whether by burning coal or oil or by nuclear reactions, results in pollution of some sort, and the pollutants typically spill over to harm third parties. If society mandated a zero pollution standard, the economy would stop functioning. We couldn't even return to nature and live like cavemen because this would require building fires, which create pollution.

If we "think one owner"—the economy as whole owns all of the sources of pollution—then we are in the position of the town with the copper smelter. There will generally be a trade-off: more output for the economy will generate benefits, say as measured by an increase in consumer's surplus, but it will also generate more pollution. The "owner" of the economy, namely, all of its citizens, will conclude that the optimal level of output will occur when its marginal benefit just equals its marginal cost.

Note, however, that when we expand from a single product, copper, to the entire economy, we also expand from one pollutant to many. This doesn't really change matters; it simply means that, for optimality, the marginal *societal* benefit of expanding output of every good or service must just balance its marginal *societal* cost.

Thus basic theory of dealing with externalities is simple. But how can it be implemented when in fact the owners of the steel mills, copper smelters, semiconductor facilities, and so on, are separate from those affected by the pollutants they may create? Even if the optimal level of the various types of pollution could be determined, there would be the formidable technical problem of deciding which polluter would contribute which fraction of the optimal level. And there is the additional problem of policing the polluters to ensure that they produce no more than their respective fractions.

For at least a couple of decades, economists have been vigorously championing a system of marketable pollution rights as a solution to this problem. Various systems have been proposed which differ in the details. But the main idea is again a simple one. The economy as a whole through its elected representatives and expert technicians decides on the optimal level of pollution, firm by firm, or at least makes a first try at deciding on this level. Each firm's pollution level then becomes a *pollution right* for that firm. The crucial feature of the plan is that this right can be *sold* or *traded*.

How would this plan work? We can assume that the elected representatives and their experts would not be able to do their job perfectly. Their initial allocation of pollution rights would appear very generous to some firms and hopelessly inadequate to others. As a result, a market for pollution rights of the various sorts would be formed. Firms who got a generous allocation of rights would sell them to those who got an inadequate allocation. The trades through the market would cease when the marginal opportunity cost of a pollution right was the same for every firm.

Note that I said "marginal *opportunity* cost" in the preceding sentence. Why? Because firms would have an incentive to sell their pollution rights and correspondingly reduce their pollution levels whenever this would increase profits. But to reduce levels they might have to raise new capital to buy more expensive equipment, change technologies, hire more skilled workers, or a myriad of other steps. In a word, to create more pollution rights, the firm would have to forgo the benefits of doing other things, and thus opportunity costs would enter into its decision.

But an attraction of marketable pollution rights is that they give a firm incentives to explore these possibilities, and the firm is in the best position to make this exploration. Presumably it knows all of the subtle matters affecting its production and marketing decisions better than anyone else, including government officials. Most importantly, similar incentives do not exist in a nonmarket system to control pollution, wherein government officials set standards and also enforce them.

As Crandall (1983, 74–75) points out, there are other advantages as well. For one, a marketable rights system eliminates the current distinction in the law between old and new sources of pollution. Currently, a new production facility is generally held to more stringent pollution standards than an old one, on the grounds that it can take advantage of the most recent and best technology.[5] This argument has been challenged and has generated controversy, a controversy that disappears under a marketable rights scheme. New firms in fact have an incentive to use the best and most efficient technology and needn't argue with government officials as to what that is; likewise, old firms have an incentive to install new and better technology whenever that is more efficient than keeping old technology.

For another, with marketable rights, prices are mobilized to perform their usual information conveying role, information that can be used in a variety of ways for policy making. For example, we can almost be certain that the representatives' and experts' initial allocation of rights or, equivalently, their setting of initial standards, will be imperfect and will require adjustment. With a scheme of marketable rights, the market for rights establishes the cost of further reduction in a pollutant—a state or the federal government could reduce the quantity of the pollutant simply by buying rights from the market and retiring them. Thus marketable rights give a direct measure in dollars of the cost of changing existing levels of pollution; by contrast, with a standard-setting scheme, government officials have no way of knowing the costs and benefits of a change in standards until after the change is made.

Lack of Information

Another standard argument for government intervention in the market-place is that the market does not yield us the information to make good choices of doctors, dentists, lawyers, barbers, morticians, taxi drivers, dispensers of alcholic beverages, and so forth, and it would be inefficient for each of us to have to gather such information on our own. Instead, to remedy this market failure, we instruct the government to license practitioners of these and other trades and professions, thereby protecting us from incompetents.

As Friedman (1982) points out, licensing is only one form of giving us such protection, and is in fact the third and most intrusive form of government regulation in a chain of three different forms. The first is registration. Examples are the registration of automobiles, pedigreed dogs, and in some states, the registration of firearms. Registration can be with a government or private agency, with the government using registration mainly as a way of collecting all taxes due it; as long as the taxes are paid, the penalties for nonregistration are usually mild.

The second is certification, common in medical specialties; again, certification typically does not directly involve the police power of the state in economic transactions. Any licensed medical doctor can advertise as a plastic surgeon, even though he or she is not a "board certified" plastic surgeon. If the doctor performs bad plastic surgery, the doctor's patient can sue for damages, but the state will not prevent the doctor from doing the plastic surgery, nor subject the doctor to criminal penalties for practicing it.

Licensure, the third form, does directly involve the police power of the state. Only licensed medical doctors are allowed to practice medicine. The unlicensed practice of medicine is a criminal act, subject to criminal penalties. Unlike the two previous cases of monopoly and externalities, there is little detailed economic theory to guide policy on the optimum way to cure the failure of the market to provide adequate information, although there is an extensive economics literature that points out the economic *inefficiencies* of licensure.

In a nutshell, economists have observed that the initiative for licensing occupation X usually comes from occupation X. Likewise, after occupation X succeeds in licensing itself, invariably the state licensing boards for occupation X are composed of members of occupation X; the principal occupation X society or organization usually choses the members, with the governor routinely rubber-stamping the choice. Finally, the usual justification for establishing a licensing procedure is to protect the public, although it is often not obvious why the public needs protection. Or, if it is, why licensure, rather than registration or certification, is necessary. As Friedman mentions (1982, 139), states license, for no clear reason, one or more of the following: egg graders, guide dog trainers, pest controllers, yacht salesmen, tree surgeons, well diggers, tile layers, and potato growers. Furthermore, the requirements for licensure sometimes seem excessive; for example, to acquire a barber's license in Arizona, one must receive 1,450 hours— roughly nine months—of full-time instruction at an accredited barber school.

All of this has led many economists to conclude that much of licensure is simply a means for an occupation to form a cartel, a cartel that the occupation can easily control and that will present high barriers to those who wish to enter the occupation. This allows the cartel's members to set prices at monopoly levels and make monopoly profits. Friedman (1982, chap. 9) argues forcefully that certification would give the public all the protection it needs, while at the same time reducing the monopoly power of the cartels that licensure has created and increasing economic efficiency.

## 13.4  Cautionary Note

In this chapter I have tried to show the basic economic forces that are at the heart of theoretical models of economically efficient government intervention and regulation. As mentioned at the outset, there are a number of such models; although they have in common the elements that led to the derivation of lump-sum taxes as first best and Ramsey regulated prices as second best, they differ in the details of the descriptions of a firm's markets and the interactions of the firm with the rest of the economy. The reader is cautioned that these differences can be significant. For example, in the derivation of the Ramsey formula we assumed that a consumer's gains or losses depended only on the units of a commodity that the consumer consumed and not on the units that others consumed (in economists' jargon, we assumed the absence of consumption externalities). In reality, having a telephone is obviously worthless unless someone else has a telephone, and, as one might suspect, consumption externalities play an important role in telephone pricing. Indeed, the notion that the value of telephone service to me depends on the number of persons I can talk to was historically an important element in the "value of service" concept in traditional telephone rate making. When consumption externalities are important, the Ramsey formula for a public utilities prices must be modified.

Likewise, in deriving the simple Ramsey formula, we have assumed that prices outside of the regulated sector are everywhere equal to marginal costs. The importance of this assumption is brought out in chapter 15, which discusses at length the crucial importance of whether or not gainers are able to compensate losers. All the assumptions underlying the Ramsey formula must be kept firmly in mind in applying it, as chapter 15 emphasizes in its general discussion of economically efficient prices for the regulated firm.

## Exercises

1. What goals are often cited as justification for the government to regulate or otherwise interfere with the working of the free market?

2. Summarize the heart of the argument for a lump-sum tax as being least distortionary or "first best."

3. In what sense are Ramsey taxes "second best."

4. Suppose that the price of a good plus the tax on it is $10/unit and a tiny tax increase of $0.01/unit of the good is imposed. By means of a demand-supply diagram, indicate the effect of this tax on (a) the marginal consumer of the good, and on (b) the inframarginal consumer of the good. Indicate these effects for a tax decrease of $0.01.

5. In terms of consumer's surplus, what property characterizes Ramsey taxes? Reproduce the diagrammatic conditions for Ramsey prices for the case of two goods, each having straight-line demands and constant marginal costs.

6. What is the Ramsey prices formula for a "natural monopoly"? How is it similar to the Ramsey taxation formula?

7. Describe how the purchase by the town residents of the town's copper smelter "internalizes" the smelter's pollution externality. How does this purchase relate to the "think one owner" insight that emerges from a study of Coase's (1937) theorem on externalities?

8. Discuss the properties of marketable pollution rights, including their information conveying role.

9. Summarize Friedman's (1982) claim that occupational certification would give almost all of the advantages of occupational licensure with only few of its disadvantages. Do you believe this claim?

# 14     Interest Group (Positive) Economic Theories of Regulation: Incentive-Compatible Regulation

*[A]s recognized by both the framers of the Constitution and modern scholars of public choice, all political systems provide interest groups with an incentive for "rent seeking," that is, manipulation of collective action for private benefit....[Rent seeking] can lead government agencies to make decisions that benefit a particular interest group even though they are costly to society as a whole.*

Annual Report of the Council of Economic Advisers, 1994

## 14.1   Basic Approach

The discussion in the previous chapter of economists' normative approaches to regulation and government intervention may seem sterile, abstract, and have little relation to reality. Terms like *Pareto optimality, economic efficiency, gains through exchange* are hardly household words and are usually not in a politician's lexicon. Not surprisingly, economists' admonitions about "what should be done about it" that are based on economic efficiency seem rarely to be followed, at least at the level of detail suggested by the standard economic efficiency normative theories.

In this chapter we consider the attempts by economists and political scientists to formulate *positive* theories of regulation and government intervention, theories that attempt to describe realistically what *is* rather than what *ought to be*. These are generally known as "interest group" theories of regulation and government intervention to distinguish them from the normative, "public interest" theories taken up in the last chapter.

At first glance, all of our work on understanding economists' attempts at creating normative theories of government intervention might seem in vain. We might think that, in developing interest group theories, an entirely new approach is called for. This is not the case, in fact, just the opposite. Economists have made great strides at understanding politics and government by applying the methods and tools they know best. Perhaps, most importantly, in approaching these problems, economists have retained their assumption of the twin pillars of human behavior: (1) people tend to act in their own self-interest; and (2) they tend to seek and benefit from gains through exchange.

## 14.2  Theory of Public Choice

As is true with most innovations, the roots of public choice theory can be traced back to a number of persons, including Adam Smith; however, the seminal book that gave birth to public choice as a major field spanning economics and political science is *The Calculus of Consent*, written in 1962 by James Buchanan and Gordon Tullock. Since its publication, both authors have made further major contributions to the public choice field, with Buchanan receiving the 1986 Nobel Prize in economics for his efforts.

In order to give the reader a flavor of the public choice approach, following paragraphs of this section outline some of the main ideas contained in *The Calculus of Consent*. Subsequent sections take up the specific topic of rent-seeking, first introduced by Tullock, and the Stigler-Peltzman and Becker approaches to regulation and government intervention in the marketplace.

Constitutional Level of Collective Choice

In approaching the problem of the choice of public or collective goods, Buchanan and Tullock (1962) distinguish between rule making and operating within a given set of rules. Decisions on the rules that a group will use for making collective choices are considered to be at the *constitutional* stage. Both from a normative and positive point of view, they argue that constitutional decisions must be unanimous; otherwise, the group is faced with an infinite regress problem. That is, if constitutional decisions are not unanimous, by what rule are constitutional choices to be made, and how is the group to decide on this rule? If the choice of the rule is by other than a unanimous vote, by what more basic rule is the voting procedure to be arrived at, and so on. Thus in public choice theory, unanimity acts like a "primitive" or "undefined term" in mathematical or justice theory. Not surprisingly, individuals are assumed to approach constitutional decisions in a manner akin to that of the Harsanyi-Rawls primitive notion of "original position," that is, "the individual will not find it advantageous to vote for rules that may promote sectional, class, or group interests because, by presupposition, he is unable to predict the role that he will be playing in the actual collective decision-making process at any particular time in the future" (Buchanan and Tullock, 1962, 78).

## Constitutional Collective Choice, Voluntary Exchange, and Choice

Once the group has decided on its constitution or the rules by which it will make its collective choices, there is left the problem of whether or not an individual will prefer to use the group process for decision making or will prefer some other process. This choice, of course, depends on the benefits and costs associated with the various options available. Buchanan and Tullock (1962) distinguish among three possibilities: (1) individual or private action, (2) voluntary exchange, or (3) collective choice.

The principal costs associated with collective action or voluntary exchange are the costs of organization. Even if the group has decided on a decision-making rule such as majority vote, the costs of bringing an issue to a vote, the time spent on deliberations in committee, and the costs of information gathering may be considerable. On the other hand, if the choice is left in individual hands, there may be considerable external costs inflicted on others as a consequence of one individual's actions.

Which of the possible organizational forms prevails depends of course on the particular circumstances. For example, you will probably wish to choose the color of your new car by yourself rather than have this decision voted upon by a group; both the costs and the benefits of making a decision on car color through some voluntary exchange with others are minimal. Within a firm, the allocation of office space may very well be left to individual department heads, who may best do the allocation through "horse-trading" among themselves. Finally, classic public goods, such as police and fire protection and national defense, are usually best decided upon through collective action. One might imagine a society organized so that everyone contracts for his or her own private police protection, but in practice, the legal difficulties and costs of private police arrangements would be formidable, and one individual's zealous private police force might turn out to be a considerable annoyance to others.

Hence, having decided upon the rules of operation by unanimous agreement, we can expect that modes of decision making will depend on circumstances, and anything from individual choice to collective choice can be expected.

Time Element, Vote Trading, and Logrolling

The functioning of a legislature is a complex process. As Buchanan (1976, 23) says:

The political unit contains many persons, many potential voters-taxpayers-beneficiaries, and fiscal decisions are made through a very complex political process which involves parties, pressure groups, political entrepreneurs, periodic but sometimes infrequent elections, legislative assemblies operating under complicated rules and with ordered committee structures, and bureaucratic hierarchies.

The realities of the legislative process give rich opportunities for the realization of gains in trade through voluntary exchanges. In particular, two effects are at work in legislatures that are absent from the theoretical efficiency models we have considered in previous sections.

First of all, we have by and large considered once-and-for-all decisions. In a legislature, decisions are not necessarily made at a single point in time but are stretched over some finite length of time. Second, decisions are not generally made in isolation but are part of a process of continual decision making on a variety of interrelated issues. This allows legislators representing different groups to profit from mutually advantageous exchanges. Such exchanges popularly go under the pejorative terms of *logrolling* or *vote trading*, but, as Buchanan and Tullock (1962) remark, it is no accident that the practices have developed and flourished as part of the democratic process, nor should they necessarily be condemned out of hand as morally reprehensible. They are in fact exactly what the theory of public choice would predict and are the consequence of various groups' trying to effect decisions as expeditiously as possible.

As we discuss in chapter 15, the difficulty of arranging for winners to compensate losers, that is, for direct side payments to take place, may seriously impede the attainment of Pareto efficiency in the regulated sector. Direct compensations or side payments are of course equally difficult in matters of taxation and other legislative actions. On the other hand, as Buchanan and Tullock (1962) point out, however politically difficult direct compensations may be to arrange, logrolling and other practical forms of exchange may make *indirect* compensation relatively easy.[1]

## 14.3   Rent Seeking

The above very brief synopsis of some of the ideas of *The Calculus of Consent* paints a picture of complex interactions among legislators to effect gains through trade. Of course, the legislators are not the only parties to the interactions. Every legislative body, down to the level of the town council, is surrounded by pleaders of self-interest, from professional lobbyists to ordinary citizens seeking redress of some grievance in the name of simple justice. Legislators achieving gains through trade are in effect substituting for a market; indeed, the ideas from public choice apply generally to nonmarket institutions.

For example, it is often observed that managers within a large corporation spend the bulk of their time in meetings. Much of this activity consists of arranging gains through exchange with their peers, subordinates, or superiors. The governance mechanism of any institution must provide for such trades to take place if the institution is to run efficiently.

On the other hand, as the above synopsis also brings out, the complex activity within legislatures and other organizations to achieve gains through trade takes time and resources, and the same is true within other nonmarket institutions. It is easy for the process to get out of hand, to assume a life of its own, with many more resources being spent on lobbying, logrolling, and the like than is efficient. If the institution is not subject to the discipline of the market, or is only weakly subject to that discipline, as is the case with legislatures, government institutions, and monopoly firms, this danger looms large. The worst case is when an institution gets totally consumed with internal fights; its members devote all of their time and energy fighting rivals within the institution rather than doing their jobs.

Although inefficiencies within a government institution or a monopoly firm are often observed and commented on, Tullock (1967) was the first to incorporate them into an analytical framework, developing a method to quantify their effect. Again, Tullock's basic insight is a simple one, illustrated by the standard price-quantity diagram for pricing by a monopoly firm, as shown in figure 14.1.

For analytical simplicity, I have assumed that the demand curve is a straight line, denoted by "Demand." This, in turn yields a marginal revenue curve that is also a straight line but twice as steep, denoted by $MR$. Also, I have assumed that marginal costs are constant, denoted by the horizontal line at level $mc$. To maximize profits, the monopolist will equate marginal revenue to marginal cost, which results in a price, $p_m$, a quantity, $Q_m$, and a producer's surplus rectangle (see figure 14.1), also called "economic rent".[2] In addition, there is a "deadweight loss" given by the triangle shown in figure 14.1. That is, at prices less than $p_m$ but greater than $mc$, consumers are willing to pay more than the marginal cost of an additional unit of

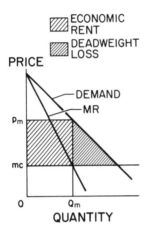

**Figure 14.1**
Tullock's economic rent rectangle

production. Both the consumer and the producer are denied the surplus in
the deadweight loss triangle; no one in society enjoys this potential benefit
—thus the term *deadweight loss*.

Prior to Tullock's (1967) pioneering paper, economists considered the
deadweight loss to be the only welfare loss due to a firm's monopolization
of a market. But suppose a firm in fact has monopoly power within its
market, and thus is able to set its price at $p_m$ if it so chooses, and suppose
further that its employees engage furiously in the sort of inefficient internal
fighting described above. Part of the firm's potential monopoly profit may
go to supporting these sorts of inefficiencies. In the limit, the entire rectangle of economic rent may be so consumed in nonproductive activity. In this
case the total welfare loss to society is not just the deadweight loss, but the
sum of the potential producer's surplus and the deadweight loss, represented by the sum of the economic rent rectangle and the deadweight loss
triangle.

Since the publication of his 1967 paper, Tullock's insight has been applied to a wide variety of economic institutions and arrangements, and
Kruger has given the activity that Tullock described an apt name—"rent
seeking". In a word, if there is economic rent to be had, someone will seek
to get it by fair means or foul.

For example, if a town limits the number of licenses to operate taxicabs,
it will create a taxicab monopoly. One expects that there will arise an
industry of lobbyists and influence peddlers who, for a fee, will facilitate the
obtaining of a coveted license. If they sell their services to the highest

bidder, those who wish a license will bid up to the economic rent rectangle for their services; or if those who already have taxicab licenses decide to sell them to the highest bidder, they can expect to receive up to this area for it. Thus New York City currently limits the number of taxicab licenses for Yellow Cabs to 11,800 and a license sells for about $140,000.[3] Tullock's argument applies not only to taxicab and occupational licensing generally but to the welfare consequences of tariffs and crimes, as well as to the infighting inefficiencies of any organization.

## 14.4 Stigler-Peltzman and Becker Theories of Regulation and Government Intervention

As we have seen, the thrust of public choice theory is to apply economists' tools to the study of politics and government. One such tool is supply and demand analysis. Stigler's (1971) insight is that this can be applied to regulation as well as to goods and services. For example, in chapter 13 we considered occupational licensing and observed that, more often than not, the demand for licensing occupation X came from occupation X itself. Who can supply the licenses? Some legislative body; in the United States, typically a state legislature. So occupation X and the state legislature make up the two sides of a demand-supply model of the regulation of Occupation X. Peltzman (1976) has elaborated on Stigler's (1971) insight to formulate a more explicit mathematical model of Stigler's theory. Peltzman assumes that what legislators and regulators can supply is the power to transfer wealth or income from one group to another; in return, they desire votes so that they can stay in office. On the other hand, any group that wishes to benefit from a transfer of wealth has to convince the electorate to do the transfer and will likely meet opposition from those who stand to lose wealth.

In symbols, let $M$ be the probable number of votes that a legislator receives, given by

$$M = \rho - v,$$

where $\rho$ is the number of probable positive votes and $v$ is the number of probable negative votes. We can expect that $\rho$ will equal the product of the number of beneficiaries from the wealth transfer and the probability that the beneficiaries will in fact vote positively, while $v$ will consist of the product of the number of those who will be taxed and the probability that they will vote negatively:

$$\rho = fn, \qquad v = h(N - n),$$

where $n$ is the number of potential positive voters, $N$ is the total number of potential voters, $f$ is the probability of a positive vote, and $h$ the probability of a negative vote.

This then is the bare-bones structure of Peltzman's (1971) model, but of course many details remain to be filled in. I will not attempt to spell them out in symbols but will simply describe some of the details that Peltzman supplies. For one, he assumes that the probability of support will depend on the amount of wealth or income received by each of the beneficiaries, which in turn is the total amount transferred less the amount spent campaigning to effect the transfer, including the amount spent organizing the campaign. Likewise, Peltzman assumes that the probability of opposition will depend on the rate at which the nonbeneficiaries are taxed and the amount that those in favor spend to mitigate the opposition. Peltzman then manipulates the mathematical model he obtains with these assumptions to solve for the possible equilibria and to gain insight into the relative importance of the factors that enter into the model. As we shall see in chapter 22, Peltzman's bare-bones framework is quite general and applies to a variety of situations; moreover, in a particular instance, we need not formulate the details exactly as Peltzman has and can tailor them to the case at hand.

Nevertheless, Peltzman's (1971) formulation slights an obvious element of the political process: interest groups compete with one another to get law makers and regulators to side with them; it is this aspect of the process that Becker (1983) focuses on, adopting an approach reminiscent of oligopoly theory in economics. Rather than envisioning two or more firms in the same market, each trying to maximize profits, Becker envisions two or more groups exerting pressure in order to maximize the amount of wealth transferred to them. The pressure can be of various sorts—a letter-writing campaign to try to influence a legislator's vote, contributions to politicians' campaigns for election or reelection, the promise to shift jobs into a congressman's district or the threat to remove them, and so forth. Becker does not try to quantify the pressure with some sort of measuring rod but simply assumes that it can somehow be quantified; he notes that exerting pressure requires that a group expend resources, with the costs of the additional resources eventually overtaking the additional wealth that these resources generate.

For a given amount of pressure exerted by pressure group 2, we can imagine pressure group 1 calculating the optimum amount of pressure it can bring to bear on the political process to achieve its ends. Becker calls the schedule of pressure group 1's optimal pressures as a function of the pressure chosen by pressure group 2, the "influence function" for pressure

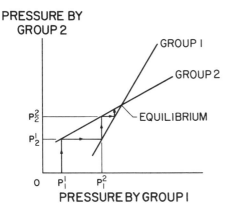

**Figure 14.2**
Group 1 and group 2's influence functions

group 1. Obviously, pressure group 2 will calculate a similar influence function that indicates *its* optimum pressure level, given that pressure group 1 exerts a given amount of pressure.

Figure 14.2 depicts pressure group 1's and pressure group 2's influence functions. Their intersection establishes an equilibrium point; at the intersection, neither group will gain by changing pressure, given that the other group's pressure remains fixed. Figure 14.2 also shows how equilibrium may be obtained. If group 1 exerts pressure $P_1^1$, group 2 will respond with pressure $P_2^1$; group 1 will then respond with pressure $P_1^2$, to which group 2 will respond with pressure $P_2^2$; and so on. For the orientation of influence functions shown in figure 14.2, where group 1's influence function is steeper than group 2's, the result will be a spiraling in to the equilibrium point. It is easily shown that if the reverse is true, the equilibrium will be unstable; a small perturbation from the equilibrium will result in a spiraling out rather than in.

As with Peltzman, Becker (1983) manipulates his model to get several interesting insights into the political process. For one, the equilibrium is not a Pareto optimum. If interest groups joined forces or colluded, they could reduce the resources they spend to exert pressure and gain the same outcome. For another, the model has interesting things to say about *free riding*, a problem that any group influencing political outcomes has to deal with. Trial lawyers hoping to defeat the imposition of a ceiling on medical malpractice awards have an incentive to free ride by letting colleagues fight the battle, while they reap the rewards of the fight. Becker's model suggests it is the *relative* and not the absolute amount of free riding that is important.

Finally, and most important, the model suggests that all of the competing pressure groups will suffer from policy moves that decrease welfare, as measured by an increase in consumer's and producer's surpluses, and will benefit from moves that increase welfare. Why? Because a decrease in consumer's plus producer's surplus decreases the potential amount of wealth to be transferred and vice versa, which means that, in spite of a lack of a Pareto optimal equilibrium, competition among pressure groups can be welfare-improving.

## 14.5   Incentive-Compatible Regulation and Government Intervention

Years ago, I heard a distinguished scientist give a talk on his plan for cities of the future. They were all to be underground in order to save the environment; also, housing was to be densely clustered together in order to save on infrastructure expenditures such as costs of sewers, transportation, heating, and illumination. Between-cities transportation networks were to be optimized with respect to cost and carrying capacity. The scientist had thought things through carefully and was proud of his work. In the question period, someone asked, "How are you going to make people live underground and do all the other things that you want them to do?" The speaker was not pleased when the audience laughed.

The anecdote illustrates an extreme example of what might be called the "utopian planning syndrome." The speaker had envisioned a set of goals for his plan; it remained only to design the perfect plan, as if he were designing a clock. In the plan, people were to act like the parts of the clock, mechanically performing their designated roles; after the clock was built, it had only to be wound, after which it would work perfectly.

As stressed in part II, people are not like the mechanical parts of a clock. They have minds of their own; they wish to follow their own agendas, not necessarily the planner's. In a word, they tend to follow their self-interest.

Unfortunately, the utopian planning syndrome is still with us. All too often, planners start worrying about self-interested behavior only when near completion of the design of their perfect clock. A current example is the welfare system, designed with the best of intentions to help the disadvantaged. Unfortunately, as now generally recognized, its design did not sufficiently take into account self-interest; as a result, under the current system, many welfare recipients lose money and health care benefits as soon as they get a job and get off the system.

How does one eliminate or at least minimize such perverse effects? Two things immediately come to mind. One is to assume self-interested behavior at the *beginning* rather than the end of the planning process. The other is to design a plan that gives people incentives to work *for* the plan's goals rather than against them. This is the idea of "incentive-compatible regulation".

The familiar "cut and choose" algorithm described in chapter 6 is an example. Suppose you are a working parent with two children. You find that your children are constantly fighting over who gets how much of a cake, an apple pie, toys, and so forth. Unable to be at home to referee most of these fights, you decree the following regulatory policy: whenever possible, all things are to be divided by the "cut and choose" algorithm. One child will cut the thing to be divided, say a cake or a group of toys, into two parts or two groups; the other child will then have first choice of which of two pieces or groups it wants. Whichever child is chosen to do the division into two will have an incentive to make the pieces or groupings as equal as possible. If the child doesn't do the dividing equitably, he or she will be left with the smaller pieces or the less desirable group.

The most prevalent incentive-compatible regulatory scheme is the free market. Although people who live in a free-market economy tend to take its incentive-compatible properties for granted, we have only to compare it with a command-and-control economy to appreciate its self-regulating features.

Nevertheless, there are instances when markets fail or the market does not achieve societal objectives, as discussed in the previous chapter, and government intervention is called for. Unfortunately, systems of regulation and government intervention have rarely been designed starting with an explicit incentive-compatible viewpoint, but history does give us examples, and the evidence is encouraging.

For example, McCraw (1984) describes the successes of several regulators—Charles Francis Adams, one of the first American railroad regulators (1869–1878); James Landis, an original member and later chairman of the Securities Exchange Commission; and Alfred E. Kahn, chairman of both the New York State Public Service Commission and the Civil Aeronautics Board. The regulatory regimes of all three were marked by what today we would call the "incentive-compatible viewpoint." They all tried to structure incentives so that, in following self-interest, economic agents under their purview acted to achieve regulatory goals, with a minimum of formal regulatory proceedings.

All three men were also aware of the potentially enormous cost of the alternative—endless, time-consuming, and expensive litigation, as well as large and expensive policing staffs, not to mention the compliance costs heaped on those being regulated. For example, Santa Monica, California, a city with a population of 87,000, currently spends $5 million enforcing its rent control ordinance. This direct cost supports a permanent staff of fifty-five persons (Johnson 1994) but does not include the legal costs of landlords appealing staff decisions, tenants suing landlords, and so forth, not to mention the maintenance forgone because the landlord is unable to recoup costs.

In chapter 21 we briefly discuss the history of incentive-compatible regulation of public utilities. More recently, we have seen the attempts to introduce marketable pollution rights in environmental regulation in order to achieve incentive-compatible regulation. And in telecommunications regulation we now have numerous attempts to replace traditional rate-of-return regulation with incentive-compatible regulatory schemes, a topic we also discuss in more detail in chapter 21.

## 14.6   Discussion

A market economy has often been compared with the human body; both are complex organisms where everything seems to influence everything else. Prick your finger and a complex chain of chemical and biological reactions are triggered off. Have coal miners go on strike and a complex chain of economic transactions ripple through the economy.

Likewise, both have marvelous recuperative properties. Whether it be a market economy or the human body, abuse it, shock it, or infect it with any number of diseases, and over time, it will recover by itself. During the Great Depression of the 1930s, many of the world's market economies seemed to be very sick. Strong medication was tried; a certain amount of improvement resulted. But many economies were overmedicated, and some came close to being "killed with improvement."

Modern medicine, having learned the dangers of too many drugs and too much surgery, proceeds carefully and cautiously; most important, it has learned to try as much as possible to mobilize the human body's self-healing capabilities. Likewise, in dealing with a market economy's failures or "diseases," modern economists have learned of the dangers of too much regulation and too much government intervention; they have also learned to proceed carefully and cautiously and that mobilizing the economy's self-healing powers can have big payoffs. Sometimes economists express this with the slogan "The market is the best regulator," meaning that, if possible, the market should be mobilized to help regulate, as exemplified by marketable pollution rights (see chapter 13). This in turn is a special case of the more general dictum "Seek incentive-compatible regulatory mechanisms."

## Exercises

1. For a group that wishes to make decisions *as a group*, how do the rules and regulations in its *constitution* differ from other rules and regulations that the group adopts?

2. What is the Buchanan-Tullock (1962) argument that, in theory, constitutions should be adopted by unanimous agreement.

3. What three modes of decision making or choice do Buchanan and Tullock (1962) identify? What determines which mode will be used?

4. In the Buchanan-Tullock (1962) theory, *logrolling* or *vote trading* are not necessarily pejorative terms. Why not?

5. Discuss "Tullock's rectangle."

6. Discuss "rent seeking."

7. Contrast and compare the Stigler (1971)-Peltzman (1976) and Becker (1983) theories of regulation.

8. Discuss incentive-compatible regulation.

# IV

# Case Studies and Applications

# 15    Introduction to Part IV

*Perceptions are realities.*

Anonymous

This chapter discusses some preliminary matters before we consider the case studies that make up most of part IV. First, we consider the problems facing the policy maker who might try to implement economically efficient policies of regulation and government intervention. To illustrate the difficulty of these problems, we give an imaginary dialogue between a regulator and his expert economic adviser. Next, we consider stakeholders and how you might recognize one if you saw one. Finally, we discuss the issue of "perceptions are realities." The data that the public uses to form political judgments are obtained from reading newspapers and magazines or watching television; knowingly or unknowingly, information gets filtered as it flows from original sources through the media to the individual, and the filtering distorts it.

## 15.1  Difficulties of Implementing Economically Efficient and Fair Policies

In applying Ramsey prices for a public utility, regulators face the problem of lack of control over all prices in the economy—a lack of control that deprives them of being able to set economically efficient prices.

An idealized example illustrates the difficulty. Suppose, as shown in figure 15.1, a regulated electric utility company sells electricity *only* to residential customers and to a large number of competitive bakeries. Suppose further that the bakeries sell their bread *only* to the residential customers, whose consumption of bread is totally insensitive to bread prices.

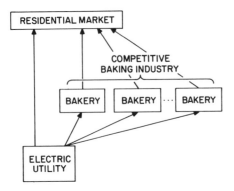

**Figure 15.1**
Electric utility that serves a competitive market and a residential market; regulators have complete control over the economy

Finally, suppose that compared to Ramsey prices, the price of electricity sold to the bakeries is too high and the price to residential users is too low. Now imagine bakeries' electricity prices are lowered and residential prices are raised so that both attain their Ramsey values. The intense competition among bakeries will then cause the price of bread to go down; indeed, we can expect the reduction in the aggregate bakeries' electricity bill to be passed through completely to the residents in the form of lower bread bills. The conversion to Ramsey prices in this case will result in an aggregate net gain for the residential users. They will have an increased aggregate electricity bill, but this increase will be more than offset by the decrease in their aggregate bread bill. Hence regulators faced with a competitive bakery industry as their only business market, together with a residential market, might in this hypothetical example convince themselves to set electricity prices at Ramsey values.

Now suppose we have the situation shown in figure 15.2, where, instead of a competitive bakery industry, there is only a single, monopoly producer of bread. Further, suppose that the bread monopolist sells to two residential markets, residential markets I and II, but that our utility sells electricity only to residential market I; moreover, suppose that the demand for bread is sensitive to price changes.

The proper course of action for the utility's regulators is not obvious. The decrease in electricity prices charged to the monopoly bakery will not necessarily all be passed through to the residential users of electricity; the monopoly bakery may partially siphon off some of the decrease as an increase in its profit. Hence the price reduction will probably have more

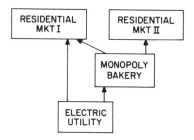

**Figure 15.2**
Electric utility that serves a monopoly market and a single residential market; regulators have only partial control over the economy

complicated effects. The lowering of its unit costs will cause the bakery to lower the price of bread, which will result in an increase in demand for bread and an increase in the baker's profits. If demand is not too sensitive to price changes, the lower bread prices will result in a decrease in the aggregate or total residential bread bill. However, the decrease in the total residential bread bill may not offset the increase in the total residential electricity bill, and residents in aggregate may have an out-of-pocket loss.

This might present the regulators with a dilemma. If they are willing to treat every dollar gained or lost by the bakery stockholders on an even footing with every dollar gained or lost by the residence customers, including those outside their jurisdiction, they may opt for a change to Ramsey prices if the increase in bakery profits exceeds the residential out-of-pocket loss. On the other hand, if they attach more weight to the residential gains or losses than to those of the bakery owners, and if they are concerned *only* with the residents living within their area of jurisdiction, they may not find a change to Ramsey prices appealing. Indeed, if they are elected officials, a switch to Ramsey prices might get them voted out of office.[1] Thus, where the regulators find themselves in a world that is "second best" compared to the ideal world in which Ramsey prices apply, a straightforward switch from existing prices to Ramsey prices may be neither desirable nor politically feasible.

Pricing Reform and Compensation of Losers by Gainers

The example of the previous section brings out two other, related issues that have also been discussed in the literature of taxation and public enterprise pricing. First is the distinction between de novo taxation or pricing and taxation or pricing reform. Suppose a pricing expert is asked to design prices for a public enterprise that is to be part of a brand-new economy, now in the planning stage. Suppose further that in some magical fashion the expert can get all necessary data regarding demands and costs and can be sure that there will be no second-best problems. In this case our expert probably would have no trouble in selling decision makers on setting prices at their economically efficient values. For once these prices were established, there would be no price changes that would mutually benefit some group of customers, even if it were possible for gainers to compensate losers.

Unfortunately, the regulator is seldom given a new economy to play with. Instead of the de novo taxation or pricing problem, the regulator is faced with the question of how to improve present taxes or prices, that is, the problem of "taxation or pricing reform." If there were a mechanism for gainers to compensate losers, then matters would be straightforward. The regulator could simply arrange for the compensations to take place. Unfortunately, compensations are also rarely feasible, so that a pricing "reform" that goes from existing prices to "economically efficient" prices is bound to incur the wrath of those whose prices are increased and may be difficult to arrange.

Put in other terms, the regulator or policy maker must operate with the instruments at hand and within the given political or institutional constraints. The instruments will rarely provide for direct compensations or "lump-sum transfers" from one group to another. Prices that are economically inefficient when such transfers or compensations are available may be economically efficient when transfers are unavailable and when one considers the instruments that are actually at hand. The task of effectuating a pricing reform rather than instituting prices de novo; the lack of sufficiently flexible instruments, in particular the practical inability to arrange for compensations or lump-sum transfers; and, finally, the need to cope with political or institutional constraints—all of these difficulties, either singly or in combination, can present the policy maker with a difficult dilemma.

The Policy Maker's Dilemma

Economically efficient prices have the property that small deviations from them result in the gains from price decreases exactly balancing the losses from price increases. If prices are inefficient, there will always be possible adjustments of prices so that, in principle, gains from price decreases can be used to compensate losses from price increases. Furthermore, the gains will be more than adequate; if the compensation could be carried out, the gains could cover the losses and there would be *money left over* (recall the discussion of the Kaldor-Hicks compensation criterion in chapter 7). This "money left over" is a quantitative measure, in dollars of additional income that can be distributed to consumers, of the benefits of price adjustments accompanied by income transfers. If the price adjustments with transfers are not effectuated, these "money left over" benefits accrue to no one; they are the deadweight losses we considered in chapter 14.

A deadweight loss to an economist is like an unexploited energy source is to an engineer; in both cases lack of tools or the presence of constraints may thwart the realization of potential benefits. But the larger the potential benefits, the more justified is an effort to obtain more flexible or additional policy instruments to convert potential benefits into realized benefits. Of course, the obstacles may be so great that even herculean efforts are insufficient to bring about the conversion—a situation of great frustration to both the economist and the engineer.

Thus the policy maker must keep in perspective the difficulties discussed in the last two sections. Although these difficulties can be formidable, they do not negate the importance of the idea of economic efficiency nor do they prevent the computation of economically efficient prices, even when these prices are computed under the ideal assumptions that compensations can be arranged. These computations can be especially useful when the economist can accompany them with some idea of the deadweight losses associated with maintaining inefficient prices; in such a case, the policy maker has a quantitative measure, in terms of potential dollars of aggregate income, of the benefits forgone should the policy maker or society decide *not* to move from inefficient to efficient prices.

Deadweight losses, then, give a quantitative idea of the trade-off between achieving efficiency and achieving social or other noneconomic goals by maintaining prices at inefficient levels, although, as measured by "money left over," the deadweight loss is certainly not the only possible measure of this trade-off. As part II indicates, however, giving a precise meaning to terms like *equity, social justice,* and *fairness* is hard enough; relating them to notions of economic efficiency is harder still, especially when the policy maker must take account of how consumers *actually* view fairness, instead of how they *should* view it according to some normative moral theory.

It is useful to summarize what has been discussed thus far by means of an imaginary dialogue between a policy maker and his expert economic adviser.[2]

*Economist:*   I have just finished computing the economically efficient price levels. Here they are.

*Policy Maker:*   Thank you. I see where you have come up with some whopping price increases as well as decreases. Could you tell me again what is so great about these economically efficient prices you have computed?

*Economist:*   Well, if you were to change these prices a little bit, it wouldn't be possible for the gainers to pay off the losers and still have some money left over.

*Policy Maker:*   You mean to tell me that the prices that are being charged now don't have that property? Could I rearrange prices so that everybody could be better off than they are now?

*Economist:*   That's right. You could change the present prices so that everyone would in principle be better off.

*Policy Maker:*   But how am I going to arrange for those who get a price decrease to compensate those who suffer a price increase?

*Economist:*   I was hoping you could figure out some way to arrange that.

*Policy Maker:*   I know of no way to arrange that. In effect, what you're telling me is that I de facto already have a set of "economically or Pareto-efficient" prices, as you call them, since if I'm going to lower someone's price I have to raise someone else's. It seems to me that the prices that you've calculated are of no use to me at all.

*Economist:*   You're making a good point. You're saying that the only instruments available for you to work with are prices, and compensations from one group to another are not instruments you can juggle. In terms of instruments that you feel are available, you already have a set of economically efficient prices.

*Policy Maker:*   That's right. So what do I do now?

*Economist:*   You will have to make the final decision as to what action, if any, you want to take. I can only help you analyze the economic consequences of what you do. But first of all, let me remind you that if you could arrange the compensation, there would be the money left over after the gainers compensated the losers This left-over money could be spread among both those whose prices go up and those whose prices go down. By keeping prices where they are, you forgo any possibility of achieving this benefit. You are passively accepting a "deadweight loss."

*Policy Maker:*   That's bothersome. But I simply don't know of a way to arrange the compensations.

*Economist:*   There are some studies that might help you decide whether or not you want to change the present prices, even though you can't directly arrange for compensations. First of all, it may be that the same people subscribe to all the services. If that's the case, the compensations might take place automatically. In effect, consumers would take money out of one pocket and put it in the other. Second, recall the story I told you of the highly idealized economy with an electric utility serving only a competitive bakery industry and a residential market. In that situation, the proper compensation took place indirectly by means of the pass-through to residential consumers of the bakeries' lower costs. We could try to determine whether or not such indirect compensations would take place if you moved toward more efficient prices.

*Policy Maker:*   If you could convince me that we had your first case, so that the compensation would take place automatically at the level of the individual customer, I'd certainly want to consider changing prices toward more efficient values. But what I really have is more like your second example of the idealized competitive bakers and residential market, except what I am facing is far more complex. The industrial market that is being served isn't composed of a nice, simple competitive industry but rather of industries that span the spectrum from highly competitive to monopolistic. Likewise, the residential market is highly diversified in terms of the regulated goods and services consumed. So I think a study to trace through the effects of price changes would be difficult, and you may not be able to tell me with any certainty whether or not sufficient compensation takes place indirectly.

*Economist:*   You're right. It may be very difficult to gauge the amounts of indirect compensation. But even if I can't successfully do such a study, a sufficiently extreme deadweight loss may make you want to consider carefully whether or not inefficient prices should be maintained.

*Policy Maker:*   What do you mean?

*Economist:*   Let's take an example. In some cities water is priced at zero or near zero. At any rate, it isn't metered and the charging for water has little relationship to the cost of what is being used. As a result, in some cities there is no discipline on water usage, and a lot of water is wasted because faucets are left open to run at will, leaky plumbing fixtures are not fixed, and so on. Large, unnecessary reservoirs have been built, and millions of dollars are needlessly spent for providing water.[3] In such cases, the deadweight loss is not only the millions of dollars lost because of sheer waste but also probably millions of dollars of "left-over money" that would result if water were charged for and those who lost thereby were compensated.

*Policy Maker:*   Your water example may not be so difficult from the point of view of regulatory decision making. After all, everyone uses water, so taxpayers and water users are more or less the same. If I were a water regulator, I might argue that an increase in water prices would be more than offset by the decrease in taxes resulting from not having to build more reservoirs and other water facilities. Therefore, this would be one of those cases of "out one pocket and into another" that you mentioned earlier. That consideration would suggest instituting charges for water at economically efficient rates. On the other hand, come to think of it, if I were a water regulator, I might find myself thrown out of office if I tried to charge for something that people were used to getting "free." Isn't there anything you can advise to avoid having to raise someone's price?

*Economist:*   Well, so far we've talked only about price levels. I can also play around with price structure. By "unbundling"—working harder to charge separately for separate services and products—it may be possible to find situations where everyone's prices can be lowered without penalty to the utility.

*Policy Maker:*   Of course that would be useful. But after you've exploited all the benefits of varying the price structure, won't I probably face all the same dilemmas as before?

*Economist:*   I never said that your job was easy.

Several remarks about the above imaginary conversation are in order. First of all, to make my points I had the regulator face large proposed price changes. If only small price changes are required to reach economically efficient prices, the wrath of those whose prices are to be raised may not be very intense and may not cause a difficult problem for the regulator. Furthermore, the regulator might adopt the strategy of moving toward efficient prices in a series of small steps rather than in one large step. Hence, when the small-step option is available or when, as perhaps in the water example, the misallocation of resources is so extreme that even large price changes are obviously called for, the regulator's decision to move toward economically efficient prices may not be so difficult.

Second, I have couched the conversation in terms of an economist– public utility regulator dialogue. But the issues brought out are by no means peculiar to public utility regulation; they exist in a wide variety of contexts where policy makers have the job of directly or indirectly influencing prices. For example, suppose a national sales tax is to be imposed on some prices in a perfectly competitive economy to raise a certain sum of money for national defense. Ideally, before the necessity for the tax, all prices would be at marginal costs; the sales tax would then cause the prices to deviate from marginal cost. In fact, as was shown in chapter 13, with marginal costs as the initial prices, the analytical problem facing the policy maker's economic adviser is identical to the problem facing a public utility regulator who must set prices de novo. Moreover, the political problems would also be similar to those facing the regulator, and one can imagine an economist–policy maker dialogue similar to the one above.

In either case, the policy maker's economic adviser might be quite helpful in giving a sense, sometimes even a quantitative sense, of the trade-offs between maintaining inefficient prices and attaining noneconomic goals. Nevertheless, even with the knowledge that existing prices are inherently inefficient and contain large deadweight losses, the policy maker may still be left with difficult choices. Identifying the deadweight losses is only a starting point; policy makers usually confront much more fundamental problems than minimizing deadweight losses—they must confront stakeholders, sometimes very angry and upset ones.

## 15.2   Stakeholders

What Are Stakeholders?

By "stakeholders," I mean individuals or groups whose interests are vitally affected by some proposed legislation, regulation, or government action. Of course, a major policy change is apt to ripple through the entire economy, so that, to a degree, almost everyone in the economy can be considered to have a stake in seeing the change implemented or defeated. Increase the cost-of-living allowance to social security recipients and they will spend more at Christmas, which will increase the revenues of merchants, allowing them to hire more personnel. Those hired to fill the new jobs will probably have no inkling of their source and will not realize that they have a stake in higher cost-of-living allowances for senior citizens.

For the purposes of analysis, we shall, somewhat arbitrarily, divide those whose interests are affected by some proposed legislation, regulation, or government action into two categories—those with a vital, concentrated interest, and those with a relatively minimal interest. We call the former group "stakeholders". Typically, we associate the word "stakeholders" with a group whose interest is so large that it has organized an effort to carry or defeat the proposed action, whose effect usually represents a major change in the incomes of the group's members, either positive or negative. Examples are a regulatory commission's ruling that will change the rates that a public utility can charge, with a major impact on the utility's revenues, thus making the utility a stakeholder; legislation to limit the amount of damages resulting from a medical malpractice suit, with a major impact on the contingency fees collected by personal injury attorneys and on the malpractice insurance premiums paid by doctors, making personal injury attorneys and doctors stakeholders; and the awarding of a major defense contract to a firm in city X, with a major increase in employment in city X, and so forth, making the unemployed in city X stakeholders. In this usage, the term *stakeholders* does not include those who are minimally affected by a proposed government action.

Asymmetric Incidence of Governmental Action: Concentrated Benefits and Diffused Costs or the Reverse

Often, there is an asymmetry in the incidence of a governmental policy's benefits and its costs. Both benefits and costs may be concentrated, or one may be concentrated while the other is diffused, or both may be diffused.

For example, an increase of a few cents a month in one's phone bill may result in millions of dollars of increased monthly revenues to the phone company; the cap on medical malpractice awards may lower a typical physician's malpractice insurance premiums by thousands of dollars but may lower a typical patient's medical bill by only a few cents; and obtaining defense industry job may increase a worker's income dramatically but may increase the income tax of the typical taxpayer by only a few cents. In each of these examples, there are one or more stakeholders (in the sense indicated above), as well as individuals or groups only minimally affected (whom I do not consider to be stakeholders).

We expect that stakeholders, the affected voters with a concentrated interest, will have incentives to organize into groups. These groups will be active in efforts to lobby legislatures and regulators, to publicize their side of the story, organize letter-writing, faxing, and telephone campaigns to put pressure on legislatures and regulators, and to raise money to accomplish all of the above, while the nonstakeholders will remain inactive. As a result, we might expect the stakeholders to get their way. However, there are exceptions; if the stakeholder's benefits are too blatantly self-serving, or if entrepreneurial activists can arouse the public's attention to benefits the public is forgoing, stakeholder interests may be thwarted.

Wilson (1980, 367–372) gives a convenient scheme for classifying the effects of proposed governmental action, summarized in figure 15.3. If the stakeholders on both sides of an issue are reasonably well balanced, we can

## COSTS

|  | CONCENTRATED | DIFFUSED |
|---|---|---|
| **BENEFITS** CONCENTRATED | CONTROVERSY UNCERTAIN GOVT ACTION *Interest Group Politics* | GOVT ACTION *Client Politics* |
| DIFFUSED | GOVT ACTION *Entrepreneurial Politics* | UNCERTAIN GOVT ACTION *Majoritarian Politics* |

**Figure 15.3**
Wilson's scheme for classifying the effects of proposed governmental action

expect controversy, a lengthy public battle, with uncertainty as to which side will prevail or what sort of compromise will be reached. At the time of this writing, this seems to be the case regarding President Clinton's proposed health care plan. Wilson classifies this situation as "interest group politics," depicted as the NW cell of figure 15.3.

If benefits are concentrated while costs are diffuse, the concentrated interests are likely to become the clients of politicians who can help them, giving rise to what Wilson (1980) calls "client politics," represented by the NE cell of figure 15.3. Should there be no comparable stakeholders opposing them, the lobbying efforts of the concentrated interests (stakeholders) will likely meet with comparatively little resistance, and the outcome will likely be government action favorable to the concentrated beneficiaries. For years, agricultural interests have succeeded in getting legislation passed to subsidize the production of agricultural products, increasing benefits to farmers, while imposing diffuse costs on the general population.

If the effect of a proposed governmental action will heap large costs on a concentrated group of stakeholders, we can expect that the stakeholders will mobilize to defeat the proposal. However, as we see from the Peltzman (1976) model, defeat will occur only if there are insufficient positive votes in support. In recent years, we have seen numerous cases where, through their entrepreneurial skill, environmental and consumer activists have succeeded in organizing diffused beneficiaries into enough positive votes to overcome the stakeholders' negative votes, obtaining governmental action opposing the stakeholders' interests. Examples are the various antipollution and auto safety acts that have been passed in recent years over the objections of industry, at least in part due to activists' efforts. Wilson classifies this situation as "entrepreneurial politics," which occupies the SW cell of figure 15.3.

Finally, if both those who benefit and those who must bear costs are sufficiently diffuse, we again expect an uncertain outcome, either no governmental action or action determined by a relatively uncommitted majority vote in the Congress. For example, for years attempts to create a nationwide health care system got nowhere. No stakeholder groups or coalition of groups was able to move the issue out of the southeast corner, where the numerous bills introduced in every Congress that fail to gain sufficient support languish.[4] Wilson characterizes this corner as "majoritarian politics."

Hidden Stakeholders

The full roster of stakeholders may not be evident from media accounts of a controversy. In the United States, federal election laws ostensibly ensure that the names of stakeholders who contribute to political campaigns are made public; however, there are so many loopholes in these laws that there is once again a reform movement to change them.

For example, although the federal law limits the contributions from one individual or political action committee to $25,000 per campaign, with a further limit of $1,000 per candidate, there are no limits on how much can be contributed to a political party. Moreover, direct contributions to candidates for office are not the only way that money can influence political campaigns in favor of or in opposition to a candidate or a piece of legislation. Money can be given to pressure groups such as Common Cause, the Environmental Defense Fund, the American Association of Retired Persons (AARP), the National Rifle Association (NRA), and a host of other organizations with extensive mailing lists of persons that are apt to be sympathetic to a particular point of view. Groups like these can initiate awesome write-in campaigns; they can also spend unlimited amounts of money.

It may be politically expedient for stakeholders to be anonymous, especially if they are wealthy, a corporation, or if the public would perceive their attempts to influence legislation as too blatantly self-serving. Contributions to intermediary groups of this sort are an excellent way for stakeholders to hide their attempts to influence lawmakers from the electorate. So, for example, suppose your goal is to throw a particular congressman out of office. You can, without restriction, pour money into a group that opposes him and that will run a negative campaign of newspaper and TV ads attacking him.

Stakeholders within Stakeholder Groups

As an interest group grows in size, it evolves from an amorphous group of individuals bound by commitment to the achievement of a common end to an *organization* with a permanent headquarters, a paid staff, a monthly magazine or newsletter, an annual meeting with reports from the president and/or executive director and heads of the principal departments, and so on. Most important, the career achievements and financial well-being of the group's professional staff are coupled to the group's fortunes.

A cynical view is that the professional staff of an interest group has a self-interest in exaggerating the size of the grievances that the group seeks to redress, and in keeping the group in an agitated state. This increases the perceived value of the work that it does. A less cynical view is that the leaders are human beings, who are just as prone as the rest of us to deny the validity of any arguments that run counter to the group's position and to cite only evidence that reinforces its position. In a word, they do their advocacy work with the utmost sincerity.

Whatever the argument, the point is the same: the leadership of an interest group may have a self-interest that is not perfectly congruent with the self-interests of all members of the group. Thus we have a common phenomenon of stakeholders *within* a stakeholder group. On the other hand, it may not be easy to distinguish what the group really thinks from what its leadership believes and purports that it thinks. An example is the federal catastrophic medical insurance that the American Association of Retired Persons (AARP) advocated and vigorously lobbied for during the Reagan administration. The lobbying effort was successful, Congress passed a bill to implement the insurance, and President Reagan signed it. However, only after the bill's passage did senior citizens realize the financial burden the bill would put on them. A senior citizens' grassroots outcry erupted, demanding the bill's repeal; Congress hurriedly did just that, even before the bill could be implemented.

## 15.3   Perceptions Are Realities: The Role of the Media

I once attended a workshop conducted by experienced ex-journalists who had gone into the business of training business executives on how to deal with the media. The workshop began with each attendee's being subjected to a mock interview on his or her area of expertise. The interview was televised and critiqued, after which there was a second televised interview. The first round of interviews was uniformly disastrous. Even though the interviewers (the ex-journalists) had had only a limited time to familiarize themselves with our areas of expertise, we were putty in the their hands. They had no trouble embarrassing us with tough questions that we fielded badly, generally making each of us look like total incompetents who were trying to evade their search for the simple truth. After the critiques of the first round and some lecturing by the instructors, however, we all greatly improved in the second round of interviews. Why the difference? What secret did the instructors impart?

The instructors' message was in fact simple, and hardly a secret formula when we thought about it. Reporters are interested in getting *news*; they usually have little interest in what you think or feel about anything. If they can create some news at your expense, fine; in fact, without any detailed knowledge about you that might be turned into news, they may very well seize on trying to get you to admit something embarrassing. But as it is for almost everyone, the reporter's time is important.

These almost self-evident facts suggest a strategy for the interviewee: don't consent to be interviewed unless you have a newsworthy story to give the reporter. Then, no matter what the reporter asks, hammer away at your story. Brush aside all attempts to get the *reporter's* story out of you and carry on like a broken record about *your* story. Eventually, time will run out and the reporter will accept your story. In a word, the strategy is that *you* and *not* the reporter should control the interview. The strategy worked, at least in the workshop; the videos of our second-round interviews showed a dramatic improvement.

If the instruction in the workshop is valid, it suggests that political news is naturally filtered through the lens of those making it. Furthermore, only those who are good at making news are liable to make it—a second filter. For example, I had long wondered why only a small subset of the 535 members of Congress seemed to always appear on the nationally televised interview programs. After the workshop it occurred to me that, of the 535, a small subset had either attended a workshop like mine or through experience had learned the workshop's techniques and had become good at them. And they are the ones you can expect to see on television.

But the biases in news reporting aren't confined to politics. In fact, a small industry of scholars studies them. Perhaps most striking are the biases in reporting events involving risk of death, disease, or injury—accidents, natural disasters, exposure to hazardous materials like asbestos, exposure to esoteric diseases, and so forth. These are particularly susceptible to biased reporting because accurate reporting requires a knowledge of complex technologies and of statistics, a background few reporters have.

The large literature on the media's reporting of risk reveals the following:[5]

• Reporters tend to stress "newsworthy" events.

• Reporters tend to classify as "newsworthy" risks that are newly discovered, that are increasing from their customary level, or that have novel, dramatic, or devastating consequences.

• Truly substantial risks that are not considered newsworthy, such as risks of being overweight or ingesting too much fat, can go largely unattended by the media.

• Reporters are good at reporting specific, concrete events but not at putting them in a larger perspective. In particular, reporters pay little attention to the benefits of a risk-prevention policy in relation to its costs. Few reporters have the technical background required to give a larger perspective.

• Many stories involving some aspect of risk contain inaccurate statements, even in the most prestigious media sources.

Thus, for example, the injection of cyanide into Tylenol capsules in the 1980s brought the nationwide sale of Tylenol to a halt, even though, nationwide, the risk of buying cyanide-laden Tylenol was minuscule; thousands of tourists canceled European vacations after a single, highly publicized terrorist attack in Europe; consumers estimate the risk of lung cancer from smoking as 42 out of 100, which exceeds the actual risk by four to eight times; and individuals tend to underestimate the chance of dying from heart disease and stroke and to greatly overestimate the chance of being killed by lightning.

What comes out of the numerous academic studies is that, by and large, the media do a poor job in reporting risk, leaving the public with a highly distorted image of levels of risk, with some greatly exaggerated and others greatly minimized. Indeed, the public has little concept of the quantitative trade-offs between the benefits and costs of alternative social policies regarding risk. We return to the distorting effects of media reporting in chapter 22 in our discussion of health, safety, and environmental regulation.

## 15.4  The Stakeholders-Fairness-Efficiency Framework

The remaining chapters in this section consider applications and case studies that illustrate the concepts laid out in the first three parts of the book. All of the examples are couched in the "stakeholders-fairness-efficiency" organizational framework. Before proceeding, I wish to raise some caveats.

First of all, by listing, stakeholders, fairness, and efficiency in that order, I do not mean to imply a causal relationship. That is, the reader should not assume that once stakeholder or interest groups form that fairness arguments are trotted out as night follows day, and from them inexorably follow certain efficiency consequences. Clearly, there will be interaction among these elements and much to-ing and fro-ing. This is illustrated for example by the evolution of the federal income tax, discussed in the next chapter. Tried very successfully during the Civil War, the income tax was championed on the grounds of fairness by the populists at the end of the century but opposed by the northeastern states until economic forces caused them to abandon their opposition and to embrace it at the beginning of this century; it has provided a continual battleground of fairness arguments and coalitions of interest groups ever since.

Likewise, the history of the progressive income tax illustrates another important point: arguments in a political debate cannot always be easily classified as either fairness *or* efficiency arguments. For example, it is often argued that private individuals can more efficiently and effectively make resources flow to their highest valued uses than the government can, and therefore the fewer taxes, the better. This can be considered to be either an efficiency argument (private ownership leads to more Pareto improvements) or a fairness argument (Pareto improvements mean we are all better off or at least no worse off, and this is fair).

Finally, I do not wish to claim too much for the stakeholder-fairness-efficiency paradigm; it is merely a convenient starting point for analysis. Also, it is easier to compare two analyses when they are couched in the same framework. Furthermore, as the following brief case studies all show, after one has sorted out the main stakeholders and the main fairness and efficiency arguments, there is typically still much to be analyzed, and one may find that there are other, more fruitful methods for the next stages of analysis.

**Exercises**

1. The text argues that, because regulators do not have control over the entire economy, they are unable to set economically efficient prices. Summarize this argument.

2. Contrast and compare *de novo* taxation or pricing with taxation or pricing *reform*.

3. Discuss the statement "Because regulators rarely have the power to remove deadweight losses, the calculation of the magnitudes of deadweight losses is pointless."

4. Discuss the main points brought out by the imaginary dialogue between a policy maker and an expert economist adviser.

5. Discuss the following: asymmetric stakeholders, hidden stakeholders, and stakeholders within stakeholder groups.

6. Summarize the results of research regarding the accuracy and validity of the reporting of risk by the news medial.

# 16                              Progressive Taxation

J. K. Lasser's, *Your Income Tax*, 1984 (for 1983 taxes), Simon and Schuster, New York, $6.95, 326 pages.

J. K. Lasser's, *Your Income Tax*, 1994 (for 1993 taxes), Prentice-Hall, New York, $14.00, 511 pages.

## 16.1  Reasons to Study Progressive Taxation

Progressive taxation is the quintessential example of the stakeholder-fairness-efficiency paradigm in action; its history shows fierce battles between stakeholders, battles that were fought in the public arena mainly over "fairness," with economic efficiency as a sideshow. Further, the efficiency consequences of the various positions advocated have only been dimly perceived, partly because they are not easy to determine. Even today, many aspects of the economic efficiency consequences of taxation policy are not easy to analyze. Finally, because of lack of a consensus fairness framework, progressive taxation has been a prime example of the electorate searching endlessly for the Holy Grail of perfect fairness; the search has made progressive taxation a political battleground where a talent for fairness strategizing can pay rich rewards.

## 16.2  History

Seligman's 1908 book gives a comprehensive review of the early history of progressive taxation, starting with its roots in antiquity—Seligman's account begins with progressive taxation in Athens in 596 B.C.

   In the United States the first instance of progressive taxation is a proposal put forth in 1798, whose final form was due to Albert Gallatin (Seligman 1908, 29). The tax was on housing; houses were divided into nine classes, the lowest class with market values from $100 to $500 and the highest with values in excess of $30,000. The tax ranged from 0.2 percent to 1 percent of market value. No other form of progressive tax at the federal level was known until the Civil War, when both the Union and the Confederacy adopted a progressive income tax. In both cases, low incomes were exempt—below $600 in the Union and below $500 in the Confederacy. The maximum rates on incomes over $10,000 were 10 percent in the Union and 15 percent in the Confederacy. Individual states preceded the federal government by some twenty years, with Virginia adopting a graduated income tax in 1843.

The big firestorm over the income tax didn't erupt until the second Cleveland administration. Even though it had been lifted in 1872, the Civil War income tax was challenged as unconstitional, a challenge that only came to the Supreme Court in 1880 and that was unsuccessful.[1] In 1894 President Cleveland proposed and Congress enacted an income tax of 2 percent, with an exemption of $4,000. Because of the exemption, this was a progressive tax; the average tax rate continually increased with income, approaching 2 percent as incomes became very large.

The 1894 income tax was promptly challenged in the courts on broad constitutional grounds, including the argument that progressivity was discriminatory, as brought out in Justice Field's concurring opinion (*Pollock v. Farmers' Loan & Trust*, 1895, 596): "It [a progressive income tax] is the same in essential character as that of the English income tax statute of 1691, which taxed Protestants at a certain rate, Catholics, as a class, at double the rate of Protestants, and Jews at another and separate rate."

However, the Court's 5-4 decision to strike down the law was based on a narrow ground. Article I, Section 9, Paragraph 4 of the U.S. Constitution reads:

No capitation, or other direct, tax shall be laid, unless in proportion to the census or enumeration herein before directed to be taken.

The Court interpreted this to mean that an income tax must be apportioned proportionately to the census—for example, a state with 1 percent of the population must pay 1 percent of the tax. Because the 1894 legislation did not guarantee this outcome, the Court declared it to be unconstitutional.

The Supreme Court's 1894 decision was not made in a vacuum. The economic historians Benjamin Baack and Edward Ray (1993) point out that in 1894 the memory of the Civil War income tax was still fresh in Massachusetts, New York, and Pennsylvania. These states had provided 60 percent of the Civil War income tax revenues and were opposed to reinstating it.

But events reversed the Northeast's opposition. Between 1894 and 1908 military spending increased dramatically. The United States became a major exporter of manufactured goods and it was necessary to ensure safe shipping lanes to keep overseas markets open. The result was an increasing flow of federal revenues into the northeastern states in support of naval contracts and army arsenals, as well as veterans' pensions payments (Baack and Ray 1993, 105–107). By 1909 the coalition of interests in favor of an income tax was so broad that, by almost a unanimous vote, the Congress passed an amendment to the Constitution (the Sixteenth) to make an income tax legal.

The Sixteenth Amendment was ratified in 1913, but it did not address the constitutionality of progressivity, which was quickly challenged. The Court brushed aside the challenge in *Brushaber v. Union Pacific* (1916), and the power of the federal government to levy progressively higher taxes on income was firmly established.

### 16.3   Stakeholders

The principal stakeholder during the Civil War in both the North and South was the central government. Both the Union and the Confederacy were desperate for funds to finance the war, and a progressive income tax was a quick and politically expedient way to raise them.

By the end of the last century the Civil War income tax had been allowed to expire, but the Populist movement began the agitation to reinstate it. According to J. D. Hicks in his classic, *The Populist Revolt* (chapter 3, 1962), the movement was the result of a number of factors. The years 1887–1897 were years of severe drought in the West, an area that had been recently settled by farmers who had been lured there by railroads offering easy credit. In turn, the railroad "robber barons" had engaged in a number of shady practices in the transportation of farm products, all at the perceived expense of the farmers (the farmers were the prevailing element in the then predominantly rural economy).

On top of all of this, the federal government's "hard money" stance—strict adherence to the gold standard—had led to continual deflation. In the thirty years following the Civil War the purchasing power of the dollar increased threefold. The net effect of high interest rates and high deflation was interest rates of the order of 25 percent on farmers' loans (Hicks 1961, 90; however, see DiLorenzo 1990 for a contrary view). All of this led to the small farmers' belief that the railroads together with eastern wealth were the cause of the severe depression that had hit them in the 1890s.

The principal stakeholders were, of course, the small farmers who felt that the income tax would help redress their grievances against the eastern rich. However, the leaders of the Populist movement had their reputations and political careers at stake, a stake that was transferred to the leadership of the Democratic Party, for the Populist Party became a significant third party. In the 1892 elections it polled over 1,000,000 popular votes and 22 electoral votes; in fusion with the Democrats, it elected three governors (Hicks 1961, 267). This left the Democratic Party with the choice of opposing it, trying to join forces with it, or usurping part or all of its platform. The Democratic Party leadership chose to do some of the last, including the adoption of a progressive income tax, and the Populist movement ceased to be a force after the 1896 elections. But the result was that President Cleveland and the Democratic Party leaders became significant stakeholders in the fight to institute a progressive income tax.

As already mentioned in the previous section and recounted by Baack and Ray (1993), the story gets more complicated as we move beyond the Populists' heyday. Toward the end of the last century, the reduced imports of manufactured goods and increased imports of less-tariffed raw materials led to a decline the share of federal revenues from tariffs; federal revenues from the sale of federal lands peaked in 1888 and thereafter also declined. At the same time, federal military spending began to rise as the United States increased naval expenditures to ensure safe shipping lanes. The result was a greater need for federal revenues; a new class of stakeholders in favor of the income tax emerged.

Since the inception of the federal income tax, we have seen a similar lineup of stakeholders. The insatiable appetite for federal revenues has always provided stakeholders in favor of increasing the amount of income tax revenues. And, of course, high-income individuals have always provided stakeholder opposed to the progressive income tax or to the extent of its progressivity. But the battle of whether or not there should be an income tax has been won by its adherents; the battle now is over how progressive it ought to be.

## 16.4  Fairness

Seligman (1908) also reviews the intellectual history of the arguments in favor of a progressive income tax. They are almost all fairness arguments, in particular, arguments for application of the Formal Principle, with various subarguments being adduced in support of the principle of progressivity. The same is true for the arguments against the progressive income tax, as we have just seen in the quote from Justice Field's concurring opinion. Some of the main fairness arguments Seligman cites for progressive taxation are

• Benefit theory (also known as the "give and take" or "quid pro quo" theory). Protection is the chief function of the state, and taxes can be looked upon as the premiums one pays to a collective insurance agency that guarantees peace and order. But the greater one's property or income, the greater the benefits received. However, the benefits are proportional to "clear income", income less expenses. Hence the tax must be graduated with respect to total income in order to correspond to clear income. A variant to this theory is that one should pay according to the cost of the service that the state renders, and this cost increases with clear income.

• Equal sacrifice theory. A tax is a sacrifice and we should all sacrifice equally. However, a $1 tax for someone making $10,000/year of income is not the same sacrifice as a $1 tax for someone making $1 million/year. To equalize the sacrifice, the wealthy should pay a higher fraction of their income in taxes.

• Faculty theory. Individuals in society should contribute to society in proportion to their faculties or abilities. Income is a good surrogate for faculty or ability.

• Tax ill-gotten gains. The rich get rich primarily by exploiting imperfections in the government—bribes, hiring expensive lawyers to bypass taxes, getting inside information, and so forth. They should pay more in taxes to offset this ill-gotten advantage.

Fairness objections to these theories are typically also based on an interpretation of the Formal Principle. Some examples are

• All of the affirmative arguments rest on empirical assumptions based on flimsy anecdotal evidence. When the empirical support for the application of Formal Principle fails, then so does the validity of applying the Formal Principle. For example, how does anyone know whether the benefits of the government's protective services are the exactly the same for all persons whose income, gross or "clear," is exactly the same?

• If the Formal Principle is to be applied, it should be strictly applied. That is, if unequals are to be treated unequally, the treatment should be *strictly* proportional to relevant similarities or differences. Departures from strict proportionality are unjust.

• The espousal of progressive taxation is a high-sounding justification for the less rich to gang up on the more rich. It is blatant *majoritarianism*—the exploitation of a minority by the majority—and thus blatant utilitarianism. As such, it suffers from all of utilitarianism's ethical shortcomings, particularly its disregard for individual rights.

In addition to Seligman (1908), Blum and Kalven (1953) and Galvin and Bittker (1969) consider most of these pro and con arguments, as well as others.

Because all of the above fairness arguments, pro or con, involve interpersonal comparisons of utility, they have no validity and are beside the point to the economist who embraces the notion that interpersonal comparisons of utility are meaningless. Endless argumentation in favor of one or the other and the adducing of evidence in support of one against another are exercises in futility. All that matters is whether a given taxation scheme is efficient, or which among two schemes has the lesser deadweight loss.

Economists' theories of interpersonal comparisons of utility are arcane and beside the point to the electorate; the 1992 Presidential election was rich in strategic fairness moves and countermoves. During the campaign, both major parties employed pollsters and continuously convened focus groups, largely for the purpose of seeing which fairness themes were effective and which were not. The campaign centered on two fairness refrains— the Democrats kept chanting that the rich must be made to pay their "fair share" of taxes, while the Republicans drummed away at the Democrats' "tax and spend" policies that unfairly wasted taxpayers' money.

At the time of this writing, my impression is that, thus far, the battle has resulted in a draw. The Democrats prevailed in the election, but the "tax and spend" refrain was effective in almost defeating President Clinton's 1993 budget bill. At a minimum, it forced him to compromise extensively with members of his own party in order to get votes, compromises that may come back to haunt him. Time will tell whether he and his party will be able to recover and mount an effective presidency.

## 16.5   Efficiency

As already mentioned in chapter 13, theoreticians within the public finance subdiscipline of economics have built models of various degrees of complexity in attempts to deal with all aspects of efficient taxation. I summarize some of the main findings of this literature as it relates generally to the income tax and specifically to the progressive income tax.

At the outset, there is the question of how to define *income*. According to a traditional definition, due to Haig and Simons income in a given year is one's increase in power to consume, made up generally of what one actually consumes plus net increases in wealth. The Haig-Simons definition differs in several important respects from what is ordinarily thought of as income, and, for that matter, what the Internal Revenue Service considers to be income. Some examples of what are considered as income under the Haig-Simons definition are the following:

• indirect payments to an employee that the employee does not see, such as the employer's contribution to the employee's benefit plan to cover health care, disability insurance, and pension

• transfer payments from the government, such as unemployment insurance, social security benefits, food stamps, and aid to dependent children

• capital gains minus capital losses from the sale of assets

• for home owners, *imputed rent*, that is, the rent that the owner saves by virtue of owning his or her home[2]

Then there is the question of the total effect of a tax on an individual, called the tax's "incidence." The computation of tax incidence is not trivial, as we see immediately from the Haig-Simons definition of income. I may pay a hefty income tax, but derive an even larger "income" from the transfer payments and services I obtain from the government.

But more to the point, an accurate calculation of tax incidence requires that one trace through the complete effect of a tax change as it ripples through the entire economy. So, if the government increases the tax on cigarettes, the consumption of cigarettes will decrease, which will decrease the revenues of cigarette companies, which may cause them to reduce their workforces, which means their workforces have less money to spend, and so forth. Included in a calculation of tax incidence must be the benefits from government intervention that each individual receives. Such an analysis requires a complete general equilibrium model of the entire economy and a comparison of the economy's equilibrium state before and after the imposition of the tax.

At a broad, general equilibrium level, the goal is to design a tax that impedes as little as possible the economy's attainment of Pareto improvements. As it is often put, resources should flow to their highest-valued uses; taxes should distort the flow as little as possible. Because a tax represents a transfer of resources from the private to the public sector, a more general issue is whether private or public ownership of resources will have the

smaller distortionary effect. Put another way, both private and public institutions are imperfect and, in one way or another, can generate waste and
inefficiencies. The basic issue is which institutions can most efficiently direct
the flow of resources.

The very simple, partial equilibrium model of chapter 13 indicates that a
lump-sum or head tax is nondistortionary. The intuition is simple: marginal
conditions determine efficient outcomes, and a lump-sum tax does not
affect margins. However, as also mentioned in chapter 13, a lump-sum tax
that is the same for every individual in society, whether the richest or the
poorest, would be considered outrageously unfair. On the other hand, if
the amount of the lump-sum tax depends on income, it becomes an income
tax and is no longer nondistortionary.

How, then, how can we design an economically efficient income tax, one
whose marginal rate varies with income? Start by observing that we can
consider *leisure* as a commodity, like any other. For example, suppose you
work 2,000 hours/year at a wage of $10/hour to earn an income of
$20,000, but you have the freedom to work only 1,999 hours/year to earn
an income of $19,990. Reducing your total hours of work is equivalent to
earning the full $20,000 but using $10 of it to "buy" an hour of leisure, thus
leaving $19,990 to spend on everything else.

We can thus imagine extending the Ramsey taxation model to incorporate leisure and income. However, there are complications. For one, the
greater the consumption of leisure, the less the amount of labor available to
produce goods and services for the economy. So the consumption and
production sides of the analysis interact, an interaction that is not included
in the simple Ramsey taxation model of chapter 13. In addition, the progressive income tax levies a different tax rate at different increments of
income—it has varying *marginal rates* of taxation, something that also
requires modification of chapter 13's basic Ramsey model.

Incorporating these effects to extend the Ramsey model takes us beyond
the scope of this book. Note, however, that the results from the theoretical
literature on "optimal," that is, economically efficient, income taxation
sometimes jar with notions of "fair" progressive income taxation that we
have come to accept. An easy-to-understand jarring result is the following:
an economically efficient progressive income tax will have a *top* marginal
rate of *zero*.

To see this, imagine that all all U.S. taxpayers are rank-ordered according to income, and that the person with the highest income is Ms. Moneybags, whose income is $100 million/year. Suppose Congress decrees, and
the President agrees, that the marginal rate on incomes above $100 million

will henceforth be zero. Ms. Moneybags may very well decide that, because she can now keep everything additional that she earns, she will work harder and earn an extra $1,000/year, increasing her income to $100,001,000/year. She will be better off, the government will continue to collect the same tax revenue as before, the output of the economy will increase because of her increased exertions, and no one else will be worse off. Thus, the switch to a top marginal rate of zero is a Pareto improvement. Not so obvious is another theoretical result: an economically efficient progressive income tax will also have a *bottom* marginal rate of *zero*. Thus, if the progressive income tax schedule were designed to achieve economic efficiency, both the richest and poorest persons would be in the zero marginal tax bracket.[3] Furthermore, over a range of incomes, the economically efficient income tax would be progressive, but over a range extending to the very top income, it would be *regressive*; the marginal rates would *decrease* as income increases.

This jarring result only became known in the 1970s (see, for example, Seade 1977). We should be careful not to make too much of it. For one thing, there may be a large gap between those at the very top of the income scale and the rest of us. For another, the result pertains to *marginal* rather than to average rates. An economically efficient tax schedule may still call for high average taxes levied on the rich even though their marginal rate is low. Nevertheless, the result dramatically shows the gap between what we have been taught to be "fair" and what, at least in theory, is economically efficient.

This, then, is a bare-bones introduction to the subject of economically efficient income taxation. The reader who is interested in more detail can find it in a public finance textbook, such as Rosen (1992), or in Young (1994, chap. 7).

## 16.6   Discussion

Since the simple 1894 progressive income tax of 2 percent on all incomes in excess of $4,000, we have seen the federal income tax system grow into something of almost incomprehensible complexity. We now have an industry of accountants and tax lawyers who devote their time and brainpower to devising ways to avoid taxes.

In 1986 Congress decided that the complexity had gotten out of hand and that simplification was the order of the day. The announced goal was to reform the income tax laws to eliminate loopholes and to reduce the immense amount of personal time and money spent on preparing one's yearly income tax return. As part of this simplification, fourteen marginal brackets were collapsed into two of 15 percent and 28 percent. In spite of this simplification and the drive to eliminate loopholes, Congress passed the 1986 tax reform law only after extensive debate.[4] When the regulation writers in the Internal Revenue Service finished, the result was hardly simple, as evidenced by the continual growth in the size of *J. K. Lasser's, Your Income Tax*. In the Commerce Clearing House's publications for professional tax accountants and lawyers, the Income Tax Code comprises an eight-volume set—two volumes covering the law and six volumes covering the regulations (as compared to the 1960s' version which contained one volume for each). At the time of this writing, early in the Clinton administration, the 1993 revision of the income tax law seems to have traded off higher tax brackets for special treatments, such as a cap of 28 percent on capital gains. Thus the law seems to be retreating to the pre-1986 atmosphere of ever-increasing complexity, which augurs for still another increase in the number of volumes in the Commerce Clearing House set and still more pages in self-help guides such as *Your Income Tax*.

Much of this complexity results from the quest for "fairness." Any change in the income tax law at the federal level is almost sure to affect the income of a large number of persons. If the effect is adverse, constituents can at a minimum claim status quo property rights and will probably get a sympathetic hearing from their congressman, who, if sufficiently adept, may arrange a special exemption to redress the grievance of the constituents. But, to get the exemption, the congressman will undoubtedly have to bargain with colleagues, who seek their own exemptions for *their* constituents. And so it goes.

Furthermore, the rare-event scale effect works to complicate the tax law. A nightmare for the federal government is to have loopholes in the law that, when discovered by the media, will embarrass it. A case in point is the discovery in 1969 that 154 persons with incomes of over $200,000 (about $700,000 in today's dollars) had exploited loopholes to the point that they paid no income tax at all in 1966 (Pechman 1987). This means that congressional framers of new tax laws and the Internal Revenue Service (IRS) civil servants who write regulations to implement them must go to extra lengths to foresee and forestall rare situations that will escape taxation. For when these are discovered, and with over 100 million income taxpayers, they are almost certain to be discovered, they will not remain rare and will embarrass the IRS, Congress, or both.

The result is an enormous waste of resources, considering the time taxpayers spend filling out forms, the money they pay to accountants and tax lawyers, and the wages IRS employees receive. In 1982 these resources were estimated at $35 billion or about 9 percent of total federal and state income tax revenue (Rosen 1992, 351). Meanwhile, for the 1992 fiscal year, receipts from the social-security/medicare payroll tax of 15.3 percent were 77.5 percent of individual income tax receipts.[5] This suggests that a uniform personal income tax rate of 15.3/0.775 or 19.7 percent would collect about the same amount of revenues as the present income tax system.

All of this indicates that a Pareto improvement is possible, both because of the deadweight losses in the present system of progressively higher marginal tax brackets and because of the system's waste. Short of a complete, perfect reform, we can conceive of the following possible Pareto improvement: (1) replace the present system with a flat tax wherein everyone's *gross* income is taxed at a uniform rate of roughly 19 percent, without any deductions; (2) put to productive uses the enormous resources that are now wasted, but that would be freed up by a switch to a simple tax system; and (3) use the fruits of this improvement to pay off the losers in the switch to a uniform rate and to increase the wealth of the poorest stratum of society.

Unfortunately, there is little prospect of such a Pareto improvement happening. The present law-cum-regulations have built into them many status quo property rights. As they have in previous reform attempts, the owners of these rights would exert political pressure to maintain them. Moreover, the income tax is fertile ground for client politics (see chapter 15) as described by Herber (1988), wherein congressmen increase their chances of reelection by furthering the interests of those whom they can benefit. Most importantly, the progressive income tax doctrine seems to be deeply ingrained in the norms of American society, and for that matter, in the norms of public finance economists. In spite of its many infirmities, the fairness and justness of the doctrine in essentially its present form go unquestioned. We can expect it to continue to be a political battlefield, with victory going to the most skilled fairness strategists.

**Exercises**

1. Summarize the main fairness arguments in favor of and against the progressive income tax.

2. How does the Haig-Simons definition of income differ from that used by the Internal Revenue Service?

3. What is meant by the *incidence* of a tax? Why are most taxation models unable to calculate the total incidence of a tax?

4. Summarize the example that illustrates the theorem that in an economically efficient income tax system, the top marginal tax rate will be zero.

5. Discuss the effects of "fairness" considerations on the complexity of the present income tax law.

# 17

## Unfair Pricing I: Cross-Subsidization

MR. MEANS (Attorney for Independent Voters of Illinois): *I would inform the Hearing Officer . . . that we are moving the Commission for an order requiring cost of service study for each and every rate which the Illinois Bell Telephone Company seeks an increase in this pending matter because we feel . . . that in many respects the rate structure proposed will have the effect of causing residential telephone users to subsidize the costs of the service rendered to non-residential telephone users. . . .*

MR. STREET (Attorney for the U.S. General Services Administration): *I would like to request the we be provided with copies of those answers . . . because I strongly suspect that it will establish that the business users are in fact subsidizing the residential users. . . .*

EXAMINER TARREL: Gentlemen, would you like to take a 10-minute break?

— Illinois Commerce Commission (from transcript of docket 56831, 1971–1972)

## 17.1 Cross-Subsidization as an Issue

I have been hearing about cross-subsidization since the first regulatory conference I ever attended in 1966, where speakers lamented that there were no data on "true costs," for, if such data existed, they would clearly show that their customer group was cross-subsidizing the telephone company's other customers. Through the years, the lament has not changed.

The breakup of AT&T has made the lament more vocal and more serious; all of the telephone companies, local and long-distance, are major players in both regulated and unregulated businesses. The danger is that they will use their profits from the regulated businesses to cross-subsidize their activities in the unregulated businesses, thereby pricing their unregulated businesses below cost to gain an unfair advantage over rivals.

The issue of cross-subsidization is widespread and serious; it is a major issue in health care regulation. Unfortunately, it is also not simple. Even coming up with a definition of cross-subsidization that accords with common usage but that has the precision needed to form a coherent theory isn't easy, as the rest of this chapter demonstrates.

## 17.2  Background

The perennial lament about "true cost" reflects one of the difficulties. Chapter 3 pointed out that "costs" come in many flavors—the term *cost* embodies both "what you paid for it or are going to pay for it" and choice. In the economists' ideal world, the debate about cross-subsidization would be in terms of future or *planning* costs, not historic costs, and would reflect optimum choices as planners looked to the future. In a word, they would be forward-looking *opportunity* costs.

Unfortunately, such costs are rarely available. In times of rapidly changing technology, they may be difficult to compute; regulators typically don't have the resources to compute them and must rely on the resources of their regulatees. But, if regulators rely too much on the regulatees, there is the possibility of regulatees fudging the numbers and being less than forthcoming about the facts. Also, because no one can foretell the future, if regulators tried to implement the economists' ideal of forward-looking opportunity costs, there would be divergent opinions as to their magnitudes.

If this weren't bad enough, there are the difficulties of "fairly" apportioning overhead or joint and common costs among several services or product lines, a thorny issue both to economists and accountants. Fortunately, there is now an extensive theory that copes with these questions. The initial, substantial development of the theory was largely the work of Bell Laboratories economists in the 1970s. This development has been elaborated on by economists worldwide to produce a large literature. Although the resulting cross-subsidization theory is general, for concreteness I will use the regulation of utilities to illustrate the analysis of cross-subsidization within a stakeholders-fairness-efficiency framework. The reader will recall from the discussion of Ramsey prices in chapter 13 that, under rate-of-return regulation, a utility is constrained to make a zero economic profit,[1] and the discussion of cross-subsidization that follows will assume that this constraint is in effect. However, as the discussion will make clear, this assumption does not reduce the generality of the theory that is developed.

## 17.3  Stakeholders

The stakeholders in a typical cross-subsidization controversy in rate-of-return regulation are first of all the various customer groups that a utility serves, or the groups' representatives. For example, it is common for retired persons to appear at "rate cases" (petitions by a regulated utility to have its rates increased), either individually or in organized groups. The plea is that retired persons on fixed incomes cannot afford higher telephone, electric, gas, or water bills, and that the rates should be kept low. On the other hand, where a regulated utility has competition—an example is AT&T competing against MCI and Sprint—there are the competitors' pleas that rates be kept sufficiently high. Then there are the stakeholders that have an interest that the regulated firm be financially viable; foremost among these are the firm's shareholders, but its employees and the unions that represent them may also have an intense interest in financial viability.

Perhaps the stakeholders with the most intense interest are the politicians. In about a third of the states, regulators of public utilities are elected to office; in the remaining states and at the federal level, they are appointed. But in either case, theirs is a very visible position, with opportunities for feature coverage in the media. Regulators must therefore contend with how the media shapes the image that they present to the public, in particular, they must be prepared to deal with the age-old charge that one group of rate payers is subsidizing, or being subsidized, by another.

## 17.4  Fairness

In public utility regulation the fairness arguments have centered on the allocation of joint and common costs. For example, how should the costs of such things as heat, electricity, water, and the salary of the company president be apportioned among the various products that are manufactured in the same factory or to services that jointly use the same equipment? Noneconomists typically base their theory of "fair" cost allocation on some variant of the Formal Principle. Proration "in proportion to relevant similarities and differences" seems to be the most natural thing in the world, and one finds a tendency to prorate common and joint costs, especially if some prorating parameter is handy, like time, area, or dollars. So, the president's salary might be apportioned among the various products in proportion to the time that he or she spends on administration of them, the heating and electricity bills in proportion to the area of the factory occupied by each product line, and so on.

In the old Bell System, Western Electric, the manufacturing arm of AT&T, had elaborate prorating procedures of this sort for apportioning costs. Likewise, for purposes of regulation, it was common to prorate costs of equipment being jointly used by several services in proportion to the minutes used by each service. This is known as the "method of fully distributed costs".

Economists resisted such proration on the grounds that it had no economic basis, but not until the late 1960s did they offer a theory to replace simple proration, one that satisfied a variant of the Formal Principle and seemed to make some economic sense. To my knowledge, a pamphlet authored by AT&T's Council of Economic Advisers, Professors W. J. Baumol, O. Eckstein, and A. E. Kahn (1970), was the first such attempt; they called their test for cross-subsidization, the "burden test."[2]

It went like this. Imagine that one of the several services that the firm offers is discontinued. As a result, the firm will (a) eliminate some costs, and (b) lose some revenue. If the revenue reduction exceeds the cost reduction, that service is deemed not to have been a burden on the remaining services. Why? Because with the discontinuation of the service, the remaining services will have to generate more revenue in order to cover all their costs. Thus the imagined discontinued service cannot be a burden on the remaining services and, according to the burden test, is not being cross-subsidized by them.

Although I have described the burden test for a single service, it can just as well be applied to a group of services. But which group? If one wants a completely *burden-free* set of rates, one would have to check that every service and every possible group of services is not a burden on the remaining services. But if there are n services, the number of possible groups is $2^n - 1$. For example, if the firm offers 10 different services, there are 1,023 possible groups, and if it offers 20 different services, there are more than a million. Checking all of them to determine which, if any, are burdens is a formidable task.

The burden test is variant of the Formal Principle. Each service is treated equally in that each must not be a burden (in the Baumol-Eckstein-Kahn sense) on the remaining services. Is that the only possible sense of "equal services?" No, another obvious sense is that no service should have to pay revenues more than it would pay on a stand-alone basis. This thought gives rise to the *stand-alone cost test*. To my knowledge, this was first mentioned by Kahn (1970, 2:222), but first formalized by Faulhaber (1975).

One imagines each service and each group of services departing and going into business as a separate firm. One then asks, As a separate firm, that is, on a stand-alone basis, will each service or group have to generate higher or lower revenues in order to cover costs? According to Faulhaber (1975), if in each case the answer is higher, then in the original firm, no service or group of services are being subsidized; if in some cases the answer is lower, then some service or group of services in the original firm are being subsidized.

The stand-alone view directly corresponds to what in game theory is called "a cooperative game". In game theory jargon, each service is a player, a group of players is called a "coalition" and the group of all players a "grand coalition". If all players are better off by remaining members of the grand coalition, the cooperative game is said to have a "core". Because of this correspondence to cooperative game theory, the problem of allocating joint and common costs among the utility's services has come to be known as the "cost allocation game". The stand-alone test for cross-subsidization is in terms of whether or not a core for the cost allocation game exists. More precisely, if

revenues of each group of services $\leq$ the services' stand-alone costs,

$$(17.1)$$

then the core of the cost allocation game is said to exist. If the core exists, then no group can better itself by going on its own, and, in the Faulhaber (1975) formulation, the rate structure is said to be "subsidy-free". If it does not exist, then some group (coalition) is better off alone, and the rate structure contains cross-subsidies.

Inequality 17.1 is called the "stand-alone cost test". It is easily shown that this test can also be formulated as an *incremental cost test*, where incremental cost is the additional cost of providing a service or a group of services. That is, if

revenues of each group of services $\geq$ the services' incremental costs,

$$(17.2)$$

then the core also exists and the rate structure is subsidy-free (inequalities 17.1 and 17.2 are equivalent). Note that, as in the case of the burden test, the stand-alone or incremental cost tests applied to n services also require that $2^n - 1$ coalitions be tested. This, in fact, will generally be true for any test for cross-subsidization.

Unfortunately, a core need not exist, surprisingly, not even when the cost of a coalition of services is less than the cost of any fragmentation into smaller coalitions. This condition, a generalization of economies of scale, is technically called "subadditivity".[3] A simple example illustrates the idea of subadditivity and demonstrates that it is insufficient to guarantee the existence of a core.

Suppose there are three services that, with respect to costs, are perfectly symmetric. Stand-alone costs are given as in table 17.1. The cost structure

**Table 17.1**
Subadditive stand-alone costs

| Grouping | Stand-alone cost of group |
| --- | --- |
| Any singleton | 30 |
| Any pair of services | 48 |
| All three services | 75 |

is subadditive. If a coalition of any pair of services fragments into two separate services, the cost of providing service to the pair increases from 48 to 60; likewise, if the grand coalition of all three services fragments into three singletons, the cost increases from 75 to 90, while if it fragments into a pair and a singleton, the cost increases from 75 to 78. Nevertheless, this cost structure does not have a core—any apportionment of 75 among the three services will give an incentive for two of the three to defect from the grand coalition and go their own way.

For example, suppose the three services form a coalition and divide the total cost of 75 equally, so that each is paying 25. This means that any two are paying more than 48, a pair's stand-alone cost, and any pair will have an incentive to defect from the grand coalition. Some pair might then demand that they be required to pay less than 48, say 46 in order to remain in the grand coalition, leaving the remaining service with a bill of 29. If the pair split the 46 equally into two shares of 23 each, another instability arises: the service paying 29 can offer to form a coalition with one of the services paying 23 and go it alone at a combined cost of 48. And so on.

In a nutshell, the average payment in a coalition of two is 24, less than the average payment of 25 in the grand coalition of all three, and any allocation in the grand coalition will fail. An equal allocation will result in every pair's paying an average of 25, when on a stand-alone basis the pair need only pay an average of 24. An unequal allocation will result in some pair paying more than an average of 25, which gives that pair an even greater incentive to defect.

Note an interesting fact. Compensations (called "side-payments" in game theory jargon) of losers by winners will not remove the instability of a cost structure that has no core. Side payments are simply reallocations of cost apportionment; if a core does not exist, they cannot create one. Instead, the guarantee of a core requires an additional condition: not only must the cost structure be subadditive, but it must satisfy the *concavity condition* that successively larger coalitions incur successively smaller incremental costs.

**Table 17.2**
Incremental costs that exhibit cost-concavity

| Initial coalition size | Increment | Final coalition size | Incremental cost |
|---|---|---|---|
| No members | Singleton | Singleton | 30 (30−0) |
| Singleton | Singleton | Pair | 25 (55−30) |
| Pair | Singleton | Triplet | 20 (75−55) |

In terms of our example, suppose the cost of a pair is 55 rather than 48. Then, we can imagine starting with no services and successively adding a service to form larger and larger coalitions, with results given in table 17.2. Here, the incremental costs of the last column form a decreasing sequence, 30, 25, 20. On the other hand, if the cost of a pair is 48 rather than 55, this sequence becomes, 30, 18, 27, a sequence which first decreases and then increases; a core exists in the first case but not in the second.[4]

The literature on the cost allocation game has greatly deepened our understanding of the relationship of a cost structure to the fairness ideas underlying the intuitive notion of "cross-subsidization." However, an obvious weakness of the cost allocation game approach is that it neglects benefits. If these are taken into account, and the stand-alone notion retained, what was a subsidy-free rate structure in terms of the cost allocation game can become one that contains cross-subsidization, and vice versa, as the following example illustrates.

Consider the cost structure of 30 (singleton), 55 (pair), and 75 (triplet), which we have just seen yields a core in the cost allocation game and therefore is subsidy-free. Suppose that the benefit structure is the following: service 1 benefits = 23, service 2 benefits = 30, service 3 benefits = 40, as given in table 17.3. With this cost structure, symmetry might suggest that a "fair share" of costs is 25 for each service. Such a fee structure of 25 for each service would be in the core of the cost allocation game, and thus would be subsidy-free in terms of either the stand-alone or incremental cost tests. However, Service 1 would be unhappy because it would be paying 25 in order to receive a benefit of only 23.

On the other hand, it is easily seen that there are a number of fee schedules that would make the benefits minus costs nonnegative for all three services and any combination of them. One such is the following: service 1 fees = 21, service 2 fees = 25, service 3 fees = 29. Table 17.3 shows that, with this fee schedule, each service and pair of services has benefits minus fees that exceed stand-alone benefits minus costs. Thus, this schedule of payments would cover all costs and would satisfy the core constraints to the "benefits-minus-costs" game.

**Table 17.3**
Illustration of the benefits-minus-costs game

| Service combination | Benefits minus fees as part of the triplet | Stand-alone benefits minus fees |
|---|---|---|
| 1 alone | 2 | 0 (benefits of 23 insufficient to cover stand-alone cost of 30, so will not be provided by itself) |
| 2 alone | 5 | 0 |
| 3 alone | 11 | 10 |
| 1 and 2 | 7 | 0 (benefits insufficient to provide standing alone) |
| 1 and 3 | 13 | 8 |
| 2 and 3 | 16 | 15 |

## 17.5   Efficiency

Before the theory of cross-subsidization in terms of the burden, stand-alone, and incremental cost tests was developed in the early 1970s, most economists regarded cross-subsidization as a nonissue; there was no literature on it, and if it was mentioned at all, it was mentioned in passing as the self-evident result of muddled thinking. Cross-subsidization was seen as an artifact of regulators' being consumed with fairness and political maneuvering. In the prevailing economists' view, if regulators did their jobs properly and set prices according to correct economic efficiency principles, cross-subsidization would not occur.

Part of the reason for this view was the almost universal use by public utilities of fully distributed costing on the basis of some "fair" cost attribution parameter. Prices based on such an allocation obviously need not have any relation to economically efficient prices and in fact, can lead to serious resource misallocations. A simple example illustrates this. In a rural area, suppose there is a need for both irrigation and power. To supply these needs, the alternatives are to sink artesian wells at an annual cost of $8 million, build a power plant at an annual cost of $12 million, or build a dam that supplies both the irrigation and power needs at an annual cost of $18 million.

From the standpoint of resource use, the dam is the most efficient because it costs only $18 million, whereas the stand-alone irrigation and power facilities together cost $20 million. But suppose the proposal is to prorate the dam's costs to the irrigation and power users in proportion to the fractions of water diverted to irrigate and to generate power. If two-thirds of the water is used for irrigation and one-third for power, the irrigation users will face an annual charge of $12 million, greatly in excess of their stand-alone cost of $8 million, and they will refuse to enter into an agreement to build the dam. In this case, a cost apportionment that may appear "unfair" from a proration point of view, benefits both parties. For example, if the agreement is for the irrigation users to pay $7 million and the power users to pay $11 million, both are better off. Even though the power users pay more than the irrigation users to get access to only one-third of the water, they save a million dollars by so doing.

What about the relationship between efficiency and the burden, stand-alone cost, and benefits-minus-costs game tests for cross-subsidization? Although these tests were also basically motivated by fairness, and we shouldn't necessarily expect them to be economically efficient, nor that an economically efficient pricing structure will pass all of these tests. Indeed, in Zajac (1972) I pointed out that Ramsey prices do not necessarily pass the stand-alone cost test. Because my example was more complicated than a simpler one later proposed by Faulhaber (1975), I will use a variant of his example, which, aside from its simplicity, has the added advantage of showing that Ramsey prices do not necessarily pass the benefits-minus-costs test.

This can be illustrated as follows. Suppose an electric power company offers two services, a day service and a night service. The two services share a common generator, but each has its own staff of maintenance men, office personnel, security guards, and so forth. The demands for the services are different, with the day demand being completely inelastic and the night demand being somewhat elastic. The result is the picture shown in figure 17.1. In this example, Ramsey prices would have the day service bear all of the overhead, the night overhead as well as the day overhead and the common overhead of the generator, while the night service was priced at marginal cost, $mc_N$. Clearly, such a pricing structure would fail both the stand-alone cost and benefits-minus-costs tests; the day service customers would be better off from the standpoint of cost burden by divorcing themselves from the night customers and building their own generator, even though the divorce would result in duplicate plant. Likewise, because reducing their cost burden by ridding themselves of the night service's overhead increases their consumer's surplus, the day service customers would also be better off from the standpoint of benefits-minus-costs. Nevertheless, at least in the Ramsey sense, the day service's bearing all of the overhead would be economically efficient.

These examples raise all of the questions discussed in the imaginary conversation of chapter 15. Thus, the day and night services example

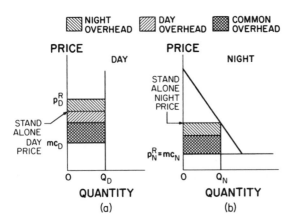

**Figure 17.1**
Faulhaber's example of Ramsey prices that are vulnerable to a rival's offering

tacitly assumes that the day and night Services have completely separate customers. If in fact the other extreme were the case, and the customers of the two services were exactly the same, then the Ramsey prices would not raise any cries of "unfair" because any unfairness would be perpetrated by the customers on themselves.

If the customer groups are not the same, we have the question of compensation. For example, suppose we start at the extreme of two separate services, with the night service priced so as to recover both its own overhead and the common overhead, as shown in figure 17.1, and with the day service also priced to cover its own and the common overhead. Then there would be an incentive for the night service to pay the day service to provide the night service's overhead. As a result, the night service would be priced at $mc_N$ (figure 17.1b), and the night service would receive the compensation back, as well as the common overhead and the deadweight loss triangle, in the form of consumer's surplus (figure 17.1b). This gain in consumer's surplus would thus exceed the payment by the amount of the common overhead and the deadweight loss triangle of figure 17.1b.

However, compensations are typically difficult, if not impossible, to arrange; moreover, in the case of three services with a cost or benefits-minus-costs structure that has no core, a subsidy-free pricing structure may be impossible to find. We are back to the imaginary conversation and all of the issues it brings out.

Fully separate subsidiaries have been proposed as a way to get around all of the difficulties of cost allocation, but this may simply change the problem from one of fair and/or efficient cost allocation to one of fair and/or efficient transfer prices. For example, in the idealized power example, suppose the day service retains the generator and creates a separate subsidiary to provide night service. At what price should the day service sell power to the night service? This again raises the question of how the cost of the generator should be apportioned between the night and day services, and we are back to the same issues.

**Exercises**

1. Ideally, what type of cost would an economist like to use in determining whether or not cross-subsidization exists? What are the practical difficulties of determining this type of cost?

2. Who are some of the principal stakeholders in a public utility "rate case" and what positions do they typically take?

3. Describe the burden test for cross-subsidization. In the general case of $n$ services, how many groups of services have to be tested to determine whether a set of rates is burden-free?

4. Describe the stand-alone and incremental cost tests for cross-subsidization. Discuss the relationship between these tests and the core of a cooperative game.

5. Discuss the concept of "cost subadditivity". If a cost structure is subadditive, is this enough to guarantee a core to the cost allocation game?

6. If a core to the cost allocation does not exist, can the resulting instability be removed by arranging for winners to compensate losers?

7. Does the existence of a core for the cost allocation game mean that the benefits-minus-costs game has a core?

8. Produce an example that shows that the proration of common costs can be economically inefficient.

9. Produce an example that shows that Ramsey prices do not necessarily pass the stand-alone cost test nor the benefits-minus-costs tests.

# 18

## Unfair Pricing II: Predatory Pricing and Dumping—Whose Ox Is Being Gored?

*[D]umping penalties have forced Americans to pay more for photo albums, pears, mirrors, ethanol, cement, shock absorbers, roof shingles, codfish, televisions, paint brushes, cookware, motorcycle batteries, bicycles, martial arts uniforms, computers and computer disks, telephone systems, forklifts, radios, flowers, aspirin, staplers and staples, paving equipment, and fireplace mesh panels. Dumping laws increasingly prevent American businesses from getting vital foreign supplies and machinery. Commerce Department officials now effectively have direct veto power over the pricing policies of over 3,000 foreign companies.*

James Bovard, *The Fair Trade Fraud*

### 18.1 Definitions

Imagine a big firm that is enjoying big profits in a number of product markets. Perhaps the big firm has a found a lucrative niche in boutique clothing stores and has established a nationwide chain of them. In city X, a little firm has established a rival boutique clothing store, offering a similar product at lower prices. What is more, the little firm seems to be succeeding. How does the big firm react?

According to common belief, the big firm will promptly cut its prices below those of its new rival. If this means a loss in this particular product market, there is no problem. After all, the big firm can offset the loss by simply raising prices in other cities where it operates, thus either driving the small rival into bankruptcy or making life so financially miserable that it will exit the business. After the big firm has disposed of its rival, it can raise prices back to their old levels or even higher, and go back to enjoying big profits.

This practice—lowering a price, even though it results in losses, with the express intent of undercutting a rival's sales or otherwise financially injuring the rival, is called "predatory pricing".

Obviously, predatory pricing is not confined to the case of *price discrimination*, that is, the firm's offering the identical product at different prices to different classes of customers based on geographic location, demographic characteristics, and so on. For example, one can conceive of a similar story for a firm that *product differentiates*, that is, produces many models of the same product, differentiated by color, quality, image, features, and so on. Again, the larger firm could use predatory pricing on any one of the models challenged by a rival.

In both of these examples, the firm has *market power*—the ability to earn positive economic profit in some markets other than the targeted market. In turn, market power gives the firm access to *financial reserves*, which can be acquired in other ways. For example, suppose a firm operates only in a single market. If it has market power in that market, over time it can accumulate financial reserves for a predatory war by simply declining to pay dividends and retaining earnings. Or, if its potential to succeed with a predatory pricing strategy is sufficiently apparent to outside investors, it can conceivably raise the reserves from external capital markets.

In whatever form, the predatory pricing story is a story of a financial war fought over time. The predator firm purposely takes losses *now* in the targeted market, on the assumption that it will be able to more than recoup these losses *later*. Presumably, a rational firm undertakes a predatory war only if it has a reasonable chance of success, that is, if its financial reserves are sufficient for the firm to weather a period of losses and if the subsequent period of profits will be sufficiently long and lucrative that the predatory campaign will have been worthwhile.

Predatory pricing needn't be confined to domestic firms. When it is practiced by a foreign firm against a domestic firm, it is called "dumping". In the dumping variant of predatory pricing, there is an added wrinkle to the story. Often, it is charged that the foreign firm's government provides the necessary financial reserves, purposely subsidizing the foreign firm in order to further global dominance. This charge can escalate an alleged dumping incident into the realm of international diplomacy.[1]

## 18.2 Background

Predatory pricing internal to the United States is an easy accusation to raise, and is often accepted by the public as a tactic that big business routinely employs. At the turn of the century, Ida Tarbell and other muckrakers accused John D. Rockefeller's Standard Oil of ruthlessly using predatory pricing to secure a monopoly on the oil business, as is brought out in

Yergin (1991). These accusations were a centerpiece of the U.S. government's antitrust suit that, in 1911, resulted in Standard Oil's breakup.

Dumping is also an easy accusation to raise; almost weekly one can read in the business press about some alleged example of dumping by a foreign industry or firm. However, a moment's thought leads one to suspect that the simple theories of predatory pricing and dumping outlined above are too simple. For example, consider the above predatory pricing story in which a big firm lowers its prices in order to drive an upstart rival small firm into bankruptcy. Suppose that there are no barriers to entry and exit, that the predator's target market is perfectly contestable. If the predator drives a rival from the scene and raises prices to their monopoly levels, won't another rival soon be tempted to enter and undercut the monopoly prices now being offered? If so, won't the losses sustained by the predator have been in vain? On the other hand, if there are substantial entry/exit barriers, isn't a better strategy for the predator to buy out the rival? For that matter, if the target market is not contestable and is therefore very lucrative, shouldn't it be relatively simple for a rival to attract the necessary capital to give the predator a run for his money? And what about recoupment by raising prices in other markets? If raising prices in these markets increases profits, why hasn't the predation firm already raised them? On the other hand, if they are at their profit-maximizing levels before predation begins, raising them in order to recoup the losses of predation will simply result in further losses (this is why economists sometimes call the recoupment story the *"recoupment fallacy"*).[2]

What about the additional wrinkle in the dumping story, that foreign governments subsidize industries to gain a global competitive advantage? First of all, proof of a cross-subsidization allegation requires that one define cross-subsidization precisely and that one produce the evidence that it has actually occurred. This raises all of the thorny issues discussed in the previous chapter.

Second, this wrinkle doesn't really distinguish dumping from predatory pricing, for a parallel situation exists in multiproduct firms. For example, suppose a firm decides to turn one of its product lines into a predator, reducing the price of the predatory product. As pointed out above in our discussion of the recoupment fallacy, if prices were set to maximize profit before predation, profits will be reduced after predation. The reduced profits will, in effect, be a tax on the firm's shareholders, akin to the tax that must be levied on the citizens of a foreign government if it decides to subsidize an industry in order to further global dominance.

All that having been said, it is clear that governments do subsidize industries, and subsidization at the government level is perhaps a more serious issue than within a U.S. firm. Indeed, it is argued that all developed nations have formed some sort of alliance between government and industry. If nothing more, developed nations all fund research and development that benefits domestic industries. Then there are the indirect subsidies. For example, for many years we had an investment tax credit that substantially benefited U.S. industries; our Japanese rivals enjoy a substantial subsidy because their employees' health care benefits are paid for by taxes rather than being added to the price of each auto. And, of course, all developed nations have elaborate schemes of agricultural subsidies. In fact, the existence of subsidies is both recognized and allowed in the latest General Agreement on Tariffs and Trade (GATT) agreement, which is meant to guide U.S. policy on dumping and, at the time of this writing, is before Congress for approval and for implementation with legislation.

## 18.3   Stakeholders

The stakeholders in domestic predatory pricing cases differ strikingly from those in dumping cases. This leads to strikingly different policy outcomes. In domestic predatory pricing cases, both the plaintiffs and defendants are typically firms based in the United States. In addition to them and perhaps their suppliers and customers, the principal players in a typical predatory pricing case are the courts.

On the other hand, in a typical dumping case, the initiator of the dumping allegation is a domestic industry or firm, while the defendant is a foreign firm. Upon initiation of the case, the U.S. Department of Commerce and, if dumping is found, the U.S. International Trade Commission, enter in the combined roles of prosecutor, judge, and jury, and thus the U.S. government becomes another major player. If the case is significant enough, senators, congressmen, and the U.S. International Trade representative may also become major players, and, for really significant cases, the White House, including the President himself, may become involved. Notably absent from the list of stakeholders is some entity that directly represents the interests of consumers. Unlike predatory pricing disputes, which are fights within the family, dumping cases become disputes wherein U.S. citizens and government officials may be pressured to rally together to fight perceived evil machinations of foreigners coming from a different culture with an intent to rob U.S. citizens of jobs.

## 18.4    Fairness/Legal Bases

Perhaps not surprisingly, the fairness and legal bases for adjudicating predatory pricing and dumping disputes have evolved in different directions, with radically different outcomes. I consider each of these in turn.

Internal Predatory Pricing

For predatory pricing cases internal to the United States, a landmark event was the publication of an article in the *Harvard Law Review* by Areeda and Turner (1975), two Harvard Law School professors. The article argued that the basis of determining whether or not predatory pricing has occurred should be the marginal cost of producing a product or service. If the firm can show that it has been pricing above marginal cost, then according to Areeda and Turner, the courts should find that no predatory pricing has occurred.

Areeda and Turner (1975) also pointed out that accounting systems are rarely set up to measure marginal cost, the cost of the last unit produced. So, from a practical point of view, Areeda and Turner's criterion may be difficult to implement. As a result, they recommended that *average variable cost* be used as a surrogate for marginal cost. Indeed, in their article, Areeda and Turner discussed various possible objections to their proposal at length, and concluded that, in spite of some infirmities, their criterion is the most legally practical and implementable.

Thus the Areeda-Turner (1975) criterion was easy to understand and was implementable. Although it generated controversy, by and large, the courts embraced its general thrust. By 1986 we find Hovencamp's *Antitrust*, a textbook for law students, stating (1986, 118), "all circuits have retained the basic Areeda-Turner AVC paradigm, although some have changed a few of the presumptions" (Here AVC stands for average variable costs and "circuits" refers to the various U.S. Circuit Courts of Appeals, the first appeal level in the federal court system).

On the other hand in the majority opinion in *Brooke Group v. Brown and Williamson Tobacco Corporation* (1993, 2587n.1), the Supreme Court has refused to resolve conflicts among the circuits on the precise cost standard that should be used to determine predatory pricing. It is worth noting that in this case both the plaintiff and the defendant agreed that average variable cost was the relevant cost measure; thus the question of whether or not Areeda-Turner was the proper cost standard was moot and only the recoupment issue faced the Supreme Court. The Court took notice that the parties had agreed on the cost standard. It then squarely faced the re-coupment question, stating that, in addition to showing that the defendant had priced below the relevant cost, the plaintiffs had to meet a second condition (p. 2588):

> The second prerequisite to holding a competitor liable under the antitrust laws for charging low prices is a demonstration that the competitor had a reasonable prospect, or, under §2 of the Sherman Act, a dangerous probability, of recouping its investment in below-cost prices.... Recoupment is the ultimate object of an unlawful predatory pricing scheme; it is the means by which an unlawful predator profits from predation. Without it, predatory pricing produces lower aggregate prices in the market, and consumer welfare is enhanced. Although unsuccessful predatory pricing may encourage some inefficient substitution toward the product being sold at less than its cost, unsuccessful predation is in general a boon to consumers.
>
> That below-cost pricing may impose painful losses on its target is of no moment to the antitrust laws if competition is not injured: It is axiomatic that the antitrust laws were passed for the "protection of *competition*, not *competitors*."

Thus the plaintiff faces formidable hurdles if he or she is to prevail in a predatory pricing suit. Since Areeda-Turner, some plaintiffs have convinced juries that predation has occurred and has injured them; not surprisingly, they have almost always lost in the appeals courts. As the above quote indicates, a simple fairness criterion seems to be driving the courts' actions —customers should be able to enjoy the lowest possible prices, and consumer welfare should be enhanced.

International Dumping

By contrast, the starting point for dumping cases is the *fair market value* (FMV) of an imported good, defined to be an estimate of its market value in the country in which the good is manufactured (the "home country"). The Department of Commerce (DOC) uses three methods to determine FMV: (1) if available, the home country market value; (2) if this is unavailable for whatever reasons, the price at which the product is sold in a third country; and finally, (3) if neither of the first two methods is available, the "constructed value," a value calculated by DOC's technicians from cost data, usually an estimate of cost of production plus increments to cover overhead and accounting profit.

As the previous chapter has shown, the allocation of common and joint costs such as overhead and accounting profit is beset with conceptual difficulties and is the subject of a large literature in both economics and accounting. The DOC bypasses these difficulties by arbitrarily tacking 10 percent onto costs to cover overhead and 8 percent to cover accounting profit. Thus, if competition has forced a foreign manufacturer's accounting profit to under 8 percent, in constructing the home fair market value, the DOC assigns the manufacturer's product 8 percent nevertheless.

However, the complications do not stop with these issues. Here are some others:

• After a foreign "fair value" is computed it must be translated to a price in U.S. dollars. But currency exchange rates change daily.

• There may be quality differences between the product sold in the home country and the product sold in the U.S.

• Prices may fluctuate over time, both in the home country and the U.S. markets.

• It may not be clear which prices are wholesale and which are retail, both in the foreign and domestic markets.

• In countries with command-and-control economies there is no "fair market value" simply because there are no markets.

If the Department of Commerce finds that dumping has occurred, and the International Trade Commission finds that the dumping has caused "material harm," duties are assessed to nullify the dumping margin that the DOC has calculated.

The above is a bare-bones description of finding of a dumping violation and remedying the violation with an assessment of duties. The interested reader can find an extensive description of the mechanics of a dumping inquiry in Murray (1991). The same volume, edited by Boltuck and Litan (1991), contains a number of critiques of U.S. dumping law and its implementation, including a defense of U.S. practice by Stewart (1991). A somewhat more lively, polemical critique can be found in Bovard (1991). Suffice it to say, the volume's consensus view, as well as Bovard's view, is that the process has many built-in biases that favor a positive finding of dumping.

A frequently cited example of such a bias is the Department of Commerce method of determining whether dumping has occurred and its extent. To illustrate the DOC method, idealize the situation so that there are no foreign currency fluctuations and assume that, over a six-month period, 100 units of a product are sold at identical prices both in the home country and in the United States. Further, assume that for the first three months 50 units were sold, both in the home country and the United States, at a price of $1.40 but that, in the final three months, competitive pressures have forced the firm to lower its price to $1.00 per unit. The average price of the

100 units sold over the six-month period is $1.20, and the DOC takes this to be the fair market value. In the DOC's procedure, *all* of the 100 sales in the United States are compared to this average; the 50 U.S. sales at a $1.00, *below* the average, are considered to be *dumping infractions*, with a dumping margin of $(1.20 - 1.00)/1.00 = 0.2$. On the other hand, the 50 U.S. sales at $1.40, *above* the average, are considered to have *zero dumping margins*. Thus the DOC would calculate that there were 50 sales with a 20 percent dumping margin and 50 with a zero margin, for an average dumping margin of 10 percent. In a nutshell, this procedure assigns a positive dumping margin to all U.S. sales below the six-month average in the home market, and a zero dumping margin to all U.S. sales above the six-month average. Thus, any fluctuations in price in the home country or in the United States, for any reason—currency fluctuations, change in tastes or in labor costs, and so forth—will bias the result in favor of a positive dumping finding. In the past, an average dumping margin of only one-half of one percent (0.5% or 0.005) has resulted in a positive dumping finding, but recently GATT has raised the minimum threshold from 0.5 percent to 5 percent, and at present writing, ratification and implementation of the GATT agreement is before the Congress. In any event, it is not surprising that Murray (1991) reports that in the 1979–1986 period, during which time the 0.5 percent threshold was in effect, the Department of Commerce–International Trade Commission process resulted in positive antidumping determinations in over 80 percent of cases that U.S. industries or firms initiated.

Thus, unlike predatory pricing cases internal to the United States, where a positive finding of predatory pricing is rare, positive findings in dumping cases are routine. The quote from Bovard at the beginning of this chapter gives a flavor of the result.

## 18.5   Efficiency

The courts' present policy on predatory pricing is marginalist and, as such, would seem to promote economic efficiency. The same cannot be said of the U.S. policy toward dumping. "Fairness" to U.S. firms, and the direct preservation of U.S. jobs seems to drive the policy; fairness to customers and indirect job consequences tend to be ignored. Higher prices to U.S. consumers and indirect job losses because of higher input prices are the result. For example, Bovard (1991, 97) points out that the U.S. machine tool industry employs 70,000 persons, but 4 million U.S. workers work in manufacturing industries that use machine tools. More expensive machine tools mean more expensive manufactured goods, which are then less competitive on world markets. A policy that keeps U.S. machine tool prices high in order to save some of the 70,000 jobs may easily end up costing many more jobs in the industries that use machine tools.

Dumping is a classic case of concentrated benefits and diffused costs. A U.S. firm or industry can reap large benefits by making a dumping charge; the costs are spread over a large body of consumers and other firms that use the allegedly dumped product as an input. Not surprisingly, dumping policy is fertile ground for client politics (see figure 15.3). The outcome is what the student of public choice would expect.

Perhaps more surprising is the outcome of domestic predatory pricing litigation. Since the Areeda-Turner (1975) article, the promotion of economic efficiency has seemed to drive the courts' actions or at least to have been the outcome of them. This is by no means automatic; the courts are perfectly capable of ignoring efficiency and catering to attractive fairness arguments, especially arguments that small businesses are being harmed by the economic power of big ones. We shall see this in chapter 20 on the Supreme Court's struggles with antitrust policies with respect to bigness of firms.

And, of course, there is always the possibility of a sea change in the courts' views. The Areeda-Turner (1975) article is an application of elementary price theory, at the level one finds in textbooks aimed at junior economics majors. As such, it is based on a number of simplifying assumptions and envisions a relatively unchanging, certain world with adequate information. Its publication brought forth a number of attacks, based on more sophisticated economic models, which cast doubt on the Areeda-Turner criterion and argued that predatory pricing could be a sound strategy after all.

Perhaps Selten's (1978) "Chain Store Paradox" article has triggered the most significant literature of this sort. Selten modeled predatory pricing by imagining an incumbent whose twenty chain stores in sequence, one after the other, become vulnerable to entry by a rival. The model further assumes that the incumbent can either cooperate with the entrant challenging a particular store, thereby reducing profit at that store somewhat but not entirely, or can fight entry, thereby reducing profit to zero. Selten argues that if he were the incumbent, he would fight entry at the outset. This would signal to future would-be entrants that, should they dare to attempt entry, they could expect promptly to be driven out of business by the strong incumbent. Selten further argues that an informal survey of colleagues shows that his intuition is widely shared.

Paradoxically, the formal game-theoretic model Selten (1978) devised does not yield this result. Instead, logic dictates that both the incumbent and would-be entrants would use *backward induction* to predict what would happen should entry occur at all twenty stores. At the last, the twentieth store, it would not pay the incumbent to fight because there would be no opportunity for later recoupment. But both the incumbent and the entrants would figure this out. Hence at the *second-to-last* store to be challenged, both would know that the last store was not going to be challenged, with the result that the incumbent would not fight the second-to-last attempt at entry either. Working backwards, logic dictates that the incumbent not fight at any stage, and hence, Selten's view that he has uncovered a paradox.

A number of game theorists promptly took up the challenge presented by Selten's "chain store paradox" in attempts to show that it was not a paradox, and that Selten's (1978) intuition was correct after all. For example, Kreps and Wilson (1982) subsequently showed that Selten's "logical" deduction from his model was a consequence of his assuming perfect information. With imperfect information, predation could in fact be a viable strategy.

## 18.6 Discussion

The fairness view in dumping policy differs radically from the courts' view in domestic predatory pricing cases. In domestic predatory pricing cases the stress is on preserving the positive effects of the competition—low prices, incentives to innovate in order to cut costs and to introduce new products, and so on. In dumping cases the stress is on "fairness" to U.S. firms, especially the fair preservation of status quo property rights to jobs, not fairness to the consumer. The threat of the direct loss of U.S. jobs to foreign firms is potent and gets action from the political process.

On the other hand, the future may bring about changes. For one, although the United States has led the world in instigating and litigating dumping charges ever since the 1979 GATT agreement, on which U.S. dumping policy is based, other nations have started to follow the U.S. lead. According to Boltuck and Litan (1991, 5), Australia, Canada, and the nations of the European Community, have increasingly prosecuted dumping infractions; we can expect Mexico and other developing nations to follow suit. If the increases in dumping findings continue throughout the world, we will eventually find ourselves in a back door trading war, in spite of "pro-trade" treaties like NAFTA. On the other hand, world trade is so important to the global economy that nations may realize that they are headed toward a disastrous equilibrium and reverse direction, adopting agreements that put the initiators of dumping actions more in the position of plaintiffs in U.S. predatory pricing cases. Only time will tell the final outcome.

Likewise, one of the Clinton administration's first forays into the predatory pricing arena concerned Northwest Airlines' threat to enter Minneapolis-Reno and two other markets with lower prices than presently charged by Reno Airlines, a fledgling, small carrier. News accounts indicated that the administration reacted quickly and negatively to Northwest's threat, and pressured Northwest to the extent that it abandoned its plan to challenge Reno. We may see the current administration, armed with suitable theory provided by economists and game theorists, mount an effort to reverse the policies of previous administrations and the courts. Again, only time will tell.

At bottom, the issues are the familiar ones brought out in the imaginary conversation between the policy maker and the expert economist adviser in chapter 15. The policy maker has only a limited number of instruments available to increase economic efficiency. So, for example, if a foreign government is foolish enough to subsidize U.S. sales at below cost, U.S. consumers should be delighted. In fact, they would undoubtedly be happy to share the benefits of lower prices with the displaced U.S. workers.

This immediately suggests a policy whereby the United States welcomes foreign goods sold here below cost and then compensates displaced U.S. workers either in cash or through retraining programs. But cash payments immediately raise difficult political problems of how large and to whom, and displaced workers are forced to face the indignity of losing jobs and the trauma of starting over again in a new line of work and perhaps even in a new city. The result is that proposals to retrain workers have their own political difficulties. The recently concluded NAFTA agreement includes extensive retraining provisions, but these did not mollify the U.S. workers who potentially would be displaced. Instead, labor unions united into a coalition to try to defeat NAFTA; the resulting political battle was one of the most intense and emotional in recent times.

Thus, the lack of instruments means that strict Pareto improvements are unavailable, only approximate ones. If the policy maker takes a utilitarian view, the course is clear: adopt policies where, even in the short run, overall societal benefits outweigh overall societal costs. Then, hope that in the long run, everyone, or at least almost everyone, will benefit. The political problem is to deal with those who lose in the short run—the owners of small businesses who perceive that giant corporations have predatorially priced them into bankruptcy or the workers who are out of a job because of perceived dumping of foreign goods on the U.S. market. As the NAFTA experience indicates, those who lose in the short run will not be easily persuaded of the fairness of a policy that promotes long-run economic efficiency.

**Exercises**

1. Discuss the role of financial reserves in the predatory pricing story. What are the sources of financial reserves?

2. Describe the Areeda-Turner (1975) test for predatory pricing.

3. Who are the main stakeholders in a domestic predatory pricing case? In an international dumping case?

4. In an international dumping case, what is "fair market value" and how is it determined?

5. In international dumping cases, what is "constructed value?" In determining constructed value, how does the Department of Commerce deal with overhead costs and accounting profit? What other complications arise in the determination of constructed value?

6. Which is more probable, (a) that a plaintiff will prevail in a domestic predatory pricing case, or (b) that the Department of Commerce will find that a dumping violation has occurred?

7. Discuss Selten's (1978) "chain store paradox".

8. Discuss the statement "If a foreign government is stupid enough to subsidize one of its industries to sell in the United States below cost, U.S. consumers should welcome the subsidy and encourage the foreign government to subsidize even more."

# 19

# Evaluating Assets Fairly: The Example of Public Utility Regulation

— *Our goal is to introduce socialism throughout the world, except for Hong Kong.*
— *Why spare Hong Kong?*
— *Because we must have free markets somewhere in order to determine prices and values.*

Joke allegedly told by Soviet economists in the 1970s

## 19.1  Value of an Asset

What is a bicycle, automobile, or home worth? If you live in a big city where there are markets with many buyers and sellers of these items, their worth is easy to establish. But when markets are "thin," with few buyers and sellers, the answer may not be simple. It gets more complicated when the market or depreciated value of an asset depends on government policy, for then the stakeholder-fairness-efficiency triangle comes to the fore and, in the evaluation of assets, government policy and the market become intertwined. The history of public utility regulation provides an excellent illustration. In this chapter we take up this history, as well as the modern economic efficiency views of how to deal with issues of public utility asset valuation.

## 19.2  Background and History

Fair Return on the Fair Value of Assets

The Fourteenth Amendment to the U.S. Constitution was a result of the Civil War. It was targeted at southern states who might deny former slaves fundamental civil rights. But 1898 saw a novel application of the Fourteenth Amendment. The alleged victims of state mistreatment were not former slaves, nor were they even human "persons." They were corporate "persons"—railroads that felt that the state of Nebraska was confiscating their property without due process.

Before Nebraska acquired a regulatory commission, the state legislature of Nebraska set intrastate railroad rates by statute, passed in 1893, the year of one of the worst depressions the United States has ever seen and also a time when the U.S. was still in its post–Civil War *deflationary* period. The statute reduced intrastate railroad rates by an average 29.5 percent from the rates in effect. The railroads sued to overturn the reduced rates, claiming that their stockholders' property was being confiscated without due process. Nebraska counterargued "that so long as the rate fixed by the law will pay the operating expenses [of the railroads] when economically administered, and something in addition thereto, the power of the court ends, and the extent to which rates must produce profits is one of political policy" (Jones 1967, 103).

When the suit (*Smyth v. Ames*, 1898) reached the Supreme Court, the Court ruled in favor of the railroads. Justice Harlan's opinion affirmed the applicability of the Fourteenth Amendment and concluded that "the basis of all calculations as to the reasonableness of rates to be charged by a corporation maintaining a highway under legislative sanction must be the *fair value* of the property being used by it for the convenience of the public.... What the company is entitled to ask is a *fair return* upon the value of that which it employs for the public convenience." (*Smyth v. Ames*, 546–547; emphasis added).

*Smyth v. Ames* established the principle that states must "fairly" and not arbitrarily exercise their police powers in regulating utilities, but it quickly became apparent that the decision seemed to be circular and to solve nothing. For how is the value of any asset determined? By the asset's earning power. Who determines earning power? The regulatory body when it sets a "fair return." Fair value was to be determined by the fair return that was to be set on the basis of the fair value!

Put in other terms, in a free-market economy, values are set by the interaction of supply and demand; without markets, there exists no value yardstick. *Smyth v. Ames* said nothing about markets; it envisioned regulators working in a closed system, sealed off from markets, and in such a closed system, there is no way to determine value. Eventually, twenty-five years after *Smyth v. Ames*, this obvious observation entered into the Supreme Court's deliberations in a famous 1923 Brandeis dissent.

The case was again brought under the Fourteenth Amendment, with Southwestern Bell claiming that rates set by the Missouri Public Service Commission were confiscatory. The majority opinion, applying *Smyth v.*

*Ames*, found for Southwestern Bell, ruling that Southwestern Bell's property had been unfairly valued. In his concurring dissent, Brandeis (*Missouri Ex. Rel. Southwestern Bell v. Missouri Public Service Commission*, 1923) attacked the foundations of *Smyth v. Ames*. Stating that it was "legally and economically unsound," he first pointed out the impossibility of determining value in the absence of markets:

It is impossible to find an exchange value for a utility, since utilities, unlike merchandise or land, are not commonly bought and sold in the market. (p. 292)

Then he pointed out the inherent circularity in *Smyth v. Ames*:

Nor can the present value of the utility be determined by capitalizing its net earnings, since earnings are determined, in large measure, by the rate by which the company will be permitted to charge; and, thus, the vicious circle would be encountered. (p. 292)

But how was the vicious circle to be broken? How were regulators to remedy the absence of markets to set values? Brandeis tackled these questions by first rejecting fair value determined, at a given point in time, by what it would cost, at that time, to reproduce the utility's plant—a method officially recommended in 1916 by the American Society of Civil Engineers. In times of deflation, this "reproduction cost" would steadily decline, resulting in a loss to investors; in times of inflation, the reverse would be true. Instead, Brandeis advocated what today would be called the "original cost" method:

The adoption of the amount prudently invested as the rate base and the amount of the capital charge as the measure of the rate of return would give definiteness to these two factors [fair value and fair return] involved in rate controversies which are now shifting and treacherous, and which render the proceedings peculiarly burdensome and largely futile. The rate base would ... be fixed, for all time, subject only to increases to represent additions to plant, after allowance for the depreciation included in the annual operating charges. The wild uncertainties of the present method of fixing the rate base under the so-called rule of *Smyth v. Ames* would be avoided.... (pp. 306–307)

Brandeis 1923 dissent did not repeal *Smyth v. Ames* and "fair value" rate making was the norm until 1944, when the *Hope* case reached the Supreme Court. This case involved the Hope Natural Gas Company's challenge to a Federal Power Commission rate ruling. Because a federal regulatory authority's action was in dispute, the Fifth rather than the Fourteenth Amendment to the Constitution was relevant. But otherwise the issue was familiar, the claim that a utility's shareholders' property was being confiscated without due process.

Justice Douglas's (*Federal Power Commission v. Hope Natural Gas Co.*, 1944) majority opinion made three major points. First, it acknowledged the "vicious circle" inherent in "fair value" rate base valuation:

"[F]air value" is the end product of the process of rate-making not the starting point as the Circuit Court of Appeals held. The heart of the matter is that rates cannot be made to depend upon "fair value" when the value of the going enterprise depends on earnings under whatever rates may be anticipated. (p. 601)

Second, the Court refused to be tied down to rate making by a specific formula. Instead, arguing for the majority, Douglas spelled out a set of general principles to guide rate making:

From the investor or company point of view it is important that there be enough revenue not only for operating expenses but also for the capital costs of the business ... the return to the equity owner should be commensurate with returns on investments in other enterprises having corresponding risks. That return, more-over, should be sufficient to assure confidence in the financial integrity of the enterprise, so as to maintain its credit and to attract capital. (p. 603)

Third, Douglas asserted that, nevertheless,

rates which enable the company to operate successfully, to maintain its financial integrity, to attract capital, and to compensate its investors for the risks assumed certainly cannot be condemned as invalid, *even though they might produce only a meager return on so-called "fair value"* (p. 605; emphasis added).

The Court concluded that, on the basis of these general principles, the Federal Power Commission had awarded Hope Natural Gas adequate returns and denied its claim of unconstitutional confiscation of stock-holders' property.

In *Hope* the Court cleverly substituted one set of fairness principles, "capital attraction" and "compensation for like risk," for another set, "fair return" on "fair value." Because the new principles subsumed the old, regu-lators were free to repeal *Smyth v. Ames*—and thus the Supreme Court avoided having to reverse itself—or they could continue to abide by it. Most chose to follow Brandeis's "prudent investment" or, in the current jargon, "original cost" method of regulation.[1] This required only that the original cost of assets and depreciation schedules be known, and did not require expert testimony on current market value of assets, or on the cost of either reproducing them or replacing them with newer technology. The original cost method was much cheaper and less speculative; in Brandeis's words, it avoided "rate controversies which are now shifting and treacher-ous, and which render the proceedings peculiarly burdensome and largely futile."

Although most jurisdictions chose to interpret *Hope* as a license to abandon "fair value" regulation, not all did, and the *Hope* decision's "capital attraction" and "compensation for like risk" twin pillars leave much room for interpretation. In addition, the value of an asset on a firm's accounting books also depends on depreciation policy, which turns out to be a thicket of issues that are a replay of the issues raised by *Smyth v. Ames*. We turn to this next.

Depreciation (Capital Recovery)

The treatment of depreciation in rate-of-return regulation is confounded by the existence of numerous views of what depreciation accounting is supposed to accomplish. Three common ones are

*View 1.* Depreciation accounting is for the purpose of forcing a firm to save money to replace equipment when it wears out or becomes obsolete (save-for-replacement depreciation).

*View 2.* Depreciation accounting is a method of allocating capital expenditures over time (accounting depreciation).

*View 3.* Depreciation accounting should reflect the decrease in market value of equipment (economic depreciation).

View 1 accords with the "fair value" concept of *Smyth v. Ames* and was the basis of the Supreme Court's first principal depreciation ruling, handed down in 1930. The case involved a street car company, United Railways and Electric Company of Baltimore. The Maryland Public Service Commission required that depreciation be based on original cost (view 2). United Railways argued that it should be based on the current value (called "present value" in the decision) of the equipment (view 1), and that the Commission's erroneous method had led to confiscatory rates.

The Court held for United Railways, basically accepting its theory of depreciation of assets. Brandeis (*United Railways v. West*, 1930) vigorously dissented. On the basis of extensive references to the accounting literature and usual business practices, he argued that the Court should have upheld the Maryland Commission, noting that

an annual depreciation charge is not a measure of the actual consumption of plant during the year. No such measure has yet been invented.... The main purpose of the charge is that irrespective of the rate of depreciation there shall be produced, through annual contribution, by the end of the service life of the depreciable plan, an amount equal to the total net expense of its retirement. (pp. 262–263)

Brandeis went to quote from a report of the Chamber of Commerce of the United States:

"The replacement theory substitutes for something certain and definite, the actual cost, a cost of reproduction which is highly speculative and conjectural and requiring frequent revision. It, moreover, seeks to establish for one expense a basis of computation fundamentally different from that used for the other expenses of doing business." (p. 266)

With his dissent in *United Railways*, Brandeis completed the essentials of the theory of rate base valuation that he first offered in his *Southwestern Bell* dissent of 1923, a theory which was basically affirmed by the *Hope* decision.[2] It is also the basis of the more refined normative theory that economists have recently proposed and that we discuss in section 19.5.[3]

### 19.3   Stakeholders

In the United States, public utilities—electric power, telephone, water, and gas companies—tend to be capital-intensive. In a typical rate case, for example, a regulatory proceedings where the utility petitions to increase its rates, a great deal of money is at stake, and the case attracts the interest of numerous stakeholders. The case is typically argued before an administrative law judge, with testimony introduced by the utility and the staff of the regulatory agency. Many states also appoint a "people's counsel" to officially represent the consumer, and the counsel or a retained expert may also testify. But, in addition, any person, groups of persons, or institutions that can demonstrate a significant interest in the outcome can petition to be "intervenors" and can testify.

Likewise, a difference of a few cents in telephone rates may mean many millions of dollars difference in revenue to the telephone company. And, also the members of the public utility commission—in about a third of the states they are elected—have a political stake in appearing to protect the rate payer from the public utility's economic power, often perceived to be enormous. Finally, even though utilities are "natural monopolies," there are substitutes for what they offer—natural gas can be substituted for electricity, bottled water for tap water, and so on; rivals have an interest in keeping the utility's rate high as contrasted with consumer groups, who have an interest in keeping the rates low.

The result is that in a typical rate case with many millions of dollars riding on the outcome, a large number of parties may have a vital interest in the case's outcome. For example, for a regulatory proceedings involving

U.S. West Communications, the telephone utility serving me, the following, incomplete, list of stakeholders immediately comes to mind:

Arizona Corporation Commission (our public utility regulators)

AT&T, MCI, Sprint (long-distance carriers that rent access to U.S. West's local switches)

Residential Utility Consumers' Organization (Arizona's "people's counsel")

Communications Workers of America, United Brotherhood of Electrical Workers (the main unions representing telephone workers)

Common Cause

Association of Retired Persons of America

Consumer Federation of America

Resellers (companies that lease lines from the telephone company to sell specialized services)

Terminal equipment vendors

Terminal equipment manufacturers

## 19.4  Fairness

Chapter 11 discusses at length what appear to me to be the principal fairness issues that arise in public utility regulation, and I will not repeat the discussion here. Briefly, more often than not, the complaints are about *unfair* treatment by the utility or regulatory commission. They generally fall into one of six categories, as summarized by the six propositions of chapter 11: (1) economic rights are being denied, (2) the Formal Principle is being violated, (3) status quo property rights are not being honored, (4) the government has failed in its role as an insurer of last resort, (5) a small minority has thwarted the conferring of large-scale benefits on the majority, and (6) the utility is being allowed to exert undue monopoly power.

## 19.5  Efficiency

A Bare-Bones Normative Theory

As a starting point of a discussion of efficient utility regulation, we need a normative theory. The normative economic theory presented here is a refinement of the basic structure outlined by Brandeis in *Southwestern Bell v. Missouri Public Service* (1923) and in *United Railways v. West* (1930).

To comprehend the theory's basic ideas it is useful first to formulate the theory for the simplest, bare-bones case, with distracting details omitted.[4] For this purpose, imagine that the stockholders of a utility simply act like a bank, loaning the utility money to buy a single asset, with the loan to be paid back over the asset's life, which is known. When, and only when, the asset dies, the mortgage will be completely paid off. Also assume that the going rate of interest varies over time, but, at any given time, is known.

In other terms, the bank (stockholders) write an *adjustable rate* mortgage for the value of the asset, with interest paid every period on the remaining balance at the current going rate (to be determined by the regulators). The face value of the mortgage is exactly the purchase price; if it were more, the stockholders would obtain a windfall profit, if it were less, the stockholders would not be fully repaid. So far, this mortgage sounds commonplace, however it differs from ordinary mortgages in a significant respect: the principal can be paid back on *any time schedule that the utility and its regulators negotiate*, as long as the mortgage is fully repaid when the asset dies.[5]

As simple as this theoretical model is, it yields important insights. For example, suppose the stockholders have a ready stock market on which to trade their shares. In a perfect world, we would expect that:

1. the stock market price of a share of a utility's stock would reach an equilibrium in which it equalled the value shown on the utility's books of account—its "book" value;

2. a stock market price not equal to per share book value would indicate that the regulators were granting a rate of return that was either above or below the going interest rate.[6]

Thus, in a perfect world, the regulators need not pick the "fair return" out of thin air; they have a readily available data source—the stock market —that will reveal it. Furthermore, the model clearly shows that the regulators play an endogenous and not exogenous role in rate making. By incorrectly setting the "fair return," they will either over- or underreward stockholders. Perhaps most significantly, the "vicious circle" of *Smyth v. Ames* disappears. The "fair value" of the firm's rate base is simply and unambiguously its book value, the amount of principal that remains to be paid on its mortgage.[7] Although this simple model carries us far, there still remains the question of depreciation (capital recovery), as well as a number of other issues to address before the theory is complete.

Elaboration of the Bare-Bones Normative Theory

A firm, of course, does not typically buy a single asset that it keeps until the firm ceases operation. Rather, it buys a continual stream of assets of different service lives; it may float new stock or bond issues to raise funds for major capital expenditures needed to construct new or replacement plant. Because we are focusing on equitable treatment of shareholders, let us continue to ignore debt financing, at the same time assuming a known, but time-varying interest rate. We also assume that, if the firm retains funds, it can place them in a bank account and earn the going interest rate on them. In other terms, we assume a perfect world without financial frictions. In such a world we expect that all financial investments will be equivalent and that any money saved, whether kept internally in the firm or invested externally, will compound at the going interest rate.[8]

Figure 19.1, due to Sinden (1979), is a convenient summary of the cash flows of a firm.[9] At the upper node, the firm's revenues divide into three streams: one flows into depreciation (payments on principal), another to pay operating expenses, and the third to pay interest on the remaining balance, which converts into dividends and/or retained earnings. In turn, the depreciation and retained earnings flows join the flow of new money (money raised from the sale of new stocks and new bonds) to form additions to the firm's cash reservoir, out of which funds are provided for the construction of new plant.

As a benchmark, figure 19.2 gives the slimmed-down version of figure 19.1 that corresponds to the bare-bones normative model. In this case, the

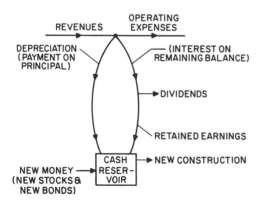

**Figure 19.1**
Sinden cash flow diagram

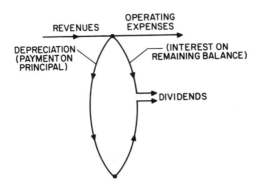

**Figure 19.2**
No retained earnings; investors paid back principal plus interest as dividends

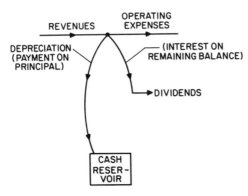

**Figure 19.3**
Interest on remaining balance paid as dividends; principal (depreciation) accumulated to build a reserve for new equipment

revenue stream goes to pay operating expenses and interest on the mortgage's remaining balance, while depreciation is the repayment of principal. The interest is joined by the depreciation flow to form the dividend flow.

Figure 19.3 depicts a more realistic case, where depreciation flows to the cash reservoir. Here the stockholders' dividends constitute a "fair return" on their investment (interest on the remaining balance on the mortgage) and do not include any repayment of principal.

From figure 19.3 it is clear that, at the end of an asset's service life, the amount of depreciation accrued in the cash reservoir will simply be the asset's purchase price and will not have any particular relation to the price of a replacement asset. For example, the asset might be a computer bought

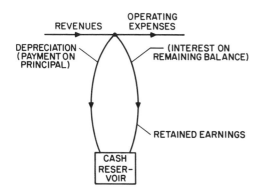

**Figure 19.4**
No dividends paid; principal and interest accumulated to build new equipment reserve

at $10,000 three years ago, now being replaced by a more powerful machine that costs only $2,000. Or it may be one of five machines that cost $5,000 each and require fifteen workmen to operate being replaced by a single machine that costs $50,000 and requires one person to operate.

Still another case is shown in figure 19.4. Where the firm pays no dividends and the entire "interest on the remaining balance" flow becomes retained earnings. These in turn flow into the cash reservoir, where, together with depreciation, they accumulate over the life of the asset. In this case, the stockholders' investment in the firm is identical to their having put their money into a bank at compound interest for the life of the asset. For example, suppose the asset's purchase price is $V_0$, the life of the asset is $T$ years, and over the life of the asset the interest rate is a constant value, $r$. At the end of the asset's life, the amount accumulated in the cash reservoir will be $(1 + r)^T V_0$.

Economically Efficient Depreciation

Consider first, "economically efficient depreciation," that is, an allocation of capital expenditures over time that is economically efficient. To keep matters simple, we again consider the bare-bones situation depicted in figure 19.2 of a firm that goes into business with a single asset. Also, we assume that our mythical firm lives for only two years, and that there is perfect foresight—over the firm's lifetime the firm and its regulators know the interest rate (assumed to be a constant value, $r$), as well as the firm's demand schedule and costs. Finally, we assume that the firm has no period-by-period fixed cost, but that its period-by-period marginal cost is a constant, $mc$.

In each period, then, the revenue in figure 19.2 is $pQ$, where $Q$ is the firm's output, and $mcQ$ corresponds to the firm's operating expenses. But, as outlined above, the regulatory contract allows the firm and its regulators to adopt any plan of payment of the principal (depreciation) that they wish.

Suppose that the firm goes into business at time $t = 0$, and that the regulators wish to set the prices in years 1 and 2, $p_1$ and $p_2$, so that they are economically efficient, how would they do it? The problem is reminiscent of the Ramsey problem for efficient multicommodity taxation or multiproduct pricing for a regulated firm, and we get closely related results. Except in this case, we don't have several different products but, rather, several time periods. Also, we do not have the requirement that the tax revenue or overhead coverages (prices in excess of marginal costs) of the several commodities or products cover the total tax requirement or total overhead. Instead, we now have the requirement that prices in excess of marginal costs must cover depreciation as well as interest payments. Finally, we have to include the time value of money—a dollar at the end of year 1 will only be worth $1/(1 + r)$ at $t = 0$, and a dollar at the end of year 2 will only be worth $1/(1 + r)^2$ at $t = 0$.

To see that economically efficient depreciation is closely related to Ramsey pricing, consider first what happens if the price in year 1 is slightly increased while that in year 2 is slightly decreased. Suppose the inframarginal change in consumer's surplus from year 1's price increase is $\Delta CS_1$ and from year 2's price decrease is $\Delta CS_2$. For simplicity, assume that effects of these price changes occur at the ends of years 1 and 2. Then, at time $t = 0$, the changes in consumer's surplus will have the values of $\Delta CS_1/(1 + r)$ and $\Delta CS_2/(1 + r)^2$, respectively; if prices are economically efficient, these will have to just balance:

$$\Delta CS_1/(1 + r) + \Delta CS_2/(1 + r)^2 = 0. \tag{19.1}$$

At the same time, the slight price increase in Year 1 will slightly increase the amount available to the firm in year 1 to cover depreciation and interest, call this "D&I coverage." Likewise, a slight price decrease in year 2 will slightly decrease year 2's D&I coverage. Denote these slight changes in depreciation and interest coverage by $\Delta D\&I_1$ and $\Delta D\&I_2$. If we again assume that their effects occur at the ends of years 1 and 2, they will have the values at $t = 0$ of $\Delta D\&I_1/(1 + r)$ and $\Delta D\&I_2/(1 + r)^2$. If prices are economically efficient, these must also just balance:

$$\Delta D\&I_1/(1 + r) + \Delta D\&I_2/(1 + r)^2 = 0. \tag{19.2}$$

Now, divide equation 19.2 into equation 19.1 to get the relation:

$$\Delta CS_1/\Delta D\&I_1 = \Delta CS_2/\Delta D\&I_2, \tag{19.3}$$

which is exactly the same as equation 13.2 except with $\Delta D\&I_1$ and $\Delta D\&I_2$ replacing $\Delta TR_1$ and $\Delta TR_2$.

Because equation 19.3 is the same as equation 13.2, the diagrammatic construction of figure 13.2 again pertains if $p_1$ and $p_2$ are interpreted as prices in years 1 and 2. That is, we again have the requirement that the ratios $DA/AD'$ be the same for both time periods. On the other hand, the requirement that the tax revenues collected from all commodities be equal to the total required tax or that the sum of overhead coverages be equal to the total overhead is now replaced with a more complicated requirement—at time $t = 0$, the discounted values of the $D\&I$ coverages recoveries must equal the purchase price or initial value of the asset, $V$:

$$V = D\&I_1/(1 + r) + D\&I_2/(1 + r)^2. \tag{19.4}$$

If, for example, the demand schedules are the same in years 1 and 2, then the diagrammatic construction immediately tells us that the economically efficient prices must be the same in both years, say $p$. Equation 19.4 in this case becomes:

$$V = (p - mc)[(1/1 + r) + (1 + r)^2]. \tag{19.5}$$

This can be solved for $p$ to give:

$$p = mc + [(V(1 + r)^2/(2 + r)]. \tag{19.6}$$

Because the $D\&I$ coverage, $p - mc$, is the same for each period, we find in this case that economically efficient depreciation yields the equivalent of a level payment mortgage. As every homeowner with such a mortgage knows, the repayment of principal, in our case the depreciation, *increases* in each subsequent period. We easily verify this fact for the two-period case. At the end of the first period, the interest due is $rV$, which means that the amount of principal repaid (depreciation) is

$$(p - mc) - rV = V/(2 + r). \tag{19.7}$$

The remaining principal must be repaid at the end of the second period. This is given by

$$V - (V/2 + r) = (1 + r)V/(2 + r). \tag{19.8}$$

Thus the second period's depreciation is $(1 + r)$ times that of the first period.

Most conventional depreciation schemes call for either level or declining depreciation allowances. That economically efficient depreciation may call for *increasing* rather than level or declining allowances makes it appear strange, and, in fact, it has been primarily only of academic interest.

Economic Depreciation

With the use of conventional depreciation methods, the "book" value of an asset—as shown on the firm's books of account—may have little relation to its resale value. This means that the firm's books of account may give the shareholder a poor idea of the market value of an asset or, for that matter, of the entire firm. More importantly, to the extent that book values are used in decision making, conventional depreciation can lead to resource misallocation. Equipment may be worth nothing on the firm's books, which might suggest that it should be replaced, when in fact it has considerable market value, and equipment whose book value is high might be technologically obsolete and might have a market value of zero.

It is often suggested that "accounting depreciation" should be replaced by "economic depreciation." That is, the market value of an asset should be determined, period-by-period, and this decrease should be the depreciation charge.[10] The accounting profession has resisted economic depreciation on at least two grounds: (1) estimates of market value might be speculative and subject to manipulation, and (2) the sum of the market values of individual equipments does not necessarily reflect the value of the entire firm as viewed by the stock market. Even in the most rudimentary "theory of the firm," at least two "factors of production" are inputs into the firm—"capital," or long-run assets, and "labor," or short-run assets. The yearly value of the firm's workforce may far exceed its yearly wage bill and may reflect years of accumulated experience in cutting costs and making the firm's production processes efficient. Also, such things like managerial talent, intellectual property (patents, copyrights, trade secrets), future prospects of the industry in which the firm operates, and other factors might cause the stockmarket to place a higher or lower value on the firm as whole than the sum of the market value of its assets.

Nevertheless, when the market value of equipment steadily decreases, our normative model has no problem accommodating economic depreciation. The amount depreciated per period is simply the decrease in the equipment's market value during that period. This depreciation continues until the equipment is worthless, at which time the face value of the "mortgage" has been completely repaid.

Should the value increase, our normative model would result in negative depreciation, which in the bare-bones version would have the shareholders paying rather than receiving money. However, a more practical obstacle suggests that there is little point in further pursuing this apparent theoretical infirmity of the model: U.S. accounting practice does not allow negative depreciation or the up-valuing of assets.

## Depreciation When Competition Exists

In the absence of competition, Brandeis depreciation allows great flexibility in the regulatory contract; the regulators and firm can spread the costs of assets over their service lives in any fashion that is convenient. Depreciation then reflects the convenient repayment of "principal" on the loan advanced by the stockholders. As inspection of the upper node of a Sinden diagram shows, the prices and associated revenues charged for the utility's products are a residual or, in the jargon of public utility regulation, a "revenue requirement"—simply the sum of depreciation, the utility's operating costs and "fair return" (interest on the loan).

On the other hand, if the regulated utility faces competition because other, unregulated vendors offer a close substitute for its services, the utility's prices or revenues are no longer a residual; they are exogenously set. In other terms, the utility together with its regulators are no longer "price makers" but instead are "price takers." In this case, depreciation rather than the prices becomes the residual and may or may not be sufficient to pay back the "principal" over an equipment's service life.[11] This situation constrains the flexibility of the regulatory contract, a constraint that can be especially troublesome in the face of rapid technological change that renders equipment obsolete.

In theory, with sufficient foreknowledge of new, cheaper technology coming on line, the regulatory apparatus can easily accommodate technological change; in practice, new technology and competition can present the apparatus with jarring political challenges. To illustrate, consider an extreme, fanciful example. Suppose five years ago, a telephone company installed new equipment that it expected would last twenty years. The company learns that, five years from now, halfway through the service life of its equipment, almost costless mental telepathy service is certain to be available. Although the mental telepathy service will yield distorted, lower-quality transmission, regulators will undoubtedly find it impossible to deny this service to those who want it. Even if the mental telepathy service is offered, the telephone company expects that there will still be a market for its present, higher-quality service, but it also expects that political pressures will not allow its service to be deregulated. As a result, the company foresees that, in five years, its equipment will be worth only 10 percent of its purchase price. Because the equipment is being uniformly depreciated over twenty years at 5 percent per year, in five years it will have a book value of 50 percent, rather than 10 percent of its purchase price.

Economic depreciation would anticipate mental telepathy and would require regulators to accelerate depreciation to 13 percent per year for the next five years. Added to the 25 percent depreciation already taken, this would depreciate the equipment by 90 percent at the end of the tenth year of service life, when mental telepathy arrives. The telephone company's book value would then be just its market value; more important, the company could then switch to a depreciation rate of 1 percent per year for the remaining ten years of service life of its equipment, a rate that would result in competitive prices.

On the other hand, an increase of depreciation from 5 percent to 13 percent per year would cause, for the next five years, a sudden jump in revenue requirements and a concomitant jump in prices, which might be politically unacceptable, especially in the five years before mental telepathy becomes a reality. If, however, regulators choose to ignore the inevitable introduction of the competitive, unregulated mental telepathy service and refuse to change their rate-setting practices, five years from now the utility will find that it cannot price competitively and that its market disappears.

The situation is all the worse, the less lead time the regulators and utility have. In the extreme case where a new technology instantaneously makes the utility's equipment worthless but still functioning, economic depreciation says that depreciation of the residual book value of the utility's equipment should also be instantaneous, something that is even more difficult for regulators and the utility's customers to accept.[12]

### Exercises

1. In rate-of-return regulation of public utilities, what is the "vicious circle" referred to by Brandeis in 1923?

2. In the *Hope* case, what new set of fairness principles did the Supreme Court lay down for the regulation of public utilities? How did these relate to the "fair return on a fair value" principle of *Smyth v. Ames* (1898)?

3. Discuss the common views of what depreciation accounting is supposed to accomplish.

4. Discuss the stakeholders in a typical public utility rate case.

5. Describe the bare-bones normative model of asset valuation discussed in the text. In this model, what is the "fair value" of a utility's asset? What happens to the "vicious circle" inherent in the *Smyth v. Ames* (1898) decision?

6. Discuss the cash flows depicted in the four cases shown in figures 19.1–19.4.

7. Mathematically derive public utility prices in the case of economically efficient depreciation and show their relation to the Ramsey prices of chapter 13.

8. Discuss economic depreciation, including it characteristics when competition exists.

# 20

## The Supreme Court's Struggle with Mergers and Breakups

*No action by this court can resurrect the old single-line Los Angeles food stores that have been run over by the automobile or obliterated by the freeway.... Today's dominant enterprise in food retailing is the supermarket.*

Justice Potter Stewart in dissent (*United States v. Von's Grocery*, 1966)

### 20.1 Introduction

Starting with the passage of the Sherman Act in 1890, the Supreme Court has struggled with the question, What limits should the government put on the size of a firm and how the firm conducts its business? The act itself was deceptively simple; according to its framers, it simply codified what was already in the common law, that "restraint of trade" and "monopolization" were illegal. In fact, the Sherman Act and the follow-on Clayton Act of 1914 triggered off a series of cases that created new law and that caused the Court to struggle with both economics and fairness. The cases form a fascinating history of this struggle, a struggle with no end in sight.

### 20.2 Background and History

As we have already discussed in chapter 5, in the period after the Civil War, technological breakthroughs led to the emergence of gigantic firms with tens of thousands and even hundreds of thousands of employees. To a large extent, this change was the result of the merging of small firms. One path of combination was first to form a trust, wherein the holders of stock in the firms transferred their voting power to a small group of "trustees." The trustees then had the power to control all of the member firms, of course in the process muting or destroying competition between them. From the trust form, it was then a small step to create a new corporation that embraced all of the business formerly done by the separate firms.

The result was firms of gigantic size, and hence, of gigantic economic power, or at least that was the perception.[1] Also, most of the gigantic firms were headquartered in the East, and, as we saw in chapter 16, the perceived economic power of the eastern "capitalists" and their Wall Street allies was the target of intense hatred by small farmers and businessmen and was a large factor in the creation of the Populist Party. The hatred was fed by the muckraking literature of the day, such as Charles Francis Adams's 1869 exposé of the alleged greed and amoral conduct of railroad tycoons[2] and Ida Tarbell's devastating attack on similar practices of Standard Oil.[3]

Such was the "trust-busting" setting for the passage of the Sherman Act. The first two sections contain the meat of the act:

*Section 1.* Every contract, combination in the form of trust or otherwise, in restraint of trade or commerce among the several States, or with foreign nations, is declared to be illegal. Every person who shall make any contract or engage in any combination or conspiracy hereby declared to be illegal shall be deemed guilty of a felony....

*Section 2.* Every person who shall monopolize, or attempt to monopolize, or combine or conspire with any other person or persons, to monopolize any part of the trade or commerce among the several States, or with foreign nations, shall be deemed guilty of a felony....

The language of the Sherman Act is thus simple and by the same token, vague; it wasn't long before the Supreme Court was called upon to give it more precise meaning and to develop a methodology for dealing with "restraints of trade" and "monopolizations."

As Bork (1978) points out, the bulk of the conceptual issues arose before 1914, but the various puzzles that the issues brought to the surface took much longer to solve. And the formation of puzzles and their solution continues to this day.

Degree of Restraint

If one literally banishes all "restraint of trade" from commerce, one banishes the free-market economy. After all, doesn't every businessman seek to "restrain the trade" of rivals so that he can flourish. This came out early in the *Trans-Missouri* case of 1897. Justice White's dissenting decision in that case points out that a literal reading of the act would seem to make illegal (*United States v. Trans-Missouri Freight Assn.*, 1897):

all those contracts which are the very essence of trade, and would be equivalent to saying that there should be no trade, and therefore nothing to restrain. (p. 351)

The Court assumed that Congress did not have such a literal reading in mind, as is evident from the congressional debates preceding the act.[4]

## "Good" versus "Bad" Restraints

If some restraints of trades are needed to have a market economy, how does one distinguish between "good" and "bad" restraints of trade? Price-fixing quickly became a test bed for this question. Prior to the Sherman Act, price-fixing was common. Firms in the same business would decide that it was only fair that none of them should price below a certain floor price in order to forestall "ruinous" competition, so they would enter into a contract specifying a schedule of floor prices that each party to the contract would agree to. However, under common law, such contracts were unenforceable.[5]

After passage of the Sherman Act, the federal government filed a number of price-fixing cases. Price fixers now faced a much more serious prospect than that their contract was unenforceable. If price-fixing was adjudged to be a "restraint of trade" under the act, the price fixers could go to jail. So much for the act's simply codifying the common law!

In two of the first price-fixing cases, *United States v. Trans-Missouri* (1897) and *United States v. Addyston Pipe* (1898), the accused freely admitted that they had fixed prices but offered a defense: their prices were just and reasonable. The Court rejected this defense and made price-fixing a "per se" violation of the act. That is, to prevail in a price fixing case, the plaintiff had only to show that the defendants had price-fixed, and did not have to prove evil intent on their part or that their actions would have bad consequences.

Although the Court early on summarily disposed of overt price-fixing, other issues of "good" versus "bad" restraint of trade were tougher, as the next puzzles bring out.

## "Bigness" versus "Monopolizing"

Is sheer "bigness" a reason to conclude that a firm is "monopolizing" and hence, under the Act, should be broken up into smaller, competing firms? In his dissent in *Northern Securities* (1904), Justice Holmes argued that nothing in the act spoke to "bigness" or "greatness" of a corporation as justifying its dissolution, and using size as a criterion was dangerous. The case involved the attempted merger of the Great Northern and Northern Pacific Railways, two large railroads that extended in parallel lines across the northern tier of states from the Great Lakes to the Pacific. The majority of the Court disallowed the merger as a violation of the act.

Prefacing his remarks with the sentence, "Great cases like hard cases make bad law," Holmes (*Northern Securities v. United States*, 1904) went on to say, [T]here is a natural inclination to assume that it [the Sherman Act] was directed against certain great combinations" (p. 402). But the Court had to be careful; whatever it ruled would apply to all corporations, great or small. Repeating White's refrain in *Trans-Missouri*, Holmes concluded that if the Court accepted the government's argument in this *Northern Securities*, then

there is hardly any transaction concerning commerce between the States that may not be made a crime by the finding of a jury or a court. (p. 403)

Nonetheless, large trusts or combinations continued to be in the public eye, perceived to be actual or potential abusers of monopoly power, and two landmark cases of 1911 saw the beginning of federal government activism to dissolve them. In both cases, *Standard Oil of New Jersey et al. v. United States* and *United States v. American Tobacco Co.*, the Court ordered the dissolution of companies that, at the end of the nineteenth century, had evolved into giant corporations.

The Justice Department alleged that Standard Oil had engaged in a long list of nefarious business practices, or "dirty tricks," reminiscent of Tarbell's accusations. These allegations were recapitulated in the Court's decision (*Standard Oil*, 1911, 42–43):

Rebates, preferences and other discriminatory practices in favor of the [Standard Oil] combination by railroad companies; restraint and monopolization by control of pipe lines, and unfair practices against competing pipe lines; contracts with competitors in restraint of trade; unfair methods of competition, such as local price cutting at the points where necessary to suppress competition; espionage of the business of competitors, the operation of bogus independent companies, and payment of rebates on oil, with the like intent; the division of the United States into districts and the limiting of operations of the various subsidiary corporations as to such districts so that competition in the sale of petroleum products between such corporations had been entirely eliminated and destroyed; and finally ... the "enormous and unreasonable profits" earned by the Standard Oil Trust and the Standard Oil Company as a result of the alleged monopoly; which presumably was averred as a means of reflexly inferring the scope and power acquired by the alleged combination.

The government's case in *American Tobacco* was similarly based on a long list of perceived nefarious practices that led to the formation of the American Tobacco Corporation.

The *Standard Oil* decision did not attempt to formulate any more "per se" criteria for restraints of trade and monopolization. Instead, the Court suggested that certain restraints of trade are "reasonable" and only if "reasonableness" were violated was there an antitrust violation. The test for reasonableness has three parts: (1) Is the firm is engaging in practices that the have been ruled as per se illegal? If it is, the Court needn't inquire further into intent or resulting market power. However, if the practices are not per se illegal, then the remaining two parts of the test, sometimes called the *inherent intent* and *inherent effect* tests, must be examined. These are, (2) Was there an intent to monopolize? and (3) Was the firm's resulting market power, or more generally, the structure of the market in which the firm operated such that monopolization was the result? Thus, according to the rule of reason, if a firm has avoided committing a per se illegal act, such as price-fixing, did not intend to monopolize, and its actions did not result in sufficient market power to significantly curb competition, then it will not be guilty of an antitrust violation.

In both *Standard Oil and American Tobacco* the Court held that the firms had failed the three-part rule-of-reason test and ordered their dissolution. On the other hand, nine years later, in *United States v. United States Steel Co.* (1920), the Court ruled that U. S. Steel had passed the rule-of-reason test and upheld a lower court's decision dismissing the government's case to dissolve it.

### "Naked" versus "Ancillary" Restraints

Does it make a difference how size was attained? Justice Taft already addressed this issue in *Addyston Pipe* (1898), arguing that the law should distinguish between "naked" restraints of trade, whose sole purpose was to suppress competition, and "ancillary" restraints of trade, which were a by-product of normal business practices. Among normal business practices allowed under common law were partnerships and exclusive arrangements between suppliers and those who deliver a final product of service to a customer. The common law had, in Taft's new terminology, adjudged these to be "ancillary" rather than "naked" restraints of trade. Holmes addressed the issue again in his *Northern Securities* (1904) dissent, pointing out that had one railroad company built both of the lines built separately by the Great Northern and Northern Pacific Railroads, there would have been no objection.

But the size issue refused to remain settled, and the *United States v. Aluminum Corporation of America et al.* (1945) and *United States v. United*

*Shoe Machinery Corp.* (1953) cases brought it to the fore. Bork (1978, 165) argues that there were two influences at work. One was the passage in 1914 of the Clayton Act. Two principal aims of the act were to prevent mergers and exclusive arrangements between a manufacturer and a supplier, for example a contract between a maker of widgets and the XYZ steel company that the widget maker will buy all of the steel that it needs exclusively from XYZ. However, Congress artfully worded the act so that mergers and exclusive dealings were illegal only if they "substantially" lessened competition.

Nevertheless, according to Bork (1978), the Clayton Act inspired the theory that

exclusionary practices need not involve a deliberate intent to gain monopoly power and may, in fact, seem to the persons employing them to be perfectly normal behavior. The result, inevitably, was to expand the category of behavior that made large size itself impermissible. (p. 165)

The second influence cited by Bork was the Court's ignoring of productive efficiency. For

once efficiency is ignored, there appears to be no difference between a cartel and a company. They both eliminate competition internally. Since cartels are illegal regardless of market power, companies should be outlawed, no matter how small. That the principle has not been taken to this logical conclusion does not make it intellectually more respectable, nor has it prevented the principle from wreaking havoc where it is applied. (p. 165)

I will not attempt to analyze the *Alcoa* and *United Shoe* decisions. Both are complex cases and interpretations of the decisions vary widely. According to Bork, the reasoning in both cases was muddled and full of internal contradictions, simply rationalizations for curbing bigness. Needless to say, not all scholars of antitrust agree with Bork.

"Incipiency" Doctrine

Should the government act only after illegal restraint of trade or monopolization have occurred, or should it take preventive action, forestalling such illegal acts in their infancy? This was a primary issue in the Warren Supreme Court decision in *Brown Shoe* (1962).

The 1914 Clayton Act, which banned mergers that "substantially" lessened competition, was ineffective because of a loophole. If firm A wanted to acquire firm B, it bought firm B's assets rather than its stock, an action that the Court ruled did not violate the Clayton Act. The Cellar-Kefauver

Act of 1950 closed this loophole. *Brown Shoe* involved the merger of the Brown and Kinney Shoe companies. The Court disallowed the merger, basing its decision on the Cellar-Kefauver Act. But more significant for our story, in doing so, it made new doctrine concerning "incipiency."

The Court's decision (*Brown Shoe Co., Inc. v. United States,* 1962) was based on two assumptions of fact which, in today's era of the "downsizing" of large corporations, seem to be shockingly without empirical foundation, nothing more than beliefs. The first was that there was a "rising tide of economic concentration in the American economy." The second was that

[i]nternal expansion is more likely to be the result of increased demand for the company's products and is more likely to provide increased investment in plants, more jobs and greater output. Conversely, expansion through merger is more likely to reduce available consumer choice while providing no increase in industry capacity, jobs or output. (p. 345n.72)

The Court also analyzed Congress's intent. According to the Court, Congress intended merger standards under the Clayton act to be more severe than those under the Sherman Act; further, Congress felt that "local control" and the protection of small business was desirable, and that economic concentration might pose a threat to "other values." But most significant, the Court introduced "incipiency" as a criterion, again justified as being part of Congress's intent. In fact, the merger of Brown and Kinney Shoes would have created a firm that at most controlled 5 percent of the nationwide retail shoe market. The Court saw this as alarming:

If a merger achieving 5% control were now approved, we might be required to approve future merger efforts by Brown's competitors seeking similar market shares. (p. 343–344)

Subsequently, in *United States v. Von's Grocery Co.* (1966), a merger of two Los Angeles supermarket chains that created a chain with 7.5 percent of the Los Angeles market, the Court again ordered dissolution. The combined effect of *Brown Shoe* and *Von's Grocery* was essentially to foreclose major mergers until the Reagan administration.

## 20.3 Stakeholders

The main stakeholders in governmental policy toward mergers and allowable size of firms have been the executives of firms that wished to merge, the firms' stockholders, owners of small firms who felt threatened by large firms and by national chain stores, and politicians, especially those who stood to gain by opposing the "big business" in favor of the small businessman. Often, the consumers' interests took second place.

## 20.4  Fairness

Starting with the debates leading to the Sherman Act, two main fairness themes occur repeatedly: the curbing of monopoly power and the little fellow's status quo property rights, with the latter usually being justified on the basis of preserving American values. We have already seen the power of the former in our discussion of the progressive income tax in chapter 16, and in our discussion of public utility regulation in chapter 11. Martin (1988, 54) argues that the debates leading to the passage of the act show that Congress was intent mainly on dispersing economic power and not allowing it to become overly concentrated in few hands, and that it was less concerned with protecting small businesses. DiLorenzo (1990) takes strong exception to this view, and argues that protection of small businesses was in fact the act's primary intent.

Whatever the correct historical interpretation, the Court early on took notice of the argument that small business is entitled to status quo property rights, especially in order to preserve "American values." Arguing for the majority, Justice Peckham (*United States v. Trans-Missouri Freight Assn.*, 1897) remarks that large business combinations may in fact be able to realize economies that would result in price reductions to the consumer but that

[t]rade or commerce under those circumstances may nevertheless be badly and unfortunately restrained by driving out of business the small dealers and worthy men whose lives have been spent therein and who might be unable to readjust themselves to their altered surroundings. Mere reduction in the price of the commodity dealt in might be dearly paid for by the ruin of such a class. (p. 323)

Judge Learned Hand picks up this theme again in *United States v. Aluminum Corporation of America et al.* (1945):

We have been speaking only of the economic reasons which forbid monopoly; but, as we have already implied; there are others, based upon the belief that great industrial consolidations are inherently undesirable, regardless of their economic results.... Throughout the history of these [antitrust] statutes it has been constantly assumed that one of their purposes was to perpetuate and preserve, for its own sake and in spite of possible cost, an organization of industry in small units which can effectively compete with each other. (pp. 428–429)

But the Warren Court's *Brown Shoe* and *Von's Grocery* cases perhaps most intensely applied the "protection of the small businessman" argument. Again, in reviewing the Court's actions, the tenor of the times is important to remember. The post-World War II era until the mid-1960s saw the solidification and expansion of giant U.S. businesses. The big three automobile companies—General Motors, Ford, and Chrysler; major oil companies—Exxon, Gulf, Shell; and giants such as AT&T, IBM, and Procter & Gamble all seemed to prosper and, if anything, to keep getting progressively bigger. Galbraith's best-seller, *The New Industrial State* (chapters 18–20), argued that these giant corporations did not respond to the market, but the market responded to them; in effect, General Motors designed an automobile and then commissioned its marketing folks to make the public want to buy it.

In all of this, the small businessman was at the mercy of the big corporations, especially if he had to compete with them. If the United States wasn't careful, soon gone would be the small grocery, shoe store, dress shop, haberdashery, book store, hardware store, and drug store, all to be replaced by branches of the impersonal, profit-hungry monster corporation headquartered in some distant city. A way of life would be wiped out, together with all of the basic values that it represented. The "rising tide of economic concentration" was a nightmare, a time bomb, and it was the duty of Court to defuse it. At least this is the impression given by the majority decisions in *Brown Shoe* and *Von's Grocery* (but note also Justice Stewart's quote at the beginning of this chapter).

Of course, the concern over fairness to the small businessman and protecting "values" slights fairness to the consumers. Consumers are interested in getting what they want at the lowest price, and they consider it the height of unfairness to have to pay more than is necessary. But ensuring the lowest price to the consumer is what economic efficiency is all about, a topic we turn to next.

## 20.5   Efficiency

We have remarked that the turn-of-the-century Supreme Courts faced most of the main conceptual issues of antitrust, but they faced them without the economic tools of analysis and concepts that are commonplace today. Fortunately, two of these concepts—consumers' and producers' surpluses, and barriers to entry/exit—go a long way to helping us analyze the puzzles that the Court faced and continues to face.

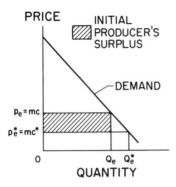

**Figure 20.1**
Effect of a merger in a competitive market

Consider the first puzzle listed above: how to distinguish between "good" and "bad" restraints of trade and monopolizing. To illustrate the analytical use of consumers' and producers' surpluses, I assume the idealized case of identical firms in a perfectly competitive industry, one where entry into or exit from the industry is costless. As we have seen in chapter 2, we expect the equilibrium price in this industry to be at marginal cost, $p = p_e = mc$, and each firm's output will correspondingly be at $Q_e$ (figure 20.1). The effect will be that the sum of consumers' and producers' surpluses will be maximized (in the special case drawn in figure 20.1, the producers' surplus is initially zero).

Now, suppose that two of the identical firms in our story find that by merging they can decrease costs from $mc$ to $mc^*$, thereby shifting their marginal cost curves downward. If they merge, we can at first expect the rest of the firms in the industry to maintain their price at $p_e$. At first, this will mean that the merged firms will each continue to produce the output $Q_e$ and will enjoy the producers' surplus shown by the shaded rectangle in figure 20.1.

But, unless the merged firms have a patent, copyright, or trade secret, we can expect the remaining firms in the industry to imitate the firms that merged; they, too, will discover that there are economies to be had through merging, and will start to form larger combinations in order to cut costs and lower their respective marginal cost curves. The final result will be the new equilibrium, shown in figure 20.1. with an equilibrium price and output of $p_e^*$ and $Q_e^*$. The result will be lower prices and greater output to the consumer, an increase in consumer's surplus, and, in the example at hand, all firms once again earning no producer's surplus.

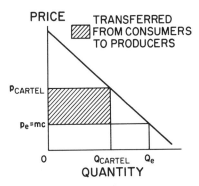

**Figure 20.2**
Effect of a cartel

Something like this is in fact the story of the birth of supermarkets. By merging, small grocers found that they could increase their buying power with suppliers and thus negotiate lower costs for the produce, meats, canned goods, and so on, that they sold. But the story is also more complicated because they did this in response to the threat from A&P, the first of the supermarket chains. Also, they found that they could get buying power without merging but by forming buying associations. In any event, the public benefited by enjoying lower prices and consuming a greater output.

By contrast, suppose the individual firms in our story formed a cartel that had the power to completely block entry into its business. Suppose further that the firms negotiated a price-fixing agreement at a price considerably higher than $p_e$, say $p_{cartel}$ in figure 20.2. This would result not only in a higher price to the consumer but also a restriction in output from $Q_e$ to $Q_{cartel}$. In addition, it would result in a transfer of the shaded area from consumers' to producers' surplus.

As simple as these two examples are, they illustrate the fundamental difference between "good" and "bad" restraints of trade and monopolization. In the first case, the firms merged in order to get some monopoly power and gain a competitive advantage over rivals. Their goal was to "restrain trade" and "monopolize." Nevertheless, their merger immediately resulted in an increase in producers' surplus without any decrease in consumers' surplus, price, or output. Ultimately, as in the history of the supermarket movement, lower prices, higher output, and an increase in consumers' surplus resulted over the entire market; the merger was a "good" restraint of trade and monopolization.

On the other hand, in the cartel story, we saw a curtailing of output and consumers' surplus, an obviously "bad" restraint of trade and monopolization. Empirically, this seems to have been the case with Standard Oil. After the 1911 breakup, shares in the member companies of Standard Oil approximately doubled in price, and the shares of one of them, Standard Oil of Indiana, tripled in price. According to Yergin (1991, 113), the breakup more than doubled John D. Rockefeller's personal worth to $900 million dollars (about $9 billion in today's dollars). Thus, presumably, the breakup not only increased competition and resulted in greater output, but also increased the rewards to shareholders or producers' surplus.

The key then to differentiating "good" from "bad" restraint of trade and monopolization is whether prices go down, while consumers' surplus and output go up, or whether the reverse is the case. In a word, the key is whether or not a proposed merger or break up of an existing firm is liable to increase economic efficiency or decrease it.

This insight is crucial and allows us to categorize many of the Supreme Court's actions without much further analysis. For example, in reading excerpts from the debates leading to the Sherman Act given by Martin (1988, 48–55), Sherman and other senators seemed intuitively to grasp the character of "good" versus "bad" restraints of trade; they went to great lengths to argue that the act would not rule out partnerships and other good combinations, nor would it penalize businessmen who were successful by virtue of their entrepreneurial skills. Similarly, Taft's *Addyston Pipe* decision shows an intuitive grasp of the importance of economic efficiency.

On the other hand, by the time of *Brown Shoe* and *Von's Grocery*, the Court seems to have lost this intuition. Indeed, regarding *Brown Shoe*, Bork (1978, 198) says:

The Court carried to drily logical extremes the notions of exclusionary practices, incipiency, and the social purpose of the antitrust laws. That this produced a result incompatible with any concern for competition appeared to bother the Court not at all.

In a word, the Court was more concerned with fairness than with efficiency, to the point that it signaled that it would prohibit any merger that it was asked to rule on.

One can argue that our static economic efficiency example is simplistic, that the real world is dynamic and risky and that a complete welfare analysis has to take this into account. Perhaps a deeper analysis would reveal that the Warren Court was promoting economic efficiency after all. This is indeed a valid objection and accords with some of the arguments made by Owen and Braeutigam (1978) that we considered in chapter 11, but it can be taken too far.

There are many arguments against a policy that too stringently prohibits mergers. For one, a common situation is an individual entrepreneur who in middle age finds himself with a profitable business built on expertise accumulated over many years. Should he die, the expertise dies with him, and the value of his firm will plummet. On the other hand, rivals can make use of his expertise and are approaching him to merge. A merger allows him to mix his equity and human capital with that of a larger firm. Should he merge and then die, his heirs would get stock in the larger firm, which would be worth considerably more than the value of his unmerged firm. As one entrepreneur told me, such a merger allowed him to "capitalize his equity." Mergers to "capitalize equity" depend on the freedom to merge without undue governmental interference. Denial of such mergers violates the "rewards should be proportional to contributions" variant of the Formal Principle and can be considered unfair.

But denial also impedes economic efficiency. If, for example, all mergers are prevented, the incentive to build a business and then "capitalize equity" will disappear. On the other hand, giving entrepreneurs the ability to merge stimulates the creation of liquid capital markets, thereby increasing incentives to start new ventures. The result is to cause resources to "flow to their highest valued uses."

## 20.6   Present-Day Merger Policy

During the last several decades, professional economists have had an increasing influence within the Department of Justice and the Federal Trade Commission, the two federal agencies charged with the responsibility of formulating antitrust policy and enforcing it. In 1984 they were instrumental in formulating the latest in a series of Department of Justice antitrust guidelines. We review these briefly here.[6]

The Hart-Scott-Rodino Act requires that an acquiring firm in a major merger must notify the Department of Justice and the Federal Trade Commission prior to the acquisition. One of these agencies then takes responsibility to evaluate the proposed merger, following a five-step protocol.

*Step 1:*  By means of the cartel concept test, define the market in which the merged firm will find itself. This test consists of imagining ever-expanding cartels until one is found that can profitably raise prices by 5 percent for a year. For example, if a cartel were formed of all of the Exxon stations in

Tucson and the cartel raised prices by 5 percent for a year, would the cartel still be profitable? If the answer is no, add all of Texaco stations to the hypothetical cartel and ask the same question. If the answer is still no, add all of the Chevron stations and ask the same question, and so forth. Eventually, the hypothetical cartel will have enough market power that the answer will be yes. This hypothetical cartel then defines the market.

*Step 2:* Using the Herfindahl-Hirschman Index (HHI), evaluate the postmerger market share and the change in HHI caused by the merger. The HHI is simply the sum of the squares of the market shares of all the firms in the market. So, if there are four firms with market shares of 10, 20, 30, and 40 percent, the HHI is $10^2 + 20^2 + 30^2 + 40^2 = 3000$. If the smallest and largest propose to merge, the postmerger HHI becomes $50^2 + 20^2 + 30^2 = 3800$ and the proposed merger would increase the HHI by 800. If the postmerger HHI is below 1,000, the merger will generally not be challenged. If it is above 1,800 and the change in HHI is 50, it generally will be challenged; if the change in HHI is above 100, it will certainly be challenged except in extraordinary circumstances. Here, "challenged" means that the government will deny the merger unless the outcome of steps 3 to 5 indicates that it should be allowed.

*Step 3:* Determine the ease of entry into the market. Entry is considered easy if, within twenty-four months, enough new capacity can be anticipated to be brought on line to make a 5 percent price rise unprofitable. If entry is sufficiently easy, the merger may be allowed.

*Step 4:* Analyze the possibility of collusion in the market should the merger be allowed. Evidence of collusion, explicit or implicit, will lessen the chances that the merger will be allowed.

*Step 5:* Analyze any remaining efficiency consequences of the merger. Is it possible that, in spite of failure to pass steps 1–4, efficiency gains not considered in steps 1–4 may be so overwhelming as to justify the merger?[7]

This is a bare-bones description of the guidelines. The interested reader can obtain a copy of the guidelines from the Department of Justice. Also, Breit and Elzinga (1989) excerpt main sections from the guidelines.

Significant is the absence from the guidelines of any discussion of "fairness," or protecting the small, worthy businessman in order to preserve "values." The guidelines are concerned mostly about curbing excessive market power in order to give competition a chance to do what it is supposed to do. However, perhaps because the guidelines were formulated during Republican administrations, they have been attacked as being too lenient toward allowing mergers and too favorable to big business and not sufficiently protective of small businesses. At bottom, we have a familiar conflict. On the one hand, we have the utilitarian view, captured currently by the guidelines, that overall benefits to society should be paramount; on the other hand, we have the individual rights view, captured by the fairness notion, that the small businessman is entitled to status quo property rights. It remains to be seen whether or not the guidelines can retain their emphasis on efficiency, to the almost total exclusion of the rights viewpoint.

**Exercises**

1. Upon passage of the Sherman Act in 1890, what was the dilemma facing the Supreme Court as regards the interpretation of the term *restraint of trade*?

2. Prior to the passage of the Sherman Act, how did American common law treat contracts or agreements wherein a group of firms agreed to fix prices for goods or services that they each provided?

3. Contrast and compare the terms *per se illegal* and *illegal by the rule of reason*.

4. What were the principal aims of the Clayton Act of 1914? What modification of the Clayton Act was contained in the Cellar-Kefauver Act of 1950?

5. Discuss the history of the Court's changing views with regard to the issue of the size of a firm and how its size was attained. Your discussion should consider the *Addyston Pipe* (1898) decision, the *Standard Oil* and *American Tobacco* decisions of 1911, the *Aluminum Corporation (ALCOA)* (1945) decision, and the *United Shoe* (1953) decision, as well as the *Brown Shoe* and *Von's Grocery* decisions of the 1960s.

6. The Warren Court is said to have introduced the "incipiency" doctrine into antitrust law. What is this doctrine? What were the consequences of its application in the *Brown Shoe* (1962) and *Von's Grocery* (1966) decisions? What was the consequence as regards the Warren Court's rulings on merger cases?

7. What is the main fairness controversy in U.S. antitrust law?

8. What are the Department of Justice guidelines for antitrust policy? Do they focus on economic efficiency or fairness?

# 21

**Attempts to Break out of the Regulatory Straitjacket, Fairly**

*When it comes to self-interest, you've got two basic options: you can mobilize it, or you can police it.*

Anonymous

## 21.1 Historical Setting

It is almost a century since the landmark 1898 *Smyth v. Ames* Supreme Court decision created "rate-of-return" regulation of public utilities (also called "cost-of-service" regulation). In the intervening years, rate-of-return (ROR) regulation has become more refined, detailed, and ritualistic; it has spawned an industry of attorneys and expert witnesses who specialize in serving it, as well as an army of critics who have pointed out its shortcomings and who have suggested reforms.

One of the perceived shortcomings of rate-of-return regulation has been its treatment of costs. Firms, regulated or unregulated, must plan as they face the future, and such plans must take into account *future* or *projected* cash outlays. Past cash outlays are of interest only insofar as they are useful for projecting future ones. To cite the example of chapter 2, if there is a sudden increase in gasoline prices from $1 to $2 per gallon, and if the $2 per gallon price is expected to persist, this is what a firm will use in projecting the costs of its car and truck fleet. The $1 per gallon price is history and of no consequence in the firm's plans.

In the face of rapid technological change, sudden changes in costs of raw materials, or changes in a utility company's demand patterns, history may be a poor guide for the projection of future costs. The high inflation of the 1970s led to regulators' being increasingly sympathetic to the use of "future test years" as the bases of establishing costs, and to some extent future projections were incorporated into the regulatory process.

Nonetheless, traditional rate-of-return regulation has had difficulties coping with sudden, radical cost changes and the associated speculative process of forecasting their consequences.

But this is only one of many problems. As was pointed out in chapter 14, rapid technological change and U.S. accounting practices can lead to woefully insufficiently rapid depreciation of the utility's plant, leaving the utility with rates that are far above those of rivals offering alternative, substitute services or products. Even in times of normal technological change, there may be honest differences of opinion between regulators and the utility as to proper depreciation rates, which can lead to endless and costly squabbling and bickering.

From a modern viewpoint, the problem with ROR is much more fundamental. Its viewpoint is "fairness" to ratepayers and shareholders, to be attained by expert, disinterested regulatory bodies acting solely in the public interest. It is thus a classic example of an attempt to apply the public interest theory of regulation, as discussed in chapter 13. Experience has shown that the public interest theory often does not work as planned for a simple reason; it ignores the fact that regulatory bodies are made up of human beings. Because of this fact, economists have increasingly embraced some variant of an interest group theory of regulation.

However, in telecommunications, policy makers have also increasingly rejected rate of return regulation and have begun intensive searches for something to replace it with; they have done so for two basic reasons. First is the breakup of AT&T and the partial deregulation of the telecommunications industry that followed. Second are the consequences of the three "order-of-magnitude" technological changes that led to the breakup, changes like the ones that revolutionized the structure of U.S. industry at the turn of the century—the digital revolution stemming from the invention of the transistor, the fiber optics revolution stemming from the invention of the laser, and the revolution in logical processes stemming from software development. In turn, these three technological breakthroughs have spawned the creation of an enormous infrastructure of computer programs and networks linking them, resulting in the gradual marriage of computing and telecommunications. The consequences will affect almost every aspect of human existence; it takes no great soothsayer to predict global, massive changes.

Policy-making groups that are particularly affected by these changes are state public utility regulators. Prior to the breakup of AT&T, national telecommunications policy was essentially formulated by a coalition of AT&T, the Federal Communications Commission (FCC), and the leadership of the National Association of Railroad and Utility Commissioners (NARUC). The NARUC leadership ostensibly represented state regulators in federal matters, leaving the states with relatively smaller issues to worry about.

The breakup created a new regulatory federalism. Each state, in concert with a few other states, suddenly found itself having to regulate a Regional Bell Operating Company (RBOC), one of the major U.S. corporations in its own right. What's more, because the RBOCs could go into nonregulated businesses, the regulatory problems were more complicated. On top of all this, the technology was changing at breakneck speed. Meanwhile, the state regulatory commission was usually expected to confront this whole new set of circumstances with the same, inadequate staff it always had. No wonder that many state regulatory commissions quickly started to search for a streamlined, more effective method of regulation! Some commissions have taken the lead and others have decided to take a wait-and-see stance, but the regulation of telecommunications is clearly entering a new phase.

## 21.2   Stakeholders

In chapter 19 we considered a long list of stakeholders in a traditional telecommunications rate case. As the technology changes with breathtaking speed, so does the list of stakeholders. At the time of this writing, cable television companies have shown an interest in invading telephone services, and vice versa. U. S. West and Telecommunications, Inc. (TCI) have already developed a successful joint venture in the United Kingdom that provides a combined telephone–cable television service to subscribers. But the "modified final judgment" (MFJ) that settled the AT&T antitrust suit and led to the AT&T breakup prohibits U.S. West and the other RBOCs from forming similar joint ventures in the United States, although most observers consider it a matter of time before this will be possible and before cable companies will be viable competitors for telephone business.

In addition, the RBOCs are all active in the cellular mobile telephone business, a business which, under the MFJ, they can engage in outside the area of their regulatory franchise. Thus, in many major cities the two cellular franchises that by FCC regulations are available are both owned or partially owned by an RBOC, one by the local RBOC and the other by a foreign RBOC. The same is true of terminal equipment (equipment on the customers' premises). The RBOCs cannot manufacture terminal equipment, but they can sell it, either within or without their jurisdiction; as a result, RBOCs are direct competitors in the terminal equipment business as well.

Thus, in telecommunications, local regulators are supposed to control a menagerie of stakeholders, while at the same time allowing the full benefits of unfettered competition to flow to the public. Theirs is not an easy job.

## 21.3   Fairness

If anything, the traditional charges and countercharges regarding cross-subsidization are heating up. At center stage is the charge that the franchised local telephone monopoly is using its regulated services to subsidize its nonregulated ones. At the same time, the perennial problem of cost determination has become harder. No longer is it only the issue of "fairly" allocating overhead costs and estimating problematic future, *planning* costs; regulators are having to cope with typical competitive pricing strategies: loss leaders and other forms of promotional pricing, price discrimination by volume or customer class, introduction of new products and services at a dizzying speed, and the formation of joint ventures, with new stakeholders continually appearing over the horizon. At the same time, the business stakeholders are busy demanding a "level playing field," while the "people's counsels" and customer groups continue to oppose any increases in prices of "basic" telephone services in order to protect the small ratepayer.

In a word, we have the standard, version 1.0 charges of excessive monopoly power and violation of the Formal Principle, but a new arena of fairness argumentation has appeared—jobs. No regulator wants to be charged with letting some other state siphon off jobs, and the states are eyeing each other nervously as they contemplate the emerging computing-cum-telecommunications world. A regulatory climate in state X which allows it to lose jobs to state Y will be viewed as being unfair to the workforce in state X.

This, then, is the background behind initiatives to replace traditional rate-of-return regulation of telecommunications.

## 21.4   Efficiency

From the normative standpoint, economists currently accept the normal, human motives of the players in the regulatory game, as cynical as this may sometimes seem, and set as their goal the design of regulatory mechanisms that, in the face of these motives, will attain societal goals as efficiently as possible. Ideally, such a mechanism should be fully "incentive-compatible"; in following their individual self-interests, all the players should be motivated to work toward the socially optimal outcome.

*Incentive-compatible* is a modern term, and a modern literature in regulatory economics has sprung up to implement and study the concept it conveys. However, the search for a more efficient alternative to rate-of-return regulation of natural monopolies is old. In his historical review of regulatory schemes, Schmalensee (1979, 68) points out that in 1848 John Stuart Mill discussed the theory of allowing firms to bid for a franchise to provide a natural monopoly service, and that, from 1826 to 1851 many French railroad franchises were awarded on the basis of competitive bids for the lowest fares. More recently, in the 1960s and early 1970s Demsetz, Stigler, and Posner all proposed franchised bidding schemes (Schmalensee 1979, 69).

The motivation for franchise bidding schemes is to encourage cost-minimizing behavior by the franchisee, and to cut the costs of regulation by streamlining it. A scheme that tries to do this is the automatic fuel adjustment contract for electric utilities, introduced in the United States in 1917, in common use in the 1920s (Schmalensee 1979, 110), and once again in vogue. Automatic fuel adjustment contracts recognize that a substantial cost to an electric power company is the cost of fuel, and that this will vary from time to time, beyond the utility's control. The regulators and the utility agree to forgo lengthy and expensive hearings to establish that a change in the price of fuel mandates a change in the electricity rates; instead, they agree to a formula that converts a fuel price change into changes in the utility's rates.

Franchise bidding schemes and fuel adjustment contracts are important, but, in this chapter, we concentrate on more recent developments in incentive-compatible regulation. The next section considers some theoretical developments, and the following section the recent implementation, in numerous jurisdictions, of various attempts at incentive compatible schemes to regulate telecommunications.

Theoretical Proposals for Alternatives to Rate-of-Return Regulation

Economists increasingly view regulation as a collection of principal-agent contracts. There are many ways that principal-agent relations enter into regulation. For example, a public interest theory of regulation would consider a regulatory body as a principal and the utility its agent, whereas an interest group theory of regulation might have the roles reversed, with the utility acting as the principal and the regulatory body acting as its agent.

While many important principal-agent relations occur in public utility regulation, the current theoretical literature has focused on modeling the regulator as the principal and the utility (or its management) as the agent. The literature accepts what is perceived to be a fundamental information asymmetry—the utility will typically have more information than its regulators, especially cost information, which it is in the utility's interest not to reveal. In the face of this information asymmetry, the literature tries to invent incentive-compatible regulatory schemes.

The number of invented theoretical mechanisms is large, and we can only consider three representative ones.[1] These are the Loeb and Magat (1979) scheme, which creates a subsidy to the utility based on consumers' surplus, the Vogelsang and Finsinger (1979) scheme, which theoretically drives the firm to Ramsey prices, and the Linhart-Radner scheme, (1992) which provides "price caps"—time-varying ceilings on the prices that the utility can charge.

Loeb and Magat's Subsidy Scheme

The Loeb and Magat (1979) scheme assumes that the regulators know only the utility's demand curves. To illustrate the scheme, consider first that (1) the utility produces only one product, (2) demand for this product is a straight line, and (3) the firm's marginal cost of producing this product is a constant value, as shown in figure 21.1a.

Suppose the firm charges the price, $p$, resulting in the consumers' surplus given by the triangle, $DAp$ in figure 21.1a. The Loeb-Magat proposal is the following: *Let the firm chose $p$, and have society pay the utility the consumers' surplus, $DAp$, as a subsidy.* Why is a subsidy desirable? Because the firm will

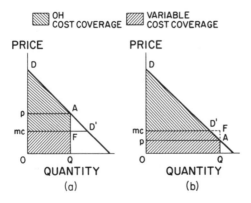

Figure 21.1
Loeb and Magat's subsidy scheme for incentive-compatible regulation

then have an incentive to set its price equal to marginal cost—the first-best, socially optimal value.

To see this, consider figures 21.1a and 21.1b. Here, as in chapter 13, we examine how the firm covers costs; in addition to "overhead coverage", I have introduced the concept of "variable cost coverage"—an amount of revenue available to cover the firm's variable costs. Because we are assuming constant marginal costs in each market, the required variable cost coverage is represented by the rectangle, $mcFQO$.

If price exceeds marginal cost, as in figure 21.1a, the firm has the entire trapezoidal area, $DAFmc$, available to cover its overhead—the rectangle $pAFmc$ from revenues and the triangle $DAp$ from the subsidy. If it decreases its price to $mc$, it still covers its variable costs but, because it receives all consumers' surplus as a subsidy, it increases its overhead coverage to the triangle $DD'mc$.

On the other hand, figure 21.1b shows the situation when the firm prices below marginal cost. Its overhead cost coverage is again the triangle $DD'mc$, but its variable cost coverage, $mcD'AQO$, is insufficient to cover the variable cost by the amount of the triangle $D'FA$. Thus, it will have to rob some funds from the overhead coverage triangle $DD'mc$ in order to cover its variable costs. Its best situation is when price is just at marginal cost; then variable costs are completely covered, overhead coverage is at a maximum, and nothing must be taken from it to help cover variable costs. At this point, the reader may feel that the Loeb-Magat (1979) scheme is ridiculous—the subsidy simply heaps undeserved profits on the utility. Of course, Loeb and Magat recognize this and suggest two methods of bringing utility's profits in line.

The first method is to put the utility up for auction. If each bidder is equally well informed, each will realize that, should it be the winning bidder, it will want to set price equal to marginal cost and each will be able to calculate the maximum subsidy. Presumably, the auction will cause the bids to rise until the winning bid is such that, including the subsidy, the firm will just break even. The result will then be that the firm will charge the first-best price but will make no excess profit. Note that although we have considered the case of a single product, the result is the same for a multiproduct regulated firm, which would price at marginal cost in each of its markets.

The second method is to have the regulator give the firm only a portion of the consumers' surplus as a subsidy. For example, in figure 21.1a, the regulators could subtract from the total consumers' surplus, $DD'mc$, the upper triangle, $DAp$, giving the firm the trapezoidal area, $pAD'mc$, as a subsidy. Ideally, the amount of the subsidy decrement would be adjusted so that the net subsidy just covered the firm's overhead and the firm was regulated to make a zero economic profit. In theory, because only the decrement and not the total subsidy was preset, the firm would still be motivated to maximize the total consumers' surplus from which the decrement was to be subtracted. This would once again induce the firm to set price at marginal cost and would result in a first-best solution.

The Vogelsang-Finsinger Adjustment-to-Ramsey-Prices Scheme

Imagine, in period 0, that a natural monopoly is totally unregulated and that it sets its prices so as to reap maximum profits. At the beginning of Period 1 it is suddenly regulated. The regulators assume that it is impossible for them to get the firm to produce accurate cost projections. On the other hand, the firm's costs in period 0 are a matter of record, as are its outputs. So the regulators issue an edict to the firm: *On the assumption that your last year's outputs and costs will not change, lower your prices so that you make zero economic profit.*

The firm immediately observes that, when it lowers its prices, outputs and thus costs will in fact increase and not stay the same (of course, the regulators know this, too), so it does not simply lower all prices proportionately in order to satisfy the regulators' edict. Instead, it chooses the new prices so that they maximize profit in the face of the regulators' edict.

At the end of period 1, the regulators audit the firm and find that its economic profits are still positive, so, at the beginning of period 2, the regulators issue the same edict. The processes is iterated period after period until it converges to a set of prices that result in zero economic profit.

Geometrically, we can understand the Vogelsang-Finsinger (1979) scheme by considering figures like those discussed in chapters 13 for the case of two services whose demands are linear and independent. In this case, it is easily shown that an unregulated, profit-maximizing monopolist would operate at the midpoint of the line segment $DD'$ along a straight-line demand schedule. That is, the monopoly output in each market will be one-half the output when price is at marginal cost. If we denote the monopoly outputs in the two markets as $Q_1^M$, $Q_2^M$ and the output when price is at marginal cost as $Q_1^{mc}$, $Q_2^{mc}$, then we have $Q_1^M = Q_1^{mc}/2$, $Q_2^M = Q_2^{mc}/2$, as shown in figure 21.2.

Suppose that in period 0 the monopolist operates as if it were unregulated, with the result that its prices in the two markets are $p_1^0$ and $p_2^0$, with associated outputs $Q_1^{mc}/2$ and $Q_2^{mc}/2$. In period 1, in response to the regula-

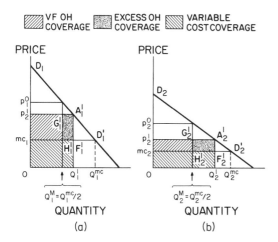

**Figure 21.2**
Vogelsang-Finsinger adjustment to Ramsey prices scheme for incentive compatible regulation

tors edict at the end of period 0, the regulated firm lowers prices so that its overhead coverage, based on *period 0's outputs*, will just cover its overhead. Call such overhead coverage "Vogelsang-Finsinger overhead coverage", labeled "VF overhead coverage" in figures 21.2a and 21.2b, and indicated by the cross-hatched rectangles, $p_1^1 G_1^1 H_1^1 mc_1$ and $p_2^1 G_2^1 H_2^1 mc_2$. However, the firm has an infinite set of period 1 prices that will generate a VF overhead coverage that equals overhead; Vogelsang and Finsinger assume that it will pick the set that will maximize its profit.

In terms of figure 21.2, the actual, profit-maximizing overhead coverage at prices $p_1^1$ and $p_2^1$ will exceed the VF overhead coverage. The result will be will be an excess, indicated by the dotted rectangles in figures 21.2a and 21.2b, $G_1^1 A_1^1 F_1^1 H_1^1$ and $G_2^1 A_2^1 F_2^1 H_2^1$, and a positive economic profit. This will result in another edict from the regulators and a further lowering of prices such that a new VF overhead coverage will just cover the overhead, calculated on the assumption that outputs and costs are price insensitive. If the result is once again a positive economic profit, the process will be repeated, and so on.

For the special case we are considering, it is easily shown that the outputs, market by market, at every stage will be in proportion to the outputs when price equals marginal cost, market by market.[2] The end result in the two markets will thus be outputs proportional to the respective price-equals-marginal cost outputs and prices that yield overhead coverages that just cover the actual overhead. But, as the discussion in chapter 13 shows, these are just the Ramsey prices!

Vogelsang and Finsinger (1979) show that the result we obtain in a special case is general: starting with any set of prices that yield an excess economic profit, if regulators issue the regulators' edict and *continue* to issue it stage after stage, the regulated firm's prices *will converge to Ramsey prices*.

## The Linhart-Radner "Price Cap" Scheme

Both the Loeb-Magat (1979) and Vogelsang-Finsinger (1979) schemes have as their goal the attainment of static, first- or second-best prices; both theoretical models underlying the schemes are deterministic and take no account of risk or chance events. By contrast, the Linhart-Radner (1992) theory, couched in a dynamic, uncertain world does not take as its goal the attainment of static economic efficiency. Instead, it assumes that regulators are interested primarily in a continual reduction of real (inflation-adjusted) prices, rather than the attainment of static economic efficiency. However, in common with the Loeb-Magat and Vogelsang-Finsinger models, the Linhart-Radner model assumes the firm has information about its demands and costs that is not available to the regulator.

Linhart and Radner (1992) explicitly put the problem in a principal-agent framework, with a hypothetical regulator as the principal and a hypothetical manager of the utility as the agent; they make several idealizations and simplifications to make the theory tractable. The regulator is assumed to focus on a *weighted index* of the utility's prices and to have as goal the control of prices over time. As the principal, the regulator wishes to constrain real prices so that they continually decrease, yet not so rapidly that the firm has no incentive to innovate and cut costs. A reasonable price rate of change is the inflation rate minus the rate of expected productivity increase by the firm, perhaps determined by extrapolation from the past or by comparison with technologically-similar industries.

Linhart and Radner (1992) point out several attractive features of their proposed regulatory scheme:

- For customers, real prices decline over time.

- For the utility, pricing flexibility is increased because its prices are not regulated, service by service; the regulators only monitor the weighted index of prices. Also, the utility has the chance to earn more than it would under ROR, but at the risk of earning less.

- For the regulators, the incentives for the utility to cut costs and to innovate are improved.

Linhart and Radner's formal model of their scheme has the manager's utility depend both on the wage the manager receives and on the actions that the manager takes, reflecting the likelihood that the manager may get satisfaction from more than just monetary compensation. A key simplification is the existence of a *cash reserve*, into which flow all of the firm's profits and out of which are paid all of the firm's expenses. Another key assumption is that the firm's productivity gain depends not only on the manager's actions but also on random factors beyond the manager's control. Finally, it is assumed that the utility must meet its franchise obligation to serve all demand.

Linhart and Radner (1992) make a drastic assumption: should the cash reserve become *negative, the manager is fired.* The manager is assumed to know this and also to know that, because the firm's productivity over time will be partly a matter of chance, so will be the manager's expected tenure. In the face of these facts, the manager is assumed to maximize the *expected discounted utility for the duration of the manager's tenure,* where the discount rate is the personal time value of money.

What happens when the cash reserve goes negative and the manager is dismissed? Linhart and Radner assume that, in effect, the firm goes into a form of bankruptcy; its "price cap" regime is then suspended for a fixed length of time, called the "recovery phase" (a period when the price caps are in effect is called an "incentive phase"). During the recovery phase, the regulators set the firm's profit per period so that, at the end of the recovery phase, the cash reserve is built up to its initial value.

These, then, are the basic ingredients of the Linhart-Radner (1992) model. Although it is a highly idealized version of how an actual price cap scheme works, it is still mathematically nontrivial, with both the cash reserve and the evolution of price varying randomly over time. Nonetheless, Linhart and Radner are able to prove two important theorems, both having to do with events when the manager's discount rate approaches zero:

1. As the manager's discount rate approaches zero, the expected value of the interval between bankruptcies approaches infinity;

2. As the manager's discount rate approaches zero, the realized long-term average rate of real (inflation-adjusted) price-decrease approaches the regulator's target rate.

Put in other terms, if the manager is sufficiently patient (has a very low discount rate), the likelihood of bankruptcy (entering a recovery phase) will be very small, and there is a high likelihood that the regulator's targeted real price decreases will be closely met. Thus the theoretical implications of the Linhart-Radner model are positive; they indicate that price cap regulation will work as desired and reinforce the intuition behind it.

## 21.5    Implemented Alternatives to Rate-of-Return Regulation in Telecommunications

A detailed review of all of the efforts to replace rate-of-return regulation in telecommunications is beyond our scope, especially since new initiatives are currently under consideration throughout the United States. I can only sketch some of the main developments at both the federal and state levels.

FCC Price Cap Regulation of AT&T

In 1989 the FCC abandoned rate-of-return regulation of AT&T in favor of keeping AT&T's rates bounded from both below and above. Lower bounds were to keep AT&T, ruled to be the "dominant firm" in the long-distance telecommunications industry, from undercutting smaller rivals by means of predatory pricing. Upper bounds, or price caps, were to provide the "incentive-compatibility" advantages enumerated in our above discussion of the Linhart-Radner scheme. Regulation-by-formula largely replaced previous lengthy, tedious and expensive regulatory proceedings. Whereas, in the past it might take over a year to effect a rate change, proposed new rates that conform to the formulas become effective in fourteen days.

Although the new form of regulation greatly streamlines the regulatory process, it is still far from simple.[3] AT&T's services are grouped into four separate "service baskets": residential and small business services, toll-free "800" services, business services (WATS, private lines, software-defined networks, and other services aimed at the large business market), and specialty services. Price cap regulation is not used for specialty services; they continue to be regulated as before.

For the other three service baskets, the conceptual starting point of the FCC's price cap regulation of AT&T is that of the Linhart-Radner theory. By formula, prices are periodically adjusted upward to take account of inflation and downward to take account of productivity gains. Each of the three service baskets has its own "price cap index" (PCI)—a weighted index of prices of services within the basket, weighted by the fraction each component service contributes to the entire basket's revenue. The gross national product (GNP) price index is used to measure inflation. At its inception in 1989, the downward adjustment for productivity was set at three percent, based on AT&T's historic productivity growth of 2.5 percent plus an additional 0.5 percent incentive inducement (called a "consumer dividend"). At the time of this writing, the downward adjustment remains at 3 percent. At least once a year, AT&T is required to calculate an "actual price index" (API), which reflects changes in prices and changes in weights that have occurred; the API must not exceed the PCI.

There are additional restrictions as well. Each individual service's rates must conform to a "service band index" (SBI). This is a $\pm 5$ percent band around the PCI for the service basket of which the individual service is a component. For example, if individual service $X$ is in service basket $N$, whose PCI increases by 2 percent, then the price change for service $X$ must be no greater than $+7$ percent and no less than $-3$ percent.

This is a bare-bones description of the FCC's price cap scheme for AT&T. More details can be found in Mitchell and Vogelsang (1991, 167–175, 264–285). Also, Beesley and Littlechild (1989) discuss the theory behind a British version of price cap regulation of telecommunications, as well as the history of its implementation.

Alternatives to ROR at the State Level

At the time of this writing, with the exception of North Carolina and Massachusetts, every state in the contiguous forty-eight has either adopted some alternative to ROR in regulating telecommunications or is contemplating it. The alternatives come in myriad flavors and varieties but consist of three basic forms: (1) a cap on prices, sometimes in the form of a cap on a price index, similar to the FCC scheme of regulating long-distance telephone, (2) a sharing by the customers and the firm of the firm's earnings, and (3) a "social contract" wherein the regulators freeze the prices of certain services, usually "basic" or "essential" services , and additionally, require that the firm invest sufficient new funds to maintain quality of service; in return, the regulators give the firm flexibility on how it prices its competitive services.

Tardiff and Taylor (1993) argue that not all of these alternatives can be regarded as incentive-compatible replacements for traditional rate-of-return regulation because not all increase the firm's incentives to operate more efficiently. In particular, of the alternatives listed above, they classify only earnings sharing, caps on a price index, and Nebraska's almost complete deregulation as incentive-compatible schemes. Figure 21.3 shows the states in the contiguous 48 that have adopted one of these schemes as of September 1993.[4]

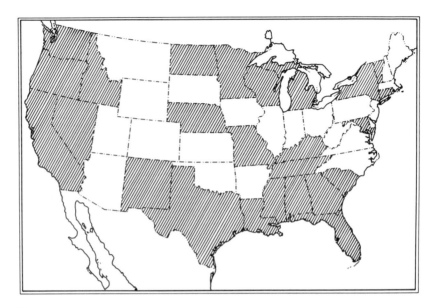

**Figure 21.3**
States (shown shaded) that have adopted some form of incentive-compatible regulation of local telephone service

## 21.6   Discussion

Incentive-compatible regulation is an idea whose time seems to have come —at least for the regulation of telecommunications. Nevertheless, despite recent, very promising experience, history suggests caution. Automatic fuel adjustment contracts were in vogue during the 1920s, only to fade away during the Great Depression, when they led to rate reductions regulators would not accept. More recently, the four-year price cap regulation of Tucson Electric Power has ended in public outcries that consumers have been fleeced, in public demands for retribution, and with Tucson Electric Power teetering on the verge of bankruptcy (Isaac 1991).[5]

As the Isaac case study of Tucson Electric Power brings out, a basic problem is the commitment a regulatory body can make, given that its membership changes over time and is subject to political pressures. Chance events beyond the control of either regulators or utility managers may sour what appeared to be a marvelous win-win agreement between them. Looking back several years later, new regulators and new stakeholders, with no personal memory of the agreement and with no commitment to it, may undo it; even worse, they may seize the political opportunity to pillory predecessor regulators for having allegedly succumbed to the utility's monopoly power.

Perhaps the differences between regulation and free-market competition are so basic that it is naive to think that a regulatory scheme can be devised that will have the incentive compatibility characteristics of competition and, at the same time, be immune to the usual strategic uses of fairness arguments in order for stakeholders to gain political advantage. On the other hand, the infirmities of standard rate-of-return regulation are so great that alternative, incentive-compatible schemes can be quite imperfect and still represent a marked improvement.[6]

## Exercises

1. Discuss the forces that are causing regulators to increasingly examine new, more incentive-compatible schemes of regulating public utilities, especially telephone utilities.

2. Discuss the fairness controversies in rate of return regulation? What new factors are influencing the treatment of these controversies?

3. Is "incentive-compatible" regulation a new idea? What are some examples of its earlier application?

4. Describe the Loeb-Magat (1979) regulatory scheme.

5. Describe the Vogelsang-Finsinger (1979) regulatory scheme.

6. Describe the Linhart-Radner (1992) regulatory scheme.

# 22

Social Regulation: A
Medley of the Power of
the Media, Efficiency,
Utilitarianism, and
Individual Rights

*On 20 January, the Democrats become the sole heirs to a phenomenon of regulation gone*
*amok. In April 1992, 59 regulatory agencies with about 125,000 employees were at work*
*on 4,186 pending regulations. The cost during 1991 of mandates already in place has been*
*estimated at $542 billion. The fastest growing component of costs is environmental regula-*
*tions, which amounted to $115 billion in 1991 but are slated to grow by more than 50*
*percent in constant dollars by the year 2000.*

Philip H. Abelson (editorial in *Science*, 8 January 1993)

## 22.1 Background

The 1970s brought the creation of four major new federal regulatory
bodies—the Environmental Protection Agency (EPA) in 1970, the National Highway Traffic Safety Administration in 1970, the Consumer Product Safety Commission in 1972, and the Occupational Safety and Health
Administration (OSHA) in 1973. In two important ways, these new major
bodies contrasted with the regulatory commissions created during the New
Deal. First, they did not focus on the "economic" regulation of prices,
quantities, quality, or entry/exit typical of public utility regulation and of
the New Deal regulatory agencies; instead, they focused on desirable social
outcomes in health, safety, and the environment. Second, they were not
designed to be a committee of regulators setting broad policy and playing
a combined legislative-judicial-executive role; instead, except for the Consumer Product Safety Commission, they were all headed by a single person
given strong police powers to enforce explicit and detailed congressional
mandates.[1] As many have observed, the result of the creation of these
agencies, as well as other social regulation at the state and federal level, has
been an explosion in social regulation (by comparison to the $542 billion
cited by Abelson in the above quote, in 1993 annual medicare and social
security expenditures were at $116 and $285 billion respectively[2]).

This explosion has caused new social regulation to swamp the deregulation in New Deal agencies begun under President Carter, with the result that regulation's fraction of the economy continues to grow. It has also given rise to a countermovement; many scientists and policy makers argue that much of the social regulation is not only expensive, but arbitrary, inconsistent, and irrational. For example, in the 1993 editorial cited above, Abelson refers to a Columbus, Ohio study chaired by Edward Hayes of Ohio State University:

[Hayes] cited the Safe Drinking Water Act, which requires that at least 133 specified pollutants be monitored. Many of the substances are not present in significant quantities in Ohio. In other instances, mandated regulatory levels are extremely tight. He cited the herbicide Atrazine. Although its average level at water intakes is far below 3 parts per billion, the city may be required to install "best available technology" for Atrazine removal at a cost of $80 million for each of two surface water plants. Hayes has stated that the action level is 3 parts per billion because the effects of massive doses to rats are extrapolated to infinitesimal doses in humans, and regulators included a thousandfold factor of safety. If the factor of safety were set at 100, then a major uncertainty would be removed, and Columbus would be more free to address real health problems in the community.

And, of course, the standard example of irrationality cited in the literature is the Delaney Clause in the 1960 Food Additive Amendment to the Food and Drug Act. This federal law mandates that *any* food additive found to cause cancer in laboratory animals cannot be used in foods. It applies regardless of how minute the amount of the additive. Also, the cancer test calls for feeding animals massive doses of the additive, and the relationship of animal tests of this sort to causes of cancers in humans is not clear.

In this chapter we consider some of the effects that have contributed to the explosion in social regulation. Most of these we have already met in earlier chapters, but social regulation is unique in that it is impacted by a such a wide variety of them—the rare-event scale effect; the Formal Principle; the influence of the media in distorting reality, causing a distorted application of the Formal Principle; and the profound ethical problems of balancing social benefits and individual rights when human lives are at stake. The chapter also tries to illustrate the application of Peltzman's (1976) theory of regulation, first, by applying the theory to a particular regulatory controversy—the regulation of swimming pools in Tucson, Arizona—and then by generalizing it.

## 22.2  Stakeholders

The stakeholders in a typical controversy involving social regulation are numerous. First of all are the professional advocacy groups, "Nader's

Raiders," the Sierra Club, the Environmental Defense Fund, and the like. Then we have the businesses that will either win or lose because of a particular social regulation. If the regulation mandates the installation of specialized new equipment, for example, scrubbers to reduce sulfur dioxide emissions of coal-burning electric power plants, manufacturers of the mandated environmental or safety equipment will obviously benefit. If the scrubbers are mandated on *all* coal-burning plants, regardless of whether they are use low- or high-sulfur coal, and thus whether they need the scrubbers or not, an unnecessary cost will be imposed on users of low-sulfur coal. This in turn will raise the price of energy in these regions, giving a competitive edge to industries in the high-sulfur coal regions.[3] Of course, the political opportunities for championing clean air, a clean environment, or increased safety are great, and we can expect politicians to become major stakeholders in social regulation. Finally, there are the consumers or groups of consumers who find themselves in the same situation. These may, of course, have interests that are quite different from the professed "consumer" groups that claim to represent them.

## 22.3   Fairness

The theoretical debate regarding utilitarianism and individual rights comes to center stage in health and safety regulation. The mainstream view in the economics literature seems to be that society should maximize expected-benefits-less-expected-costs, a variant of utilitarianism.[4] A standard argument, of course, is that society de facto has taken a utilitarian view; it routinely makes trade-offs that involve the risk of human lives,[5] and the notion that society should pursue perfect safety is a charade. If society actually had perfect safety as its goal, we would be immobilized, as we saw Harsanyi (1976) point out in chapter 9.

Nonetheless, the objection to utilitarianism that it ignores individual rights or, more generally, distributional equity is fundamental and deep.[6] Also, Broome (1978, 92) has forcefully argued that the usual benefit-cost methodology fails where a life is at stake, "[f]or no finite amount of money could compensate a person for the loss of his life, simply because money is no good to him when he is dead."

The mainstream economists' utilitarian goal of maximizing expected-benefits-minus-expected-costs will not make the objections to utilitarianism disappear; indeed, for the politician, the utilitarian view is dangerous. Policy makers who adopt it may come through as crassly ignoring individual rights and distributional equity.

This is brought out in the recent court case regarding General Motors (GM) "side-saddle" gas tanks on some of its panel trucks, tanks that can explode when the trucks are hit broadside. Walter Olson (1993) argues that the GM panel truck was not a particularly dangerous vehicle; on average, passenger cars and light pickup trucks experience more annual fatal crashes than does the GM panel truck. However, the news accounts I heard implied that GM was accused of willfully refusing to recall 5 million of such trucks because the cost of retrofitting new, safer gas tanks would have been between $0.5 and $1.0 billion. Allegedly, GM cost analysts had concluded that it was cheaper to accept the costs of negotiating settlements and litigating in the estimated few cases that would involve a fatality or serious injury. A utilitarian analyst who used the usual "cost-of-life" estimates in the economics literature of $2 to $10 million could easily come to such a conclusion.[7] The jury evidently felt otherwise. It awarded the plaintiff suing GM $4.2 million damages, which is indeed within the range inferred from cost-of-life studies; but it also awarded $101 million in punitive damages for a total of $105.2M.[8]

To the utilitarian analyst working in the world of probabilities and expected benefits and costs, individuals are abstractions to be lumped together into aggregates. But to a jury, the individual victim in a wrongful death case is far from an abstraction and has rights, explicit or inferred. The plaintiff's attorney will be sure to spell out in detail the victim's life aspirations and career possibilities in a life that is not to be. In the face of the commonly held view that the value of a human life is infinite, the utilitarian calculations of a benefit-cost analysis may seem cynical and even outrageous.

In a recent issue of *Regulation*, Belzer (1991) has reviewed risk assessment as practiced by the federal government. To say the least, the practice seems to be unsystematic, reflecting the confusion and lack of consensus in the perennial debate about utilitarianism versus individual rights; great stress is put on calculating "worst cases" or "upper bounds," and attempts are made to calculate effects on the "maximum exposed individual." All this clearly reflects a Rawlsian view and an attempt to take individual rights into account.

At the same time, in the same issue, Nichols (1991) points out that in its application of technology-based approaches, the EPA looks at cost, "although primarily in terms of potential economic impacts (particularly plant closures and job losses) rather than in terms of resources" (p. 87); he goes on to say:

Thus, the financial health of the industry in question becomes a key factor. Costly standards can be imposed on industries that are in robust financial condition or that can easily pass on costs. Industries that are less financially secure and less likely to withstand cost increases are generally subject to less stringent standards. (p. 87)

Thus the federal government's approach is neither strictly Rawlsian nor utilitarian, but a stew of approaches. We should not be surprised; a simple policy administered by expert civil servants according to formula would make politicians appear like they are abandoning their responsibilities. A utilitarian calculus might indicate that nothing needs be done, where an individual rights view might indicate immediate action, thus making the policy maker appear to refuse to act when action seems called for. More important, acting when the public perception is that action is called for is an opportunity that few politicians wish to pass up.

Given the peculiar circumstances of safety regulation, we might expect a political bias toward overreaction rather than underreaction. This is in fact Mashaw's (1979) claim:

One is often struck by the discontinuity between the evidence of social and economic malaise upon which legislatures operate and the way the legislatures define the problems they address. The evidence is usually specific, limited, even anecdotal, but the problem as defined is general. If a toxic fog appears in Pennsylvania, the problem, as defined, is somehow not that a toxic fog appeared in Pennsylvania, but air pollution control. If Corvairs are unsafe, the problem is motor vehicle safety. If a drug manufacturer in North Carolina markets an otherwise safe compound in a toxic solvent, the problem is pharmaceutical safety. (p. 44)

In Mashaw's terms, no one is a better position than politicians to satisfy the public's demand that "there oughta be a law" and to benefit from satisfying it.[9]

## 22.4   Efficiency: Toward a Positive Theory of Social Regulation

The above discussion shows a state of confusion. On the one hand, it is clear that society routinely makes trade-offs where human life is at stake—riskier occupations command higher salaries; legislatures routinely refuse to pass the tough drunk-driving laws common in Europe, even though such laws could reduce the number of fatal automobile accidents; and safety devices that are "too expensive" are routinely not mandated.

On the other hand, the trade-offs that society makes are far from systematic. If we had a rational utilitarian policy, the number of dollars expended to save one additional life would be the same for all programs, but in this regard, the government's programs are wildly inconsistent. For example,

Niskanen (1991, 13) points out that, in regulating carcinogens, the EPA currently imposes costs of over $100 million per statistical life saved while, at the same time, changes could be made in highway design that would cost less than $1 million per statistical life saved.

What is going on? We try to get a handle on the answer by analyzing a specific example—the passage of a recent ordinance in Tucson, Arizona, to childproof swimming pools. We use a public choice framework, specifically, Peltzman's (1976) theory of regulation that we considered in chapter 14. After we consider the example, we generalize it to the beginnings of a positive theory of social regulation and draw some implications from it.

Tucson's Childproofing Swimming Pool Ordinance

Because of its hot summers, Tucson, Arizona has a high density of residential swimming pools, which leads to a certain number of toddler drownings. The evidence is that a leading cause of toddler drownings is adult negligence, often exacerbated by alcohol. For example, beer in hand, the adults go indoors to watch the final innings of a baseball game; a toddler is overlooked, left at poolside unminded, and falls into the pool. In 1987, eleven toddlers under the age of six drowned in Tucson, and the following year the Tucson Town Council decided to act, appointing a blue-ribbon citizens' committee to study the matter.

After eighteen months of deliberation, the majority of the committee recommended that a childproofing ordinance be adopted that would require residential pools to be separately fenced with a fence that met minimum specifications and had a "self-locking gate."[10] Many residents, as well as the editors of the *Tucson Citizen*, were skeptical that the fences would be effective. Indeed, some argued that a fence would give a false sense of security and would undermine parental vigilance, the best toddler drowning preventive.[11] It became clear that owners of the 30,000 existing residential pools would strongly oppose an ordinance that applied retroactively and would appear in force at the public hearing for the ordinance. As a result, the ordinance was drafted to apply only to new pools to be built in the future; existing pools were exempted ("grandfathered"). This calmed the tempers of present owners of swimming pools, the hearing on the ordinance was relatively uncontroversial, and the Tucson Town Council quickly passed the ordinance.

During the proceedings, local newspapers brought out the fact that in 1989, a year in which Tucson had six toddler drownings, Phoenix, which is three times the size, had fourteen.[12] However, only twelve of the Phoenix drownings were in swimming pools. The other two were the result of toddlers falling into toilets. In neither Tucson nor Phoenix was there any movement toward adopting an ordinance requiring the childproofing of existing or future toilets.

If the main cause of toddler drownings is parental negligence, we can model the above situation by analogy with the model of student cheaters considered in chapter 5. That is, assume that in a population of $n$ parents with toddlers there is a small fraction who are negligent. If a sample of size $m$ is drawn from the population of $n$, we can expect that the probability of drawing at least one negligent parent will follow a law like the probability of a department drawing at least one cheater in chapter 5. Thus, if $n$ is the number of parents in Arizona who have toddlers and $m$ is the number in a given town, in a given year we can expect the probability of toddler drowning to be negligible in very small towns, where $m$ is small, and close to unity in very large towns, where $m$ is large. Because a toddler drowning is typically front page news, we can accordingly expect that toddler drownings will receive a disproportionate amount of publicity in large towns compared to very small ones.

If we combine this observation with that of chapter 15—the probability of a rare event that receives a lot of media attention tends to be over-estimated—we get a compound effect. If a town is sufficiently large, it is almost certain to suffer a bad rare event, and, the bad rare event will generate publicity that makes such events seem more likely than they really are. For a large town the result is a both a political opportunity, if properly exploited, and a potential political booby trap, if ignored.

To model this, following Peltzman (1976), assume that the policy makers' (in this case the town fathers') goal is to take actions that will maximize the number of the next election's favorable votes, $M$, given by

$$M = \rho - v, \tag{22.1}$$

where $\rho$ is the probable or expected number of positive votes and $v$ is the expected number of negative votes. In the case at hand, the Tucson town fathers had three main policy options available, $\Pi_i$, $i = 1, 2, 3$, each with different effects on $M$: $\Pi_1$—accept the blue-ribbon committee's recommendation and adopt an ordinance that would require childproof fences for all existing and future pools; $\Pi_2$—reject the blue-ribbon committee's recommendation and do nothing; and $\Pi_3$—adopt a childproofing ordinance that applies only to future pools. Policy option $\Pi_1$—accept the committee's recommendation—would generate the perceived benefit that the risk of a toddler drowning was greatly reduced but would heap large costs on present owners of swimming pools. Presumably this policy option would increase the probability of a positive vote by voters who do not own swimming pools, the overwhelming majority, but at the risk of generating organized opposition and a large, concentrated negative vote.

Likewise, policy option $\Pi_2$—do nothing—would generate the perception that the Town Council had, for the foreseeable future, forgone the possibility of saving toddlers' lives, which would cause many voters in favor of Policy Option $\Pi_1$ to switch from a positive to a negative vote but might leave present pool owners neutral. Policy option $\Pi_3$—adopt an ordinance that applies only to the future—stands somewhere between policy options $\Pi_1$ and $\Pi_2$. By adopting it, the Town Council appears to have done something positive to reduce the probability of toddler drownings, while, at the same time, forgoing the perceived benefit of childproofing present pools, thereby incurring some negative votes. On the other hand, it avoids heaping such costs on present swimming pool owners that they are incited to organize an opposition.

To formalize the above discussion, let $B(\Pi_i)$ be the *perceived* benefit of the removal of the risk of a toddler's drowning and $B_F(\Pi_i)$ the perceived forgone benefit, should the Town Council choose not to require childproofing of existing pools. For simplicity, assume that the perceived benefit and forgone benefits have the same value, $B$. Then $B(\Pi_i) = B$, $B_F(\Pi_i) = 0$ for $i = 1$, and $B(\Pi_i) = 0$, $B_F(\Pi_i) = B$ for $i = 2, 3$.

Further, let $\kappa$ be the cost of childproofing a swimming pool, $k$ the number of existing pools, and $A$ the extent of organized opposition to the ordinance. Assume that each of these variables will also be functions of the policy chosen, $\Pi_i$, with the level of $A$ in turn depending on the magnitude of $\kappa k$. Thus, in summary, equation 22.1 becomes

$$M = \rho(B, B_F, \kappa, k, A) - v(B, B_F, \kappa, k, A), \tag{22.2}$$

where each argument is assumed to be a function of the policy choices available, $\Pi_i$.

## Generalization of the Example

In both the example of student cheating and toddler drownings I have had human fallibility at the root of the occurrence of a rare event that led to a regulatory response. But, of course, the regulatory response can be the result of an act of nature or, as Mashaw stresses, the result of analogizing from similar events. Electricity near a swimming pool leading to an electrocution immediately brings up the general possibility that electricity near water can lead to electrocution. The prudent policy maker takes special precautions to ground electric outlets not only near swimming pools, but in kitchens, bathrooms, utility rooms, and in damp basements, *before* electrocutions occur. The point is that the discussion of section II applies, before the fact, to the forestalling of rare events as well as, after the fact, to the prevention of the repeat of incidents with bad consequences.

In particular we can expect the rare-event scale effect discussed in section II to apply before as well as after the fact. Thus, it is hardly surprising that much of the work of the new federal health, safety and environmental agencies consists of formulating detailed specifications of standards to be met by all manner of equipments in order to forestall the occurrence of bad events. Likewise, we can expect that the larger the corporation, the more assiduously it will conform to government mandates and standards regarding social regulation. Should a bad event occur because of violation of governmental mandates, the consequences in terms of large tort awards can be horrendous.

Moreover, at stake are not only the interests of the policy makers in maximizing votes. There are also the interests of the manufacturers of safety devices and equipments. In the case of the childproofing Tucson swimming pools, the fencing firms obviously had a lot at stake. Perhaps because this was so obvious, these firms did not actively campaign to fence existing pools.

According to the theory sketched above, vendors of a safety device will be successful in having use of their device mandated only if it is cheap enough. Thus at present there is no initiative to childproof toilet bowls to prevent toddlers from falling into them, but should someone invent a cheap childproofing device, it might be mandated. In the case of Tucson swimming pools, a childproofing device that was perceived to be effective and cost $20/pool might easily have been mandated for existing pools, where a fence costing at least $1,000/pool was not.

Likewise in the case of grounding of electrical appliances and fixtures, we have seen a number of mandates over the years. An example is the electrical code for plugs and wall receptacles. In the 1930s most cities mandated receptacles that would accept male plugs with two prongs of unequal width, with the wide prong connecting to ground. This design had the disadvantage that amateur electricians could easily interchange the ground and hot connections in a receptacle, with potentially disastrous results. The three-pronged plug-receptacle arrangement minimized this possibility and was soon mandated for kitchens, bathrooms and generally near a source of water, and subsequently mandated everywhere. Most recently, advances in solid-state chip technology have led to the development of the ground-fault-interrupt receptacle, which continuously checks that the currents in the hot and grounded legs of a circuit are the same, and trips a built-in circuit breaker when they are not. When the cost of the ground-fault-interrupt receptacle came down to about $10, it became mandated in most cities for bathrooms and kitchens. As its cost decreases further, it will undoubtedly be mandated for all rooms in a residence. Most importantly for the theory outlined here, each of these successive improvements was mandated for *new* construction only.

All of the above generalizations are easily incorporated into the formal model. Instead of three options, policy makers will typically have many, say $\Pi_i$, $i = 1, k$. Policy makers generalizing, either before or after the fact, to a class of possible bad events can be modeled by assigning subscripts to the arguments of the expected numbers of positive and negative votes, $\rho$ and $v$ in equation 22.2, which can be rewritten as

$$M = \rho(B_j, B_{Fj}, \kappa_j, k_j, A_j) - v(B_j, B_{Fj}, \kappa_j, k_j, A_j), j = 1, J, \tag{22.3}$$

where $J$ is the number of bad events in the more general class.

## 22.5   Implications

Some direct implications of the model are the following:

1. Public policy in social regulation will conform neither to a strict Rawlsian "maximin" or "least worst" policy nor to a strict utilitarian policy that would maximize expected-benefits-less costs. Rather it will conform to a perception-driven benefits-less-costs policy, with perceptions influenced by the publicity given to rare events, the politicking of interest groups, and the difficulty of formulating a public philosophy of dealing with uncertain, potentially fatal events. We can expect politicians to try to capitalize on this confusion of concepts, perceptions of reality, and special interests.

2. As a corollary to point 1, economists who are frustrated because policy makers do not adopt a straightforward "maximize expected-benefits-minus-expected-costs" approach to social regulation will continue to be frustrated.

3. "Grandfathering" of status quo practice will be the more frequent, the higher the cost of changing the status quo.

4. Up to a certain, critical size, large societies and organizations are more likely to enact social regulations or to obey enacted social regulations than small ones. After the critical size is reached, the probability of enactment or obeying will be only very weakly size-dependent.

5. Although policy makers will not adopt a simple "expected-benefits-minus-expected-costs" formula, costs will enter into the perception-driven, modified version referred to in point 1. Inventors of a safety device cannot expect its adoption because "the value of a human life is infinite." It will be adopted only if it is cheap enough.

6. Publicity will continue to play a large role in influencing perceptions of benefits and costs of social regulation.

7. As a corollary of point 6, social regulation can be expected to be self-limiting. Social regulations with large cost burdens but small benefits will induce political action to repeal or modify them.

## 22.6  Discussion

To my mind, social regulation to protect against the loss of human life is particularly difficult, presenting society with profound ethical dilemmas. On the one hand, I feel thankful that the rare-event scale effect makes the government go to extra lengths to issue regulations that protect me against freak accidents of all sorts. On the other hand, the rare-event scale effect also leads to large, expensive bureaucracies that I as a taxpayer do not enjoy having to pay for. I am not quite ready to accept a naive utilitarian approach to resolving this dilemma—to have social regulatory policy conducted by the formula, maximize expected-benefits-less-expected-costs. At the same time, I am aware of the costs, and perhaps paralysis, that would result if society literally put an infinite value on human life.

I know of no way to cut this Gordian knot, of no simple, "correct" moral philosophy to govern social regulation. We can expect similar dilemmas in health care regulation. As the future brings us more and more effective but very expensive medical technologies, we can only expect to confront an increasing number of Gordian knots.

## Exercises

1. Contrast and compare "economic" regulation with "social" regulation. Which form of regulation is responsible for the recent rapid growth in the societal cost of regulation?

2. What are the main arguments being advanced by those who oppose the increase in social regulation?

3. Discuss the stakeholders in the social regulation controversy.

4. What fairness controversy occupies center stage in social regulation? In general, what is the philosophical outlook of economists who specialize in social regulation? What is the philosophical outlook of the federal government, as revealed by the mandates contained in the laws creating social regulation?

5. Discuss the quote from Mashaw's (1979) writings on how legislatures approach the passage of social regulatory laws.

6. If the government followed a strict maximize-expected-benefits-less-expected-costs approach to social regulation, what marginal condition would social regulations satisfy?

7. Describe how the analysis of toddler swimming pool drownings can be modeled by analogy with the model of student cheaters used in chapter 5 to illustrate the rare-event scale effect.

8. In the case of toddler swimming pool drownings, describe how the rare-event scale effect combines with the effect of the media to create a compound effect.

9. Discuss the three main options available to the Tucson Town Council and the factors that drove the council to award present swimming pool owners a status quo property right to unfenced pools.

10. Discuss the implications of the model of social regulation presented in this chapter.

# Glossary

**act utilitarianism.** The form of utilitarianism that, in the computation of individual utilities, considers acts as the determinants of utility, for example, the act of consumption of a bundle of commodities.

**adverse selection.** Self-selection that leads to skewed populations of insured. Thus, for example, people in poor health are more likely than people in good health to seek health insurance; poor drivers are more likely than good drivers to seek automobile insurance.

**agent.** Someone who acts in the place of the principal and by the principal's authority.

**ancillary restraint of trade.** Restraint of trade that is a by-product of normal business practice.

**barrier to entry.** Anything that requires an expenditure by a new entrant into an industry, but that imposes no equivalent cost upon an incumbent.

**chain store paradox.** The paradox that a game-theoretic model of predatory pricing yields the result that predatory pricing is irrational.

**constitution.** The rules and laws that govern how an organization or institution will make rules and laws. Sometimes called the institution's "meta laws" or "basic principles".

**constructed value.** In dumping cases, a value of a product constructed by Department of Commerce officials consisting of the product's cost of production plus an allowance for overhead and accounting profit.

**consumer's(s') surplus.** The difference between what a consumer (or group of consumers) would be willing to pay to purchase a given quantity of a good and what the consumer (or group of the consumers) actually pays for this quantity.

**cooperative game.** A game consisting of a set of $n$ players who can join together to form any one of $2^n - 1$ possible coalitions. By working together, the members of a coalition can produce a given amount of net benefit to the coalition. The problem for one of the $n$ players is to decide which coalition is best to join.

**core of a cooperative game.** A core of a cooperative game is said to exist when it is most beneficial for each player to join the "grand coalition"—the coalition consisting of all players.

**cost subadditivity.** A cost structure is said to be subadditive when the cost of providing any coalition of services is less than the total cost of provision when the coalition fragments into smaller coalitions.

**cost concavity.** A cost structure is said to satisfy cost concavity when the cost of providing successively larger coalitions results in successively smaller incremental costs.

**cost.** A characteristic of a good, service, or act that involves both its price and some aspect of decision or choice.

**denial or cognitive dissonance.** The propensity of human beings to accept evidence that accords or is in consonance with their beliefs and to reject evidence that discredits their beliefs or is in dissonance with them.

**depreciation.** The decrease in the value of an asset as recorded on a firm's account books.

**dumping.** Predatory pricing when used by a foreign firm against a domestic rival.

**economic efficiency.** Economywide Pareto optimality. Also "allocative efficiency" or "Pareto efficiency."

**economic regulation.** Regulation that controls prices, quantities, quality, or entry/exit.

**economic depreciation.** Depreciation that equals the decrease in the market value of the asset over a given time period.

**economic rent.** The return to a factor of production in excess of the minimum amount to keep the factor in its present employment.

**economic right.** A right to a certain level of economic goods that are considered necessary to sustain human existence (e.g., food, shelter, clothing). In many economies, now extended to the right to a job, health care, education, energy, and communication.

**economically efficient depreciation.** A depreciation schedule that maximizes consumers' plus producers' surplus.

**externality.** A factor that affects your welfare as a consumer or your ability to produce as a producer but that is under the control of someone other than yourself.

**fair market value.** In dumping cases, the price a foreign firm charges for a product in the firm's home country.

**fixed cost.** A cost that does not vary with the amount of output.

**fully distributed costs.** The proration of cost responsibilities to products or services on the basis of some parameter such as time, area, dollars, or effort.

**fungible asset.**   An asset that can be interchanged with another asset and still retain its value. Money is the most fungible of all assets.

**GATT.**   The General Agreement on Tariffs and Trade, an international organization that negotiates trade agreements.

**Herfindahl-Hirschman Index (HHI).**   The sum of the squares of the market shares of all the firms in a given market, where the market is typically defined by the cartel concept test.

**incentive compatibility.**   In a contract, the fact that the self-interest of each party will be consonant with the self-interests of the other parties to the contract. In government regulation, this means that each person being regulated has an incentive, following self-interest, to act so as to further the government's interest.

**information impactedness.**   The suppression of information as the result of self-interested behavior.

**infuriating, contract-breaking unfairness.**   The sense of being treated unfairly that results when someone else has broken an explicit or implicit contract that you have entered into.

**institutional framing of fairness.**   The effect of institutional setting or context on how fairness is perceived and administered.

**internalization of externalities.**   Any method of causing an externality in an economic transaction to become part of the transaction.

**interpersonal comparison of utility.**   A comparison of the utilities or preferences of individuals A and B, viewed as impossible by modern economic theory.

**logrolling.**   Originally referred to the U.S. custom of neighbors helping each other by rolling logs into a pile to be burned. Now refers to legislators trading votes.

**long-run cost.**   The expense of an alternative, not in your present choice set, that eventually will be in your choice set.

**lump-sum tax.**   A tax that is independent of an individual's actions and that deprives each individual of the same amount of income.

**marginal cost.**   The amount expended to produce the last unit.

**market failure.**   An inability of a free-market economy to achieve economically efficient outcomes.

**market power.**   The ability of a firm to earn positive economic profit.

**market for lemons.**   The tendency, because of information asymmetries, for the market price to equilibrate at the value of the lowest quality items in the population of items offered for sale.

**marketable pollution rights.**   Rights owned by a firm to pollute a certain amount that the firm can sell or transfer to another firm.

**moral hazard.** The hazard that a person will not take full precautions and act ethically because any damage caused by his improper actions will be paid for by his insurers.

**naked restraint of trade.** Restraint of trade whose sole purpose is to suppress competition.

**nondistortionary or first-best outcome.** An economically efficient outcome.

**opportunistic behavior.** Self-interested maneuvering within a corporation that ignores the firm's overall interests and that may be counter to it.

**opportunity cost.** The value of a forgone benefit.

**organizational failure.** Within a firm (organization), the failure of managers to effectively perform the coordinating functions that Coase (1937) describes.

**original position.** The state of the world that is the setting of Rawls's (1971) social contract. In this state, none of us is yet born, and thus none of us knows what the future will bring.

**overhead coverage.** The amount of the firm's revenue that is available to pay overhead.

**Pareto optimality.** A state in which all Pareto improvements have been exhausted and no win-win moves exist—one economic agent can gain from an economic transaction only if some other economic agent loses from it.

**Pareto improvement.** A trade, exchange, or more generally, any economic transaction from which the transacting economic agents all benefit. Colloquially called a "win-win move."

**Parkinsons's law.** C. Northcote Parkinson's (1958) list of typical organizational failures in large firms. The most famous organizational failure is, "Work expands to fill the time available for its completion."

**perfectly contestable market.** A market into which it is costless to enter and out of which it is costless to exit.

**Pigovian tax.** A tax on externalities designed to cause socially desirable outcomes.

**predatory pricing.** The practice of a firm's lowering its prices in a given market with the expressed intent of financially injuring or disciplining a rival. Losses temporarily sustained because of lowered prices are to be recouped after the rival has been injured or disciplined.

**price cap.** A ceiling on the prices that a firm can charge. The ceiling is usually placed not on individual prices themselves, but on some price index.

**price discrimination.** The practice of charging different classes of customers different prices for the same product or service.

**price index.** A weighted average of prices.

**primary social good.**   In Rawls's (1971) theory, a good essential to existence. The main primary good is self-respect. Other essential primary social goods are rights and liberties, powers and opportunities, wealth and income.

**principal.**   The person who has controlling authority.

**principal-agent contract.**   A contract between a principal and the principal's agent.

**producer's(s') surplus.**   The difference between what the revenue that a producer (or group of producers) receives for a quantity of a good and the total variable cost to the producer (or group of producers) of producing the quantity.

**product differentiation.**   Differentiation of similar products on some dimension such as color, quality, image, features, and so forth.

**property right.**   The authority to determine both the use of a resource and its disposition.

**public good.**   A good which is nonexcludable and nondepletable.

**Ramsey taxes or prices.**   Taxes per unit or prices on a set of commodities with the property that, given the need to raise a certain amount of tax or overhead revenues, a small, tax (overhead)-revenue-preserving change from a set of Ramsey prices or taxes, will make winners just be able to compensate losers, with no money left over.

**rare-event scale effect.**   The effect that the larger the organization, the higher the probability that a rare event will strike it.

**Rawls's difference (maximin) principle.**   The notion that society should choose the social structure that, in terms of primary social goods, benefits the least advantaged the most.

**recoupment fallacy.**   The fallacy that a predatory firm can recoup losses in its target market by raising prices in its other markets.

**rent seeking.**   Activity by persons other than a firm's owners to appropriate the firm's monopoly rents, that is, the proceeds from Tullock's (1967) rectangle.

**residual claimant.**   The economic agent last in line to receive payment, who receives whatever profit remains after all other claims have been satisfied.

**risk premium.**   For a risk-averse individual, the money difference between the expected outcome of a gamble and what the individual is willing to accept with certainty in place of the gamble.

**rule utilitarianism.**   The form of utilitarianism that, in the computation of individual utilities, considers rules as the determinants of utility, for example, rules derived from laws or regulations.

**satisfying, other-regarding fairness.**   Acting fairly in the sense of being altruistic or charitable.

**second-best outcome.**   An economically efficient outcome when constraints placed on the economy prevent the achievement of unconstrained economic efficiency.

**short-run cost.**   The expense of an alternative that is in your present choice set.

**social regulation.**   Health, safety, and environmental regulation.

**stakeholder.**   A person, group, organization, or institution that has a vital interest in proposed legislation or regulations.

**sunk cost.**   An expenditure that cannot be recouped.

**target market.**   The market in which the predator lowers prices in order to financially injure a rival.

**transaction cost.**   The cost attendant to carrying out an economic transaction, for example, the cost of searching for the best bargain, the cost of investigating the credibility of the seller, or the cost of the time taken to carry out the transaction.

**Tullock's rectangle.**   A monopoly firm's producer's surplus when marginal costs are constant. This rectangle is the monopolist's economic rent and can be appropriated by persons other than the firm's owners.

**ultimatum game.**   A game, typically with two players, wherein one player is given control of some economic pie and must make a one-time, take-it-or-leave it offer to share a portion of it with the other player. If the offer is rejected, both players receive nothing.

**variable cost.**   A cost that depends on the amount of output.

**variable cost coverage.**   The amount of the firm's revenue that is available to pay variable costs.

**Vogelsang-Finsinger (VF) overhead coverage.**   The amount of firm's revenue that is available to cover overhead on the basis of the previous period's outputs.

# Notes

## Chapter 2

1. A technical point. Sometimes more than bilateral trades are needed to achieve economic efficiency. An example is Messrs. A, B, and C seated at a three-sided table. Each prefers the seat on his left, but prefers his own seat to the seat on his right. A mutually beneficial rearrangement is for each to move to the seat on the left. However, in a bilateral trade someone must take a seat on his right. So if only bilateral trades are allowed, no one will move, and the mutually beneficial rearrangement will not occur. In this book, the term *mutually beneficial exchanges or trades* is meant to include not only two-way exchanges but many-way exchanges.

2. For a more precise definition of *perfect competition*, see a text on elementary economics (for example, Baumol and Blinder 1991, chap. 25).

3. See, for example, Smith 1982.

## Chapter 3

The quotation excerpted from Leonard Read's work is reprinted by permission of the Foundation for Economic Education.

1. I am indebted to Larry Garfinkel, retired vice president of AT&T, for these data.

2. For more on the results of the Cincinnati experience with charging for directory assistance, see McSweeny (1978)

3. See Bailey (1981) for a further discussion of the importance of contestability in determining natural monopolies and what should and should not be regulated.

## Chapter 4

1. See Coase (1960).

## Chapter 5

1. For example, at the time of the breakup of the Bell System in 1984, AT&T had 364,000 employees. In the subsequent four years it went from a regulated monopoly to a competitive

firm, in the process slimming down by 25 percent to 274,000 employees. At the same time, its revenues increased by 2 percent, in spite of a general lowering of its prices (AT&T 1989).

2. The exact formula is easiest to derive by calculating the probability of getting only good guys. Let $P(G)$ be this probability and let $P(B^*)$ be the probability of getting at least one bad guy. Then

$P(B^*) = 1 - P(G)$.

But the number of ways that $m$ majors can be grouped in a population of $n$ students is $\binom{n}{m}$, out of which $\binom{g}{m}$ will be groupings of $m$ students that contain only good guys. Thus

$P(G) = [\binom{g}{m}/\binom{n}{m}]$,

and

$$P(B^*) = 1 - [g(g - 1)\cdots(g - m + 1)/n(n - 1)\cdots(n - m + 1)]. \tag{5.2a}$$

An obvious bound on $P(B^*)$ is

$$1 - (g/n)^m \le P(B^*). \tag{5.2b}$$

  Also, from equation 5.2a we can verify the validity of the approximation used in the text for small $m$, and for $g \gg m$, $n \gg m$; we get

$P(B^*) \approx 1 - (g/n)^m$.

Also,

$g/n = 1 - (b/n)$,

and for $mb/n \ll 1$, we can neglect higher order terms in the binomial or Taylor's expansion of $g/n$ to get

$1 - (g/n)^m \approx 1 - (1 - (mb/n)) = mb/n$,

which verifies the approximation of $P(B^*)$ for small $m$.

3. This follows from straightforward manipulations of inequality 5.2b of the previous note.

## Chapter 6

1. There are a set of reasonable properties or "axioms" that we would expect such a quantitative scale of satisfaction or "utility" to satisfy, and we need to assure ourselves that a scale that satisfies these properties can in fact be constructed. A discussion of such axioms and a proof that the scale will exist can be found in Varian (1991). As the text suggests, in general, it can be shown that there will be an infinite number of scales that satisfy the axioms.

## Chapter 7

This chapter is based on Zajac, "Who Wins and Who Loses? An Economic Justice Overview and Research Agenda" (1986).

1. See Flubacher (1950, 48) for more on the history of the just price doctrine.

2. The high degree of regulation in Smith's time carried over to Colonial America. For an account of regulation in the colonies as well as its antecedents in the mother country, see Hughes (1977).

3. For a fuller description of how the just price was routinely violated in the Middle Ages, see Tuchman (1978, 37–38).

4. Reminiscences by others also present at the founding are given in American Economic Association (1936), and a discussion of controversies attendant with the founding can be found in Tobin (1985).

5. See Polinsky (1972) for a discussion of the Kaldor-Hicks-Hotelling proposals.

6. Another problem with the Kaldor-Hicks-Hotelling potential compensation idea is that it places almost no accountability requirements on policy makers. Without the requirement that compensation actually be paid, policy makers can easily convince themselves on the basis of the skimpiest of data, perhaps a poorly designed survey, or even worse, a few anecdotes, that a policy move will have the property that winners will *potentially* be able to compensate losers. The policy makers can then rationalize that they are serving the public interest.

7. A landmark paper on the economists' discussions of the 1930s that led to the present focus on "Pareto optimality" is Bergson (1938). Bergson fits into a single, unifying mathematical framework all of the candidates for a societal goal that various economists had espoused and shows that they may all be derived from a meta-utility or "social welfare" function.

8. For more comprehensive critiques of the shortcomings of "Paretianism" or "economic efficiency" as the basis of policy, see Little (1957) and Sen (1987a). For an extensive discussion of the morality of a market economy, see Buchanan (1985). Hausman and McPherson (1993) offer an excellent survey of the literature at the intersection of economics and moral philosophy, as well as perhaps the most extensive self-contained critique of modern economic methodology.

## Chapter 8

Quotations from *A Theory of Justice*, by John Rawls, copyright © 1971 by the President and Fellows of Harvard College, are reprinted by permission of the publisher, Belknap Press of the Harvard University Press.

1. For a more comprehensive condensation of Rawls's *Theory of Justice* and subsequent papers, see Buchanan (1982, chap. 6) and Buchanan and Mathieu (1986).

2. An important concept to Rawls is that of the "reflective equilibrium" (1971, 20):

In searching for the most favored description of this [the original position] situation, we work from both ends. We begin by describing it so that it represents generally shared and preferably weak conditions. We then see if these conditions are strong enough to yield a significant set of principles. If not, we look for further premises equally reasonable. But if so, and these principles match our considered convictions of justice, then so far well and good. But presumably there will be discrepancies. In this case we have a choice. We can either modify the account of the account of the initial situation or we can revise our existing judgments, for even the judgments we take provisionally as fixed points are liable to revision. By going back and forth, sometimes altering the conditions of the contractual circumstances, at others withdrawing our judgments and conforming them to principle, I assume that eventually we shall find a description of the initial situations that both expresses reasonable conditions and yields principles which match our considered judgments duly pruned and adjusted. This state of affairs I refer to as reflective equilibrium.

Thus the contract arrived at in the original position is expected to be one that is in "reflective equilibrium," the result of extensive trial and error and probing of all possible eventualities by the contractees.

3. In discussing his fundamental principles, Rawls does not consistently restate them, word for word, in different parts of *A Theory of Justice*. Thus the form of the first principle quoted here from p. 302 differs from the first statement of it on p. 60.

4. Since Rawls's theory is very general, it is necessarily vague on precisely what knowledge those in the original position possess. As is the case in many other instances, it is thereby vulnerable to attack with concrete examples that seem to fall within the scope of the theory yet also seem either to contradict common sense or to lead to inconsistencies within the theory. See, for example, Arrow (1973, 252–255).

## Chapter 9

*Quotations from Philosophy of Law*, by Jeffrie G. Murphy and Jules L. Coleman, 1990, are reprinted by permission of the publisher, Westview Press, Boulder, CO.

1. See Weymark (1991) for an extensive critique of Harsanyi.

2. For a critique of Varian's notion of wealth-fairness see Pazner (1977).

3. For a concise and comprehensive survey of the present state of moral theorizing on economic justice, see Sen (1987b). For a more extensive survey, see Hausman and McPherson (1993).

## Chapter 10

1. See, for example, Timoshenko (1953) for a history of this evolution.

2. The reader should be cautioned that some moral philosophers find positive theories of economic justice or fairness abhorrent because such theories run the grave danger of confusing what the public *thinks* is just with what *is* just. Thus, simply because a majority of the public thinks that slavery is just does not make it just. And, of course, a fundamental concern of the Founding Fathers of the United States was to protect the rights of minorities from the power of the majority (even though slavery was made an exception). We need only think of the Hitler's Germany and Stalin's Soviet Union to appreciate the importance of this concern. Nonetheless, if we are to improve on how we make economic policy, I find no alternative to research on positive theories of economic justice and fairness.

3. For more on the Formal Principle and material principles of distributive justice, see Buchanan and Mathieu (1986).

4. Equity theory has evolved in many directions and now has a vast literature. For example, Jasso (1990) has developed a logarithmic metric of the degree of fairness and has extensively applied it to study perceptions of equity and justice. A recent summary of equity theory, together with a critique of it, is given by Deutsch (1985).

5. Young (1989) has offered another explanation of the equal-split phenomenon. He argues that the equal split is an obvious "focal point," that is, a possible solution to a bargaining problem that will occur to everyone.

## Chapter 11

Most of this chapter has been adapted, by permission of the International Institute for Applied Systems Analysis, from Zajac, "Perceived Economic Justice: The Example of Public Utility Regulation" (1985). Epigraphic quotation, by permission of the Institute of Public Utilities, Michigan State University, is from Sasseville (1981).

1. Chapter 713 of New York State Laws of 1981.

2. A discussion of the FCC's 1985 Lifeline Program and its 1987 follow-on, Link-Up America can be found in Mitchell and Vogelsang (1991, chap. 11), who also summarize the eligibility criteria for the Lifeline Program and Link-up America in the forty-eight states, District of Columbia, and Puerto Rico that have implemented them. Also see Makarewicz (1991) for an analysis of the effects of the Lifeline Program and Link-Up America in the states served by the Southwestern Bell Telephone Company.

3. For another, Arizona example of status quo property rights in water use, see Isaac, Mathieu, and Zajac (1991, 360–361).

4. For a more extensive discussion of the Supreme Court cases leading to *Nebbia*, see Phillips (1988, 105–109) and Gellhorn and Pierce (1987, chap. 3).

5. Unfortunately, to my knowledge, neither Owen and Braeutigam nor anyone else has developed this extended notion of economic efficiency further, nor have others undertaken empirical studies to support Owen and Braeutigam's (1978) hypothesis.

## Chapter 12

1. See Simon (1992).

2. For this example I am indebted to Walter Oi, who claims that some economists have actually had the courage to try it and have done so in an attempt to teach the importance of Pareto improvements.

3. A basic reference on cognitive dissonance is Festinger (1975).

4. See Kessel (1958) for a discussion and analysis of this case.

## Chapter 13

1. Over time, expectations have changed, with a U.S. citizen expecting more and more from the government. For a history of the evolution of these expectations, see Hughes (1977).

2. For the analytically minded, let $Q_1$, $Q_2$ be the demands in the first and second markets. Then, $\Delta CS_1 = \Delta t_1 Q_1$, $\Delta CS_2 = \Delta t_2 Q_2$ and equation 13.1a becomes

$$\Delta t_1 Q_1 + \Delta t_2 Q_2 = 0. \tag{13.7a}$$

Likewise, equation 13.1b becomes

$$\Delta TR_1 + \Delta TR_2 = \Delta(t_1 Q_1) + \Delta(t_2 Q_2) = \Delta t_1 Q_1 + t_1 \Delta Q_1 + \Delta t_2 Q_2 + t_2 \Delta Q_2 = 0. \tag{13.7b}$$

Finally, by definition, $e = (\Delta p/\Delta Q)(Q/p) = (\Delta t/\Delta Q)(Q/P)$. Using this definition together with straightforward manipulations of equations 13.7a and 13.7b yields the Ramsey formulas in the text.

3. The derivation of this diagrammatic construction follows easily from the fact that the elasticity of a point on a straight-line demand schedule is the negative of the ratio of the segment below to the segment above (i.e., in figure 13.2):

$$e_1 = -A_1 E / A_1 D_1.$$

By simple geometry,

$$t_1 / p_1 = A_1 D_1' / A_1 E.$$

Hence

$$e_1 t_1 / p_1 = -A_1 D_1' / A_1 D_1,$$

which by the Ramsey formula is constant in all markets. For a generalization of this diagrammatic construction see Zajac (1974). Note also that strictly speaking, for the case shown in figure 13.1 there will be two sets of taxes that satisfy equations 13.1 and 13.2. However each tax in one set will be higher than the corresponding tax, market by market, in the second set. The higher taxes are thus Pareto-inferior to the lower prices and can be ignored.

4. For a history of the idea of natural monopoly, see Lowry (1973).

5. There is an obvious, alternative fairness argument for why new sources of pollution are being held to stricter standards than old sources. The old sources are being accorded status quo property rights, akin to the grandfathering of existing practitioners when an occupation is first licensed.

## Chapter 14

1. For more on the theory of public choice, see Mueller (1989).

2. The term *economic rent* goes back to Ricardo, who observed that the rental price per acre that could be obtained from land was equal to the cost of production of the *marginal* acre of land, the acre which was the last to be put into production. A more productive, *inframarginal* acre of land thus earned a premium equal to the prevailing revenue per acre less the marginal cost of production for that acre. For a given farm, the total rent was equal to the prevailing price per acre less the variable cost of production on all of the farm's acres, an amount which is also equal to the producer's surplus.

3. Reported in the *Wall Street Journal*, 1 February 1993, "Hailing the American Dream."

## Chapter 15

1. For more on the theory of "flow-through" effects on public utility pricing see chapter 6 in Brown and Sibley (1986)

2. This imaginary conversation is taken from Zajac (1978).

3. The problem of wasting water because it is offered at a zero or near zero charge is often real and serious and has received many economists' attention. See Hirshleifer, De Haven, and Milliman (1960).

4. I am indebted to my student, Gary Davis, for suggesting the four-cell diagram in figure 15.3.

5. This summary is based primarily on Singer and Endrenny (1993) and on Viscusi (1991).

## Chapter 16

1. See *Springer v. United States* (1880)

2. For a fuller discussion of the Haig-Simons definition of income, see Rosen (1992)

3. See Seade (1977) for a proof of these results.

4. For an account of how client politics contorted the Treasury Department's original attempt at 1986 tax reform legislation into the bill that finally emerged, see Herber (1988).

5. Source: *Treasury News* (1993).

## Chapter 17

1. See chapter 3 for a discussion of the distinction between accounting profit and economic profit.

2. Baumol (1986, 117–119) has a more extensive discussion of the burden test, including its relation to other possible tests for cross-subsidization.

3. More precisely, suppose that $S$ and $T$ are two coalitions of services, $S \cup T$ is the coalition or union of $S$ and $T$, and $C(S)$, $C(T)$, $C(S \cup T)$ are the costs of providing $S$, $T$, and $S \cup T$. Then a cost structure is said to be sub-additive if

$$C(S \cup T) \leq C(S) + C(T).$$

The extension of simple, single-product ideas of economies of scale to the case of multiple products is tricky and requires precise definitions. So, for example, in the usual formulation pioneered by Baumol, Panzar, and Willig (1982), examples show that economies of scale do not always imply cost subadditivity. However, for our purposes, we can think of subadditivity as a generalization of the notion of economies of scale that is contained in elementary economics texts. See also Sharkey (1982) for an another extensive treatment of multiproduct cost concepts.

4. In terms of the notation of the previous note, the concavity condition can be expressed as follows:

$$C(T \cup R) - C(T) \leq C(S \cup R) - C(S),$$

where $S$ is a subset of $T$.

## Chapter 18

Quotation from *The Fair Trade Fraud*, copyright James Bovard, 1991, is reprinted with permission of the publisher, St. Martin's Press, New York.

1. The literature's terminology on predatory pricing and dumping is not uniform. For example, some authors reserve the term *predatory pricing* for the case of a single-product firm; some authors in the dumping literature consider dumping to be a form of *price discrimination* and not predatory pricing. I find these to be unimportant distinctions, as the text makes clear.

2. For a more extensive discussion of predatory pricing, see Martin (1988).

## Chapter 19

1. See Murphy and Soyster (1983, 17–27) for a state-by-state listing of the valuation bases for public utility regulation.

2. The *Hope* decision also addressed depreciation, affirming the Brandeis view and rejecting the view that depreciation should be a means of saving for replacement of worn out equipment at "reproduction" cost. See Jones (1967, 142–143).

3. For a further discussion of depreciation accounting for public utilities, including more on its history and more on the practical problems that arise, see Phillips (1988, chap. 7).

4. Some of the distracting details that will be omitted are the scrap value of an asset at the end of its service life (assumed to be zero) and the fact that operating expenses, such as taxes, may depend on capital equipment's value.

5. Greenwald (1984) calls the regulatory contract that is inherent in our (really Brandeis's) model a "basic sequential regulatory scheme" (BSRS). The essential elements of a BSRS are that the regulators promise (1) initially to value an asset at exactly its purchase price and (2) to set the "interest on the remaining balance" at a "fair," that is, market, rate. A BSRS gives the regulators freedom to spread over time the repayment of principal in any way they wish.

6. See Greenwald (1984) for a further discussion of these two points.

7. Interestingly, at the time of this writing, the savings and loan "crisis" has precipitated a debate about whether a bank's assets should be valued according to conservative accounting practices or on the basis of the assets' market values. The institutional details in banking are different from those of public utilities, and we should not automatically assume that the same regulatory methods will be appropriate to two different industries. Nevertheless, reading the arguments and counterarguments in the S&L debate generates a sense of déjà vu.

8. This "investment invariance" argument was implicitly or explicitly exploited by Frank W. Sinden in numerous internal Bell Laboratories memoranda in the 1970s. For a recent formal demonstration of the argument for the case of depreciation, see Schmalensee (1989).

9. Many different diagrams of a firm's cash flows are possible. Sinden's diagram, which reflects the accounting practices of the Bell System before its breakup, it is still a convenient representation of cash flows for most regulated firms.

10. A seminal reference on economic depreciation is Hotelling (1925).

11. A more extensive discussion of these points is given by Panzar (1986).

12. Sinden (1979) treats the case of economic depreciation in a perfectly competitive world in detail, pointing out that, in general, the introduction of technological advances will be preceded by price rises. Another treatment is given by Panzar (1986), who also discusses the allocative efficiency properties of economic depreciation and its role in regulatory proceedings.

## Chapter 20

1. For more on the emergence on the large firm, see Chandler (1977) and McCraw (1984).

2. See McCraw (1984, chap. 1) for more on Adams's muckraking efforts.

3. See Yergin (1991; 101–106) for a description of Ida Tarbell and a brief history of her work and its effect..

4. See Martin (1988, 48–55) for a discussion of the congressional debates leading to the Sherman Act.

5. See McCraw (1984, chap. 3, esp. p. 95) for a further discussion of price-fixing prior to the Sherman Act.

6. An excellent summary of the guidelines and the procedures followed by the federal government to evaluate mergers can be found in Salop (1987, 3–12).

7. Huge efficiency gains are routinely claimed for a proposed merger; just as routinely, antitrust economists treat such claims with great skepticism. See, for example, Salop (1987) for an expression of this skepticism by Salop, White (a coauthor of the 1984 guidelines), Fisher, and Schmalensee, four eminent antitrust economists.

## Chapter 21

1. For more examples of incentive-compatible regulatory schemes, as well as references to the literature on them, see Acton and Vogelsang (1989) and the accompanying papers in the *Symposium on Price-Cap Regulation.*

2. Suppose the firm's prices in period 1 are such that the VF overhead coverage equals the overhead. If changes of $dp_1^1$ and $dp_2^1$ result in new prices for which the VF overhead coverages still cover the overhead, we have

$$(Q_1^{mc}/2)dp_1^1 + (Q_2^{mc}/2)dp_2^1 = 0 \tag{21.1a}$$

At the same time, if $p_1^1$ and $p_2^1$ are the profit-maximizing prices, for small price changes they must satisfy

$$d[(p_1^1 - mc_1)Q_1^1] + d[(p_2^1 - mc_2)Q_2^1] = 0. \tag{21.1b}$$

For linear independent demands, a bit of algebra converts equation 21.1b into

$$(2Q_1^1 - Q_1^{mc})dp_1^1 + (2Q_2^1 - Q_2^{mc})dp_2^1 = 0. \tag{21.1c}$$

In turn, equations 21.1a and 21.1c imply

$$(2Q_1^1 - Q_1^{mc})/Q_1^{mc} = (2Q_2^1 - Q_2^{mc})/Q_2^{mc},$$

from which follows that $Q_1^1/Q_1^{mc} = Q_2^1/Q_2^{mc}$. The same demonstration, stage-by-stage, shows that the outputs at every stage will be proportional to the price-equals-marginal cost outputs.

3. Mitchell and Vogelsang (1991, 264–285) summarize the theory of the price indices that enter into in price cap regulation of AT&T and the actual formulas that implement it. The summary takes twenty-two pages.

4. I am indebted to Mary Wybenga and Nancy Davis of U.S. West for helping me understand the current status of alternative forms of regulation in telecommunications, and to T. J. Tardiff and W. E. Taylor for the data for figure 21.3.

5. Laboratory experiments with incentive-compatible regulatory schemes also suggest caution. For example, Cox and Isaac (1987) tried experimentally to implement a refinement of the Loeb-Magat scheme proposed by Finsinger and Vogelsang. The demand side of the market was simulated by computer; student subjects played the role of firms. To give the

students incentives to play their role seriously, any profits they earned were paid to them in actual money. The Finsinger-Vogelsang variant of Loeb-Magat posits that the firm will follow an optimal path that will converge to first-best prices. Cox and Isaac found that the student "firms" often strayed off the optimal path, and when they did, an unstable cycle leading to the firm's going bankrupt could result.

6. For an extensive theoretical treatment of incentive-compatible regulation, see Laffont and Tirole (1993).

## Chapter 22

Quotations from Phillip Abelson's work are reprinted by permission of *Science* magazine, copyright 1993 by the American Association for the Advancement of Science. Quotations from Mashaw's and Nichols's work are reprinted by permission of *Regulation* magazine.

1. For example, Nichols (1991, 91–92), discusses the 1990 amendments to the Clean Air Act:

The new law explicitly identifies 189 different individual substances or classes of substances. The EPA is directed to develop lists of categories of sources for each substance within two years of the law's enactment and to issue regulations for those source categories over ten years. . . . Similarly, the EPA must write standards for each category of new sources unless no source (or group of sources, in the case of area sources) imposes a lifetime maximum individual risk higher than one in a million.

2. According to the *Tucson Citizen*, 26 January 1993, which cites the Office of Management and Budget (OMB) as the source.

3. According the Crandall (1983), this is the scenario behind the 1977 Clean Air Act. House of Representative staffers and environmentalists formed a coalition with eastern coal producers to pressure eastern congressmen and the Environmental Protection Agency to mandate the same scrubbers nationwide, regardless of the sulfur content of the coal used by a power plant.

4. See, for example, the discussion in Viscusi, Vernon, and Harrington (1992, 609–613) and in Nichols (1991). Sometimes a distinction is made between simply making an expected-benefits-minus-expected-costs calculation and using it to dictate policy. However, in my experience, in practice, economists tend to lose sight of this distinction and simply take it for granted that a rational policy maker should try to maximize expected-benefits-minus-expected-costs.

5. For a comprehensive discussion of the trade-offs involving human lives, see Viscusi (1992).

6. To be more precise, the usual attack is on what might be called "naive" utilitarianism, which seeks the "greatest good for the greatest number." As chapter 9 points out, more sophisticated versions of utilitarianism try to cope with utilitarianism's apparent infringement of individual rights.

7. See, for example, Viscusi, Vernon, and Harrington (1992, table 20.3) for a summary of estimates of cost of life.

8. It should be noted that the case has yet to go through appeal. In 1971 a plaintiff obtained a $125 million jury award in a case involving the explosion of a Ford Pinto's gas tank (*Wall Street Journal* 1993b). In 1993 dollars this is about $375 million. On appeal, this was reduced

to $3.5 million, or about $10.5 million in 1993 dollars, a number that is not out of line with general "cost-of-life" estimates.

9. A similar point is made by Rubin (1987).

10. A self-locking gate is hung so that, when it is opened, gravity will swing it shut into a latch, sprung so as to close when the gate hits it.

11. See the *Tucson Citizen* (1989a).

12. See *Tucson Citizen* (1989b) and *Arizona Daily Star* (1990).

# References

Abelson, P. H. 1993. "Regulatory Costs." *Science* 259:159.

Acton, J. P., and Vogelsang, I. 1989. "Introduction." *Symposium on Price-Cap Regulation. Rand Journal of Economics*: 369–372.

Alchian, A. A., and Demsetz, H. 1972. "Production, Information Costs, and Economic Organization." *American Economic Review* 62:777–795.

Akerlof, G. A. 1970. "The Market for Lemons." *Quarterly Journal of Economics* 84:488–500.

Akerlof, G. A., and Dickens, W. T. 1982. "The Economic Consequences of Cognitive Dissonance." *American Economic Review* 72:307–319.

American Economic Association. 1936. "Report of the Fiftieth Anniversary Meeting." *American Economic Review* 26:319–340.

Areeda, P., and Turner, D. 1975. "Predatory Prices and Related Practices under Section 2 of the Sherman Act." *Harvard Law Review* 88:697–733.

*Arizona Daily Star* (Tucson). 1990. "Statewide Rules on Fencing Winning Support." 25 February.

Arrow, K. J. 1973. "Some Ordinalist-Utilitarian Notes on Rawls' Theory of Justice." *Journal of Philosophy* 70:245–263.

AT&T (American Telephone and Telegraph Company). 1989. *Annual Report.*

Baack, B., and Ray, E. 1993. "The Income Tax: An Idea Whose Time Has Gone and Come?" In D. N. McCloskey, ed., *Second Thoughts: Myths and Morals of U.S. Economic History.* Oxford: Oxford University Press.

Bailey, E. E. 1981. "Contestability and the Design of Regulatory and Antitrust Policy." *American Economic Review.* 71:178–183.

Baumol, W. J. 1986. *Superfairness.* Cambridge: MIT Press.

Baumol, W. J., and Blinder, A. S. 1991. *Economics: Principles and Policy.* New York: Harcourt Brace Jovanovich.

Baumol, W. J., and Bradford, D. 1970. "Optimal Departures from Marginal Cost Pricing." *American Economic Review* 60:265–283.

Baumol, W. J., Eckstein, O., and Kahn, A. E. 1970. *Competition and Monopoly in Telecommunications Services*. New York: American Telephone and Telegraph Co.

Baumol, W. J., Panzar, J. C., and Willig, R. D. 1982. *Contestable Markets and the Theory of Industry Structure*. New York: Harcourt Brace Jovanovich.

Becker, G. S. 1983. "A Theory of Competition among Pressure Groups for Political Influence." *Quarterly Journal of Economics* 98:371–400.

Beesley, M. E., and Littlechild, S. C. 1989. "The Regulation of of Privatized Monopolies in the United Kingdom." *Rand Journal of Economics* 20:454–472.

Belzer, R. B. 1991. "The Peril and Promise of Risk Assessment." *Regulation* 14:40–49.

Bergson, A. 1938. "A Reformulation of Certain Aspects of Welfare Economics." *Quarterly Journal of Economics* 52:310–334.

Blum, W. J., and Kalven, H. 1953. *The Uneasy Case for Progressive Taxation*. Chicago: University of Chicago Press.

Boltuck, R., and Litan, R. L., eds. 1991. *Down in the Dumps*. Washington, DC: Brookings Institution.

Bork, R. H. 1978. *The Antitrust Paradox*. New York: Basic Books.

Bovard, J. 1991. *The Fair Trade Fraud*. New York: St. Martin's Press.

Brandon, B. B. 1981. *The Effect of the Demographics of Individual Households on Their Telephone Usage*. Cambridge, MA: Ballinger.

Breit, W., and Elzinga, K. G. 1989. *The Antitrust Case Book*. Fort Worth, TX: Dryden Press, Harcourt Brace Jovanovich College Publishers.

Breyer, S. 1982. *Regulation and Its Reform*. Cambridge: Harvard University Press.

*Brooke Group Ltd. v. Brown and Williamson Tobacco Corporation*. 1993. 113B SuCt 2578.

Broome, J. 1978. "Trying to Value a Life." *Journal of Public Economics* 9:91–100.

*Brown Shoe Co., Inc. v. United States*. 1962. 370 U.S. 294

Brown, S. J, and Sibley, D. S. 1986. *The Theory of Public Utility Pricing*. Cambridge: Cambridge University Press.

*Brushaber v. Union Pacific*. 1916. 240 U.S. 1.

Buchanan, A. E. 1982. *Marx and Justice: The Radical Critique of Liberalism*. Totawa, NJ: Rowman and Allanhead.

Buchanan, A. E. 1985. *Ethics, Efficiency, and the Market*. Totawa, NJ: Rowman and Allanhead.

Buchanan, A. E., and Mathieu, D. 1986. "Philosophy and Justice." In R. L. Cohen, ed., *Justice: Views from the Social Sciences*, chap. 2. New York: Plenum Press.

Buchanan, J. M. 1976. "Taxation in Fiscal Exchange." *Journal of Public Economics* 6:17–29.

Buchanan J. M., and Tullock, G. 1962. *The Calculus of Consent*. Ann Arbor: University of Michigan Press.

Buckley, W. F. 1992. "If Candidates Say 'Fairness' Grab Your Wallet and Hold On." *Tucson (Arizona) Citizen*, 17 March.

Chandler, A. D., Jr. 1977. *The Visible Hand: The Managerial Revolution in American Business.* Cambridge: Belknap Press of Harvard University Press.

Cheung, S. N. 1980. *The Myth of Social Cost.* San Francisco: Cato Institute.

Coase, R. H. 1937. "The Nature of the Firm." *Economica,* n.s. 4:386–405.

Coase, R. H. 1960. "The Problem of Social Cost." *Journal of Law and Economics* 3:1–44.

Coleman, J. S. 1990. *Foundations of Social Theory.* Cambridge: Belknap Press of Harvard University Press.

Coursey, D. L., Hovis, J., and Schulze, W. D. 1987. "The Disparity Between Willingness to Accept and Willingness to Pay Measures of Value." *Quarterly Journal of Economics* 102:679–690.

Cox, J. C., and Isaac, R. M. 1987. "Mechanisms for Incentive Regulation: Theory and Experiment." *Rand Journal of Economics.* 18:348–359.

Crandall, R. W. 1983. *Controlling Industrial Pollution: The Economics and Politics of Clean Air.* Washington, DC: Brookings Institution.

Deutsch, M. 1985. *Distributive Justice: A Social-Psychological Persepective.* New Haven: Yale University Press.

DiLorenzo, T. J. 1990. "Revisiting the Origins of Antitrust." *Regulation* 13:26–34.

Eatwell, J., Milgate, M., and Newman, P., eds. 1987. *The New Palgrave.* New York: Macmillan.

Elster, J. 1989. "Incentives and Local Justice." Mimeo prepared for the Russell Sage Conference on "Local Justice and Fair Allocation," Aspen Institute, Wye Woods, MD, 15–17 December.

Elster, J. 1992. *Local Justice: How Institutions Allocate Scarce Goods and Necessary Burdens.* New York: Russell Sage Foundation.

Ely, R. T. 1936. "The Founding and Early History of the American Economic Association." *American Economic Review* 26:141–150.

Faulhaber, G. R. 1975. "Cross-Subsidization: Pricing in Public Enterprises." *American Economic Review* 65:966–977.

*Federal Power Commission v. Hope Natural Gas Co.* 1944. 320 U.S. 591.

Feinberg, J. 1973. *Social Philosophy.* Englewood Cliffs, NJ: Prentice-Hall.

Festinger, L. 1975. *A Theory of Cognitive Dissonance.* Stanford, CA: Stanford University Press.

Flubacher, J. F. 1950. *The Concept of Ethics in the History of Economics.* New York: Vantage Press.

Forsythe, R., Horowitz, J., Savin, N. E., and Sefton, M. 1988. "Replicability, Fairness and Pay in Experiments with Simple Bargaining Games." University of Iowa working paper 88-30.

Friedman, M. 1982. *Capitalism and Freedom.* Rev. ed. Chicago: University of Chicago Press.

Frohlich, N., and Oppenheimer, J. A. 1992. *Choosing Justice: An Experimental Approach to Ethical Theory.* Berekely: University of California Press.

Frohlich, N., Oppenheimer, J. A., and Eavey, C. L. 1987. "Laboratory Results on Rawls's Distributive Justice." *British Journal of Political Science* 17:1–21.

Galbraith, J. K. 1967. *The New Industrial State*, Boston, MA: Houghton Mifflin.

Galvin, C. O., and Bittker, B. I. 1969. *The Income Tax: How Progressive Should It Be?* Washington, DC: American Enterprise Institute.

Garnett, R. W. 1985. *The Telephone Enterprise: The Evolution of the Bell System's Horizontal Structure, 1876–1909.* Baltimore: Johns Hopkins University Press.

Gellhorn, E., and Levin, R. M. 1990. *Administrative Law and Process.* St. Paul, MN: West.

Gellhorn, E., and Pierce, R. J. 1987. *Regulated Industries.* St. Paul, MN: West.

Gordon, S. 1980. *Welfare, Justice, and Freedom.* New York: Columbia University Press.

Green, J. F. 1956. *The United Nations and Human Rights.* Washington, DC: Brookings Institution.

Greenwald, B. C. 1984. "Rate Base Selection and the Structure of Regulation." *Rand Journal of Economics* 15:85–95.

Harsanyi, J. C. 1976. *Essays on Ethics, Social Behavior, and Scientific Explanation.* Dordrecht, Holland: D. Reidel.

Hausman, D. M., and McPherson, M. S. 1993. "Taking Ethics Seriously: Economics and Contemporary Moral Philosophy." *Journal of Economic Literature* 31:671–731.

Hayek, F. R. 1945. "The Use of Knowledge in Society." *American Economic Review* 35:519–530.

Hayek, F. R. 1977. As quoted in transcript of the TV program "Firing Line," 11 November. Available from Southern Educational Communications Association, P. O. Box 5966, Columbia, SC.

Hechter, M. 1987. *Principles of Group Solidarity.* Berkeley: University of California Press.

Herber, B. P. 1988. "Federal Income Tax Reform in the United States." *American Journal of Economics and Sociology* 47:391–408.

Hewitt, W. A. S. 1912. "Apprenticeship, Status of." In R. H. L. Palgrave, ed., *Dictionary of Political Economy.* New York: Macmillan.

Hicks, J. D. 1961. *The Populist Revolt.* University of Nebraska Press.

Hirshleifer, J., De Haven, J. C., and Milliman, S. W. 1960. *Water Supply, Economics, Technology and Policy.* Chicago: University of Chicago Press.

Hoffman, E., and Spitzer, M. 1982. "The Coase Theorem: Some Experimental Tests." *Journal of Law and Economics* 25:73–98.

Hoffman, E., and Spitzer, M. 1985. "Entitlements, Rights, and Fairness: An Experimental Examination of Subject's Concepts of Distributive Justice." *Journal of Legal Studies* 14:259–297.

Hotelling, H. 1925. "A General Mathematical Theory of Depreciation." *Journal of the American Statistical Association* 20:340–353.

Hovencamp, H. 1986. *Antitrust.* Black Letter Series. St. Paul, MN: West.

Hughes, J. R. T. 1977. *The Governmental Habit*. New York: Basic Books.

Isaac, R. M. 1991. "Price Cap Regulation: A Case Study of Some Pitfalls of Implementation." *Journal of Regulatory Economics* 3:193–210.

Isaac, R. M., Mathieu, D., and Zajac, E. E. 1991. "Institutional Framing and Perceptions of Fairness." *Constitutional Political Economy* 2:329–370.

Jasso, G. 1990. "Methods for the Theoretical and Empirical Analysis of Comparison Processes." In C. C. Clogg, ed., *Sociological Methodology*. Washington, DC: American Sociological Association.

Jensen, M. C., and Meckling, W. H. 1976. "Theory of the Firm: Managerial Behavior, Agency Costs, and Ownership Structure." *Journal of Financial Economics* 3:305–360.

Johnson, H. 1994. "Aftershocks Jar Santa Monica's Rent Controllers." *Wall Street Journal*, 17 March.

Johnston, J. 1984. *Econometric Methods*. 3rd ed. New York: McGraw-Hill.

Jones, W. K. 1967. *Cases and Materials on Regulated Industries*. Brooklyn, NY: Foundation Press.

Kahn, A. E. 1970. *The Economics of Regulation*. New York: Wiley.

Kahneman, D., Knetsch, J. L., and Thaler, R. 1986. "Fairness as a Constraint on Profit Seeking: Entitlements in the Market." *American Economic Review*. 76:728–741.

Kessel, R. A. 1958. "Price Discrimination in Medicine." *Journal of Law and Economics* 1:20–53.

Knez, M., and Smith, V. L. 1987. "Hypothetical Valuations and Preference Reversals in the Context of Asset Trading." In A. Roth, ed., *Laboratory Experiments in Economics: Six Points of View*, 131–154. Cambridge: Cambridge University Press.

Kreps, D. M., and Wilson, R. 1982. "Reputation and Imperfect Information." *Journal of Economic Theory* 27:253–279.

Laffont, J., and Tirole, J. 1993. *A Theory of Incentives in Procurement and Regulation*. Cambridge: MIT Press.

LeGrand, J. 1991. *Equity and Choice*. London: Harper Collins.

Lewis, D. 1969. *Convention*. Cambridge: Harvard University Press.

Linhart, P. B., and Radner, R. 1992. "Price Caps." *Annals of Operations Research* 36:17–32.

Little, I. M. D. 1957. *A Critique of Welfare Economics*. 2d ed. Oxford: Oxford University Press.

Loeb, M., and Magat, W. 1979. "A Decentralized Method for Utility Regulation." *Journal of Law and Economics* 12:399–404.

Lowry, E. D. 1973. "Justification for Regulation: The Case for Natural Monopoly." *Public Utility Fortnightly* 92:17–22.

Makarewicz, T. J. 1991. "The Effectiveness of Low-Income Telephone Assistance Programmes." *Telecommunications Policy* 15:223–240.

Martin, S. 1988. *Industrial Economics: Economic Analysis and Public Policy.* New York: Macmillan.

Mashaw, J. L. 1979. "Regulation, Logic, and Ideology." *Regulation* 3:44–51.

McCraw, T. K. 1984. *Prophets of Regulation.* Cambridge: Belknap Press of the Harvard University Press.

McSweeny, A. J. 1978. "Effects of Response Cost on the Behavior of a Million Persons: Charging for Directory Assistance in Cincinnati." *Journal of Applied Behavior Analysis* 11:47–51.

*Missouri Ex. Rel. Southwestern Bell Telephone Co. v. Missouri Public Service Commission.* 1923. 262 U.S. 276.

Mitchell, B. M., and Vogelsang, I. 1991. *Telecommunications Pricing: Theory and Practice.* Cambridge: Cambridge University Press.

Mueller, D. C. 1989. *Public Choice II.* Cambridge: Cambridge University Press.

*Munn v. Illinois.* 1877. 94 U.S. 113.

Murphy, F. H., and Soyster, A. L. 1983. *Economic Behavior of Electric Utilities.* Englewood Cliffs, NJ: Prentice-Hall.

Murphy J. G., and Coleman, J. L. 1990. *The Philosophy of Law.* Rev. ed. Boulder, CO: Westview Press.

Murray, T. 1991. "The Administration of the Antidumping Duty Law by the Department of Commerce." In R. Boltuck and R. E. Litan, eds., *Down in the Dumps.* Washington, DC: Brookings Institution.

Musgrave, R. A. 1959. *The Theory of Public Finance.* New York: McGraw-Hill.

*National Conference of Catholic Bishops.* 1986. *Economic Justice for All: Pastoral Letter on Catholic Social Teaching and the U.S. Economy.* United States Catholic Conference.

*Nebbia v. New York.* 1934. 291 U.S. 502.

Nichols, A. L. 1991. "Comparing Risk Standards: The Superiority of the Benefit-Cost Approach." *Regulation* 14:85–94.

Niskanen, W. A. 1991. "Making Sense of Safety." *Regulation* 14:12–14.

North, D. C. 1990. *Institutions, Institutional Change, and Economic Performance.* Cambridge: Cambridge University Press.

*Northern Securities Company v. United States.* 1904. 193 U.S. 197.

Nozick, R. 1974. *Anarchy, State, and Utopia.* New York: Basic Books.

Olson, W. 1993. "The Most Dangerous Vehicle on the Road." *Wall Street Journal,* 6 February.

Owen, B. M., and Braeutigam, R. 1978. *The Regulatory Game: Strategic Use of the Administrative Process.* Cambridge, MA: Ballinger.

Panzar, J. C. 1986. "Economic Depreciation Principles." Unpublished manuscript.

Pareto, V. 1909. *Manual of Political Economy.* Trans. A. S. Schwier. New York: Augustus M. Kelly, 1971.

Parkinson, C. N. 1958. *Parkinson's Law*. London: John Murray.

Pazner, E. A. 1977. "Pitfalls in the Theory of Fairness." *Journal of Economic Theory* 14:458–466.

Pazner, E. A., and Schmeidler, D. 1974. "A Difficulty in the Concept of Fairness." *Review of Economic Studies* 41:441–443.

Pechman, J. A. 1987. "Tax Reform: Theory and Practice." *Journal of Economic Perspectives* 1:11–28.

Peltzman, S. 1976. "Toward a More General Theory of Regulation." *Journal of Law and Economics* 19:211–240.

Phillips, C. F., Jr. 1988. *The Regulation of Public Utilities*. 2d ed., Arlington, VA: Public Utilities Reports.

*Pollock v. Farmers' Loan & Trust Co.* 1895. 157 U.S. 429.

Polinsky, A. M. 1972. "Probabalistic Compensation Criteria." *Quarterly Journal of Economics* 5:335–358.

Pope John Paul II. 1991. Encyclical Letter *Centesimus Annus*. Boston: St. Paul Books and Media.

Rawls, J. 1971. *A Theory of Justice*. Cambridge: Harvard University Press.

Rawls, J. 1974. "Some Reasons for the Maximin Criterion." *American Economic Review* 64:141–152.

Rawls, J. 1993. *Political Liberalism*. New York: Columbia University Press.

Read, L. 1958. "I, Pencil." Irvington-on-Hudson, NY: Foundation for Economic Education.

Robbins, L. 1938. "Interpersonal Comparisons of Utility: A Comment." *Economic Journal* 48:635–641.

Rohlfs, J. H., Jackson, C. L., and Kelly, T. E. 1991. "Estimate of the Loss to the United States Caused by the FCC's Delay in Licensing Cellular Telecommunications." National Economic Research Associates, Washington, DC., 8 November.

Rosen, H. S. 1992. *Public Finance*. 3rd ed., Homewood, IL: Irwin.

Rosenberg, N. 1979. "Adam Smith and Laissez-Faire Revisisted." In G. P. Driscoll, Jr., ed., *Adam Smith and the Modern Political Economy*. Ames: Iowa State University Press.

Rubin, P. H. 1987. "The Dangers of Overstating Safety Risks." *Wall Street Journal*, 8 October.

Salop, S. C., ed. 1987. *Symposium: Horizontal Mergers and Antitrust. Journal of Economic Perspectives* 1:3–54.

Samuelson, P. A. 1957. Foreword to J. de V. Graaff, *Theoretical Welfare Economics*. Cambridge: Cambridge University Press.

Sasseville, K. E. 1981. "Comments." In *Energy and Communications in Transition*, 110–116. Proceedings of the Institute of Public Utilities Eleventh Annual Conference. Michigan State University, East Lansing.

Schlicht, E. 1984. "Cognitive Dissonance in Economics." In H. Todt, ed. *Normengeleites Verhalten in den Sozialwissenschaften*. Berlin: Duncker and Humboldt.

Schmalensee, R. 1979. *The Control of Natural Monopolies*. Lexington, MA: Lexington Books, D. C. Heath.

Schmalensee, R. 1989. "An Expository Note on Depreciation and Profitability." *Journal of Regulatory Economics* 1:293–297.

Schotter, A. 1985. *Free Market Economics: A Critical Appraisal*. New York: St. Martin's Press.

Schumpeter, J. A. 1950. *Capitalism, Socialism, and Democracy*. New York: Harper Colophon.

Schumpeter, J. A. 1954. *History of Economic Analysis*. Oxford: Oxford University Press.

Seade, J. K. 1977. "On the Shape of the Optimal Tax Schedule." *Journal of Public Economics* 7:203–235.

Seligman, E. R. A. 1908. *Progressive Taxation in Theory and Practice*. Princeton: Princeton University Press.

Selten, R. 1978. "The Chain Store Paradox." *Theory and Decision* 9:127–159.

Sen, A. 1987a. *On Ethics and Economics*. Oxford: Blackwell.

Sen, A. 1987b. "Justice." In J. Eatwell, M. Milgate, and Peter Newman, ed., *The New Palgrave Dictionary of Economics*. New York: Macmillan.

Sen A., and Williams, B., eds. 1982. *Utilitarianism and Beyond*. Cambridge: Cambridge University Press.

Sharkey, W. W. 1982. *The Theory of Natural Monopoly*. Cambridge: Cambridge University Press.

Silver, M. 1989. *Foundations of Economic Justice*. Oxford: Blackwell.

Simon, J. L. 1992. "Freer Skies Gave Us Better Service." *Wall Street Journal*, 14 October.

Sinden, F. W. 1979. "Obsolescence, Depreciation, and New Technology." *Issues in Public Utility Regulation*, 304–316. Institute of Public Utilities, Graduate School of Business, Michigan State University, East Lansing.

Singer, E., and Endreny, P. M. 1993. *Reporting on Risk*. New York: Russell Sage Foundation.

Smith, A. 1776. *An Inquiry into the Nature and Causes of the Wealth of Nations*, Reprint, Chicago: University of Chicago Press, 1976.

Smith, V. L. 1982. "Microeconomic Systems as an Experimental Science." *American Economic Review* 72:923–955.

Smith, V. L., and Williams, A. W. 1990. "The Boundaries of Competitive Price Theory: Convergence, Expectation, and Transaction Costs." In L. Green and J. Kagel, eds., *Advances in Behavioral Economics*, II, Norwood, NJ: Ablex.

*Smyth v. Ames*. 1898. 169 U.S. 466.

*Springer v. United States*. 1880. 102 U.S. 586.

*Standard Oil Co. of New Jersey, et al. v. United States*. 1911. 221 U.S.1.

Stewart, T. P. 1991. "Administration of the Antidumping Law: A Different Perspective." In R. Boltuck and R. E. Litan, eds., *Down in the Dumps*. Washington, DC: Brookings Institution.

Stigler, G. J. 1971. "The Theory of Economic Regulation." *Bell Journal of Economics* 2:3–21.

Sugden, R. 1986. *The Economics of Rights, Co-Operation, and Welfare.* Oxford: Blackwell.

Tardiff, T. J., and Taylor, W. E. 1993. "Telephone Company Performance under Alternative Forms of Regulation in the U.S." National Economic Research Associates, Cambridge, MA, 7 September.

Timoshenko, S. P. 1953. *History of Strength of Materials.* New York: McGraw-Hill.

Tobin, J. 1985. "Neoclassical Theory in America: J. B. Clark and Fisher." *American Economic Review* 75:28–38.

*Treasury News.* 1993. U.S. Department of the Treasury, Washington, DC, 28 October.

Tuchman, B. 1978. *A Distant Mirror.* New York: Knopf.

*Tucson (Arizona) Citizen.* 1989a. Editorial, 18 August.

*Tucson (Arizona) Citizen.* 1989b. "Barriers between Pools, Homes May Be Required." 23 September.

*Tucson (Arizona) Citizen.* 1993. "Clinton Appoints Wife to Key Job." 26 January.

Tullock, G. 1967. "The Welfare Costs of Tariffs, Monopolies and Theft." *Western Economic Journal* 5:224–32.

Ullmann-Margalit, E. 1977. *The Emergence of Norms.* Oxford: Oxford University Press.

*United Railways v. West.* 1930. 280 U.S. 234.

*United States v. Addyston Pipe and Steel Co. et al.* 1898. 85 Fed. 271 (6th Cir.)

*United States v. Aluminum Corporation of America et al.* 1945. 148 F. 2d 416 (2d Circuit)

*United States v. American Tobacco Co.* 1911. 221 U.S. 106.

*United States v. Trans-Missouri Freight Assn.* 1897. 166 U.S. 290.

*United States v. United Shoe Machinery Corp.* 1953. 110 F. Supp. 295 (D. Mass.)

*United States v. United States Steel Corp. et al.* 1920. 251 U.S. 417.

*United States v. Von's Grocery Co.* 1966. 384 U.S. 270.

Varian, H. R. 1975. "Distributive Justice, Welfare Economics, and the Theory of Justice." *Journal of Philosophy and Public Affairs* 4:223–247.

Varian, H. R. 1991. *Microeconomic Analysis.* 3d ed. New York: Norton.

Viscusi, W. K. 1991. "Risk Perceptions in Regulation, Tort Liability, and the Market." *Regulation* 14:50–57.

Viscusi, W. K. 1992. *Fatal Trade-offs: Public and Private Responsibilities for Risk.* Oxford: Oxford University Press.

Viscusi, W. K., Vernon, J. M., and Harrington, J. E. 1992. *Economics of Regulation and Antitrust.* Lexington, MA: D. C. Heath.

Vogelsang, I., and Finsinger, J. 1979. "A Regulatory Adjustment Process for Optimal Pricing by Multiproduct Monopoly Firms." *Bell Journal of Economics* 10:157–171.

*Wall Street Journal*. 1993a. "Hailing the American Dream." 1 February.

*Wall Street Journal*. 1993b. "GM Ordered by Jury to Pay $105.2 Million over Death." 5 February.

Walster, E., Walster, G. W., and Berscheid, E. 1979. *Equity: Theory and Research*. Boston: Allyn and Bacon.

Wenders, J. T. 1981. Testimony in *Southern Nevada Homebuilders Association, Inc. et al. v. Las Vegas Valley Water District*. Case No. A-154270, Eighth Judicial District Court of the State of Nevada in and for the County of Clark.

Weymark, J. A. 1991. "A Reconsideration of the Harasanyi-Sen Debate on Utilitarianism." In J. Elester and J. E. Roemer, eds., *Interpersonal Comparisons of Well-Being*. Cambridge: Cambridge University Press.

Williamson, O. E. 1975. *Markets and Hierarchies*. New York: Free Press, Macmillan.

*Wilk v. American Medical Association*. 1990. 895 F.2d 352 (7th Circuit).

Wilson, J. Q. ed. 1980. *The Politics of Regulation*. New York: Basic Books.

Yergin, D. 1991. *The Prize: The Epic Quest for Oil, Money, and Power*. New York: Simon and Schuster.

Young, P. 1989. "Fairness and Focal Points in Bargaining." Mimeo prepared for the Russell Sage Conference on Local Justice and Fair Allocation, Aspen Institute, Wye Woods, MD, 15–17 December.

Young, P. 1994. *Equity: In Theory and Practice*. Princeton: Princeton University Press.

Zajac, E. E. 1972. "Some Preliminary Thoughts on Subsidization." Proceedings 1972 Conference on Telecommunications Policy Research.

Zajac, E. E. 1974. "Note on an Extension of the Ramsey Inverse Elasticity of Demand Pricing or Taxation Formula." *Journal of Public Economics* 3:181–184.

Zajac, E. E. 1978. *Fairness or Efficiency: An Introduction to Public Utility Pricing*. Cambridge, MA: Ballinger.

Zajac, E. E. 1985. "Perceived Economic Justice: The Example of Public Utility Regulation." In H. P. Young, ed. *Cost Allocation: Methods, Principles, Applications*. Amsterdam: North-Holland.

Zajac, E. E. 1986. "Who Wins and Who Loses? An Economic Justice Overview and Research Agenda." In J. Miller, ed., *Telecommunications and Equity*, Amsterdam: Esevier Science, North-Holland.

# Index